Frederick W. Marks III

# Independence on Trial

## Foreign Affairs and the Making of the Constitution

Louisiana State University Press
Baton Rouge

For her without whom . . .

ISBN 0-8071-0052-8
Library of Congress Catalog Card Number 73-77652
Copyright © 1973 by Louisiana State University Press
All rights reserved
Manufactured in the United States of America
Printed by The TJM Corporation, Baton Rouge, Louisiana
Designed by Albert R. Crochet

Some of the material in this volume was previously published as "Foreign
Affairs: A Winning Issue in the Campaign for Ratification of the United
States Constitution," reprinted with permission from *Political Science
Quarterly*, LXXXVI, No. 3 (September, 1971); and "American Pride,
European Prejudice, and the Constitution," reprinted with permission from
*The Historian*, XXXIV, No. 4 (August, 1972).

# Contents

Acknowledgments   vii

Introduction   ix

I   The Problem of National Defense   3

II   The Challenge of Foreign Trade Restrictions   52

III   The National Mood   96

IV   The Culmination: Philadelphia, 1787   142

V   The Final Test   167

Epilogue   207

Bibliography   221

Index   249

# Acknowledgments

I wish to thank Bradford Perkins for his time, his energy, and the influence which he has exerted on the conception and execution of the entire book. I also express my appreciation to Robert E. Brown, Shaw Livermore, Gordon Wood, Samuel Eldersveld, Stephen Kurtz, Thomas Maddux, Allan Wilbur, Blaine Brownell, and Jerald Combs for suggestions and queries which have proved most helpful. Others to whom I owe thanks include Agnes Pope and William Ewing at the Clements Library, Walter O. Forster of Purdue University, Mary Smith and Mary Gibbs on the staff of the Purdue Library, Anna Van Williams at Columbia, Clifford Shipton of the American Antiquarian Society, and W. J. Van Shreeven of the Virginia State Library. I am also grateful to the University of Michigan and the Purdue Research Foundation for both moral and material support.

Most of all, I am indebted to my wife Sylvia Ann, who contributed to every phase of the work and provided constant inspiration.

# Introduction

The question of why Americans scrapped the Articles of Confederation in 1787–1788 to obtain a stronger central government under the Constitution is a vital one, as it determines in part the meaning of the Constitution for later generations. Generally, and especially during the past sixty years, historians have emphasized domestic considerations such as class conflict and economic gain as the leading concerns of the founding fathers.[1] But no other view of their motives and objectives has been developed in depth. The purpose of this book is to provide such a view by assessing the facts of the period in the context of foreign affairs.

1. For two interesting and perceptive historiographical introductions to the period, see Richard Morris, "The Confederation Period and the American Historian," *William and Mary Quarterly*, XIII, Ser. 3 (April, 1956); and Stanley Elkins and Eric McKitrick, "The Founding Fathers: Young Men of the Revolution," *Political Science Quarterly*, LXXVI (June, 1961). Morris divided the literature into two categories: first, the Antifederalist school led by J. Allen Smith (1907), Charles Beard (1913), and Merrill Jensen (1950); second, the nationalist school represented by George Ticknor Curtis (1854), William Henry Trescot (1857), Richard Frothingham (1872), H. Von Holst (1889), James Schouler (1894), George Bancroft (1882), John Bach McMaster (1883), John Fiske (1888), and, with reservations, Andrew C. McLaughlin (1905).

The early historians of the Confederation era, men such as George Bancroft, John Bach McMaster, and John Fiske, were virtually silent on the subject of military weakness and national pride. They wrote much about the effort to obtain a steady federal revenue but did not explain it except in terms of the need to pay off the national debt.[2] They covered commercial problems in broad detail, but did not fully

2. Bancroft, in his two-volume *History of the Formation of the Constitution of the United States of America* (New York: D. Appleton and Co., 1888), paid little attention to Shays's Rebellion, but he paid even less to problems of defense. He was silent on the role of Henry Knox, Alexander McGillivray, Joseph Brant, and Josiah Harmar. He conveyed little, if any, sense of the fierce patriotic sentiment current at the time (notwithstanding incidental references: I, 153, 258). McMaster, in his *History of the People of the United States From the Revolution to the Civil War* (8 vols.; New York: D. Appleton and Co., 1883–1913), devoted much attention to fiscal problems and to Shays (I, 281–356, 391–92), and he added a description of European misconceptions about the United States (I, 224–26); but he referred to the Indian threat only incidentally and mentioned Harmar only in connection with his defeat in 1790. The name Knox did not figure significantly. North African pirates were given only passing reference (I, 361–62) except for the negotiations with Tripoli and Morocco (I, 406–12). The issue of Spain and the Mississippi was well covered (I, 371–89, 412–16), but the reader was not alerted to the military weaknesses which determined its outcome. Fiske, in his classic study of *The Critical Period in American History, 1783–1789* (New York: Houghton Mifflin Co., 1888), devoted a scant fifty pages out of four hundred to the question of foreign relations in the years 1783–87 and said nothing of western military problems. The Jay-Gardoqui negotiations were mentioned, but not Harmar, McGillivray, or even Knox. There was only a brief reference to the sentiment of national pride and no suggestion of its importance. McLaughlin, in his *The Confederation and the Constitution, 1783–1789* (New York: Harper and Bros., 1905), devoted a short chapter to the major diplomatic problems with a brief suggestion of their impact on the reform movement (pp. 173–74). He mentioned the Barbary pirates and the Indians (pp. 82, 90) but placed his emphasis on the paper money issue and Shays's Rebellion which he viewed as "immensely" important to the reform movement (pp. 141, 166, 168). He alluded only once to the existence of national pride, and while he claimed that "our relations with Spain and England were fraught with danger" (p. 174), he did not explain why. Edward Channing's treatment of foreign problems in his *History of the United States* (6 vols.; New York: Macmillan Co., 1905–25) is also meager. He devoted only two short chapters out of six sturdy volumes to the period 1783–87 and was less informative than his predecessors. He contended that the Constitution was written because of three major factors:

describe the grass-roots pressure for a constitutional amendment which would allow Congress to regulate foreign trade.[3] In 1928, Charles Warren stated that the constitutional movement arose from a "patriotic desire for a united nation, able to take its place with the other nations of the world" and that the chief fear of the nationalists was a "dissolution of the union leaving the states open to attack by foreign power."[4] Although Warren did not explore the question of union and disunion in depth, he was correct in sensing the need for greater emphasis on the problem of national security.

Recent historians have paid little attention to foreign affairs, choosing instead to stress the friction between rich and poor. They tend to view Shays's Rebellion as the most significant and symbolic event of the period and the key to understanding the origins of the Constitutional Convention.

---

internal disorders (paper money disputes and Shays's Rebellion); the threatened secession of the Southwest over the Jay-Gardoqui proposals; and the inability of the federal government to aid colonization in the Northwest. Again there was little specific discussion of defense problems or the patriotic *zeitgeist*.

3. The earliest accounts are the best. Bancroft gave some sense of local sentiment as expressed in town meetings and did tie the Constitutional Convention to commercial distress (I, 55–56, 62–68, 146–49, 185–200, 250–60). He cited four causes for the writing of the Constitution: commercial distress; the need to hold and populate the trans-Allegheny area; the need for revenue; and the need to regulate domestic trade. McMaster also pointed out the causal relationship between general commercial distress and the success of the reform movement. He was the first to examine petitions which were filed on the state level in Virginia. He also described John Adams' frustrating efforts to obtain diplomatic redress in London (I, 204–209, 233–49, 255–59, 268, 272–79, 360–61, 366). But neither Bancroft nor McMaster gave sufficient emphasis or detail to the impact of British trade restrictions on American public opinion. Fiske stressed the problem of commerce but said nothing about grass roots impatience with state efforts to break down British restrictions or the widespread pressure for a constitutional amendment. McLaughlin argued that the issue was unimportant (pp. 71–88), and Channing ignored it entirely.

4. Charles Warren, *The Making of the Constitution* (Boston: Little, Brown & Co., 1928), 8–9.

The groundwork for this approach appeared in the early 1900s in the work of J. Allen Smith, Charles A. Beard, Arthur F. Bentley, and Algie M. Simons.[5] Edward Channing and Andrew C. McLaughlin reflected the "new history" to a degree but generally stayed within the traditional frame of reference. Gradually, however, the socio-economic interpretation of the Constitution gained popularity. Merrill Jensen adhered to it in his full-scale history of the period published in 1950.[6] Jackson Turner Main stated in 1961 that "there is a good deal of evidence to show that the division [between Federalists and Antifederalists] followed class lines." He explained that class cleavage was not the only division, but implied that it was the most significant. According to Main, "the key to the political history of the period . . . is a socio-economic division." [7] Forrest McDonald, who launched a brilliant attack in 1965 on Beard's *An Economic Interpretation of the Constitution* (1913), accepted Beard's economic orientation and did not concern himself with foreign affairs outside the area of trade except to note that "almost all" the friends of the Constitution

5. Richard Morris traces it even further back to 1871 when Henry Dawson asserted that the Federalists were exaggerating the dire state of foreign relations in order to promote their own selfish interests. In line with this, Beard and his followers went on to view the Constitution as a weapon fashioned by the rich against the poor. The ratification contest was seen as a clash of interest groups, and the reform movement was judged antidemocratic; Morris, "The Confederation Period," 148–51.

6. Jensen observed the widespread patriotic pride of the period but made no connection between this and the Philadelphia Convention. He described British trade restrictions but argued that their impact on the American economy was negligible; Merrill Jensen, *The New Nation* (New York: Vintage Books, 1965), 165–66, 193, 198. He did mention (p. 255) that "popular opinion" was inflamed, but the reader was left to draw his own conclusions since Jensen maintained that the states were doing a satisfactory job of regulating commerce (pp. 401, 407).

7. Jackson Turner Main, *The Antifederalists: Critics of the Constitution, 1781–1788* (Chapel Hill: University of North Carolina Press, 1961), 261–62, 271. He pursued the same theme in his account of *The Upper House in Revolutionary America, 1763–1788* (Madison: University of Wisconsin Press, 1967).

"were either born or educated abroad." [8] Earlier, Robert E. Brown brought forth an incisive and comprehensive attack on Beard's assumptions as well as his methods (1956), and he was seconded by Richard Morris' fine historiographical sketch of the Confederation period which appeared the same year. Brown and Morris, however, concerned themselves more with exposing Beard's weaknesses than advancing a new interpretation.

A number of recent articles have questioned important assumptions. In 1961, Stanley Elkins and Eric McKitrick suggested that what distinguished Federalists from Antifederalists was a "continental" approach to problems. They stressed the youthfulness and national experience of Federalist leaders, many of whose careers had been launched on the continental level during the Revolution. The same year, John P. Roche described the founding fathers as a small group of men distinguished by their consciousness of America's "international impotence." [9] In 1969, Robert A. Feer published a pioneer article in the *New England Quarterly* questioning the significance of Shays's Rebellion both as a cause for the convention of 1787 and as an influence on its proceedings. He could find no evidence that the rebellion was decisive or even important in deciding the state legislatures to send delegates to Philadelphia. If Feer is correct, one is led to question the priorities not only of Beard and the "new" historians but also of McMaster and McLaughlin.[10]

8. Forrest McDonald, *E Pluribus Unum* (Boston: Houghton Mifflin Co., 1965), 5. Actually, the majority of Federalists was probably born and educated at home, but the comparison in this regard between Federalists and Antifederalists is surely remarkable, as McDonald suggests.

9. Elkins and McKitrick, "Founding Fathers"; John P. Roche, "The Founding Fathers: A Reform Caucus in Action," *American Political Science Review*, LV (December, 1961), 801.

10. Robert A. Feer, "Shays's Rebellion and the Constitution: A Study in Causation," *New England Quarterly*, Vol. XLII, No. 3 (September, 1969), 393, 410. Bancroft had disposed of Shays in less than two pages in his *History of the Formation of the Constitution*. Two recent publications

The socio-economic explanation for the Constitution is still strong, however, judging from the latest book-length study of the period, which follows Beard and Jensen in claiming that "the struggle over the Constitution . . . can best be understood as a social one" for "the quarrel was fundamentally one between aristocracy and democracy." [11]

The following account of the foreign affairs of the period should be considered in conjunction with the socio-economic interpretation rather than as a substitute for it. One hopes that, in covering the diplomatic history of the years 1783–1789, it will contribute to the presently sparse scholarship in this area. At the same time it aims to go beyond factual narrative and to open new avenues of thought. It suggests, for example, that British trade restrictions affected the economy and mood of the American people more sharply than was realized by Bancroft, McMaster, or more recent historians; that Shays's Rebellion was viewed in 1786 as a sign of British subversion as well as a manifestation of domestic grievances; that the military exigencies on land and sea and the sensitivity of national pride deserve more emphasis than they have thus far received; and that the friends of the Constitution differed significantly from their opponents not only in their socio-economic status but also in their experience and knowledge of foreign affairs.

No effort is made to disparage the accomplishments of

---

have drawn attention to foreign affairs as a stimulus to constitutional reform although neither explores the connection in depth: Richard Hofstadter, *The Progressive Historians* (New York: Alfred A. Knopf, 1968), 231–37; Lawrence Kaplan, *From Colonies into Nation* (New York: Macmillan Co., 1972), 145–81.

11. Gordon S. Wood, *Creation of the American Republic, 1776–1787* (New York: W. W. Norton & Co., 1972), 476, 484–85. See also Wood's review in the *William and Mary Quarterly*, XXIV, Ser. 3 (October, 1967), 632–37. His *Creation* makes its major contribution to the literature of the period in suggesting the importance of ideas as motivating forces.

the Confederation. Such gains as the land ordinances, the reduction of the domestic debt, the assumption of federal debts by the states, and the winning of the Revolution itself cannot be overlooked by anyone who has read the accounts given by Merrill Jensen and E. J. Ferguson.[12] Nor is there any denial of the economic and social factors which may have tended to separate Americans.

One would not want to suggest that all Americans were equally disturbed by military problems or equally anxious to meet the challenge of foreign trade restrictions. Main, in his account of *The Antifederalists*, has proven otherwise. At the same time, while some Antifederalists were not seriously concerned about the posture of American foreign relations, others were as concerned as their adversaries but felt that the advantages to be gained under the new Constitution would be outweighed by risks such as involuntary taxation and overcentralization of government. Perhaps they were more cognizant of the risks, while the Federalists were more aware of possible advantages.

One final word about definitions. The term "nationalist" for the years 1781–1787 refers to those who supported a limited increase in the powers of Congress but more especially to those who favored drastic constitutional change and later called themselves Federalists. The expression "foreign affairs" is used in the broadest sense. Internal and external matters are so closely related that the distinction between them is frequently lost. The term refers to relations with the Indian nations as well as with foreign countries. It also encompasses ideas such as the American image of Europe,

12. See Jensen, *New Nation*; E. James Ferguson, "State Assumption of Federal Debt During the Confederation," *Mississippi Valley Historical Review*, XXXVIII (1951), 403–24; and Ferguson, *The Power of the Purse: A History of American Public Finance, 1776–1790* (Chapel Hill: University of North Carolina Press, 1961).

and feelings such as national pride. What Americans thought of themselves and of the world around them is often more important than actual reality in trying to explain why they acted as they did. If, for example, men generally expressed more irritation in 1786 than in previous years over British commercial restrictions, their feelings are no less significant for the fact that business was showing signs of improvement. Considerable attention is therefore directed throughout the book to what people wrote and said. One hesitates to take words at face value in all cases, especially in the realm of politics. On the other hand, it seems reasonable to assume that what was written between friends of similar political outlook is unlikely to have been mere rhetoric.

Independence
on Trial

# I

# The Problem
# of National Defense

The most elemental duty of the Confederation government, its very *raison d'être*, was the protection of the country against foreign attack. Yet Congress was singularly ill-equipped to discharge this responsibility under the Articles of Confederation.

Among the important defensive powers which the United States lacked in 1783 was the power to enforce treaties. The Articles gave Congress exclusive power to negotiate with foreign nations, including Indian tribes, but did not make treaties the supreme law of the land. There was no federal judiciary to decide cases in dispute between federal and state governments, and no coercive force to back up such a judiciary had it existed. As a result, individual states undercut congressional prerogative in foreign relations and jeopardized the security of the entire nation.

Virginia, for example, insisted on ratifying the peace treaty despite prior ratification by Congress. She then disobeyed Congress and violated the law of nations by harboring a French pirate wanted on criminal charges by the government of Louis XVI. Similarly, commissioners of the state of Georgia took it upon themselves, without congressional approval, to demand that Spanish authorities cede a number of forts and agree to a general settlement of disputed boundaries.[1] It was also common for states to negotiate their own loans from foreign countries.

In dealing with the Indians, states tended to be more rapacious than the federal government. They were more apt to close their eyes when their citizens trespassed on Indian lands or obtained lucrative trade concessions without a federal license. It was not surprising, therefore, that many treaty conferences came to naught when attended by agents of both state and nation. At a meeting with the Mohawks, the New York delegation upset congressional plans before the federal commissioners had even arrived. At another meeting in the fall of 1785 at Galphinton, Georgia, United States commissioners tried to negotiate a treaty with the Creek nation. When the Creeks did not send a representative delegation, federal agents refused to take advantage of the situation and walked out. Later, agents from Georgia appeared on the scene, met the Creeks, and drove a hard bargain (this was only one of three illegal treaties signed by Georgia in defiance of the United States). Federal agents also agreed in the Treaty of Hopewell to return land to the Cherokees which had already been sold to white settlers by the state of North Carolina. Needless to say, the Galphinton and Hopewell treaties were lame ducks from the start.[2]

1. James Madison to James Monroe, June 21, 1785, in Gaillard Hunt, (ed.), *The Writings of James Madison* (9 vols.; New York: G. P. Putnam's Sons, 1900–10), II, 146.

2. For information on the problem of federal Indian policy, I have relied heavily on Reginald Horsman, *Expansion and American Indian Policy, 1783–1812* (East Lansing: Michigan State University Press, 1967); Arthur Preston Whitaker, *The Spanish-American Frontier: 1783–1795* (Boston and New York: Houghton Mifflin Co., 1927); Samuel Flagg

There was friction between the southern states and Congress over the question of military priorities. Congress faced hostile tribes in both the North and the South. But the area northwest of the Ohio River was regarded as more critical both because of its prospective yield in land sales and because it was closer to the British outposts. Hoping to concentrate its few troops in the North and finding it impossible to protect the settlements in Kentucky or Tennessee, Congress sought to pacify the southern tribes with a liberal land policy; but such a scheme was neither successful nor popular. In addition, Indian warfare often took place on land still claimed by Virginia, North Carolina, and Georgia. Since the main burden of defending this part of the country rested on the shoulders of state militia, the states were inescapably drawn into negotiations which involved matters beyond their borders and violated congressional prerogative.[3]

Another problem stemming from congressional weakness in the area of treaty enforcement was the defense of the northern frontier. According to the peace terms of 1783, Great Britain had agreed to surrender her strategic forts in the Great Lakes area "with all convenient speed." Michilimackinac lay at the intersection of Lakes Michigan and Huron; Detroit lay at the river junction connecting Lakes Huron and Erie; and Niagara dominated the link between Lakes Erie and Ontario. Point au Fer and Dutchman's Point on Lake Champlain stood athwart the vital trade route be-

---

Bemis, *Pinckney's Treaty, America's Advantage from Europe's Distresses, 1783–1800* (Rev. ed.; New Haven: Yale University Press, 1960); and Francis Paul Prucha, *The Sword of the Republic: The United States Army on the Frontier* (London: Macmillan & Co., 1969).

3. The semi-independent state of Franklin presented a most peculiar problem since it existed in a political limbo, officially part of North Carolina, yet demanding recognition as a sovereign member of the Confederation.

tween Montreal and Albany. Oswego and Oswegatchie held the key to the western reaches of the Mohawk Valley; and Sandusky and Presqu'Isle controlled the route from Lake Erie to the Ohio River.[4] Since Congress could not fulfill its treaty commitments entailing compensation of the Loyalists and the payment of debts owed to British merchants, the British for their part would not remove their garrisons. Perhaps the garrisons would have been retained in any case for military and commercial reasons.[5] But Congress lost all moral and legal initiative when it failed to honor its commitments.

The British-held forts were of immense military value. Without them, Congress had to maintain a secondary line of defense which was not only inferior from a strategic point of view, but also costly, since it could not be supplied via the lakes. Shipments had to travel as much as three hundred miles overland. According to the hard-working secretary of war Henry Knox, there could be no lasting peace with the Indians until the two key forts of Niagara and

4. See Charles R. Ritcheson, *Aftermath of Revolution: British Policy Toward the United States, 1783–1795* (Dallas: Southern Methodist University Press, 1969), 75–79.

5. British intentions in this regard seem clear from the fact that on April 8, 1784, exactly one day before George III solemnly ratified the final treaty of peace, the British Secretary for Home Affairs ordered that all the controversial frontier posts be held indefinitely. Curtis P. Nettels and Samuel Flagg Bemis maintain that the British decision to remain on the frontier was primarily motivated by an interest in the fur trade. But Alfred L. Burt concludes that it was mainly British fear of the Indians as well as the desire to set up a buffer state that lay behind their refusal to evacuate; Curtis Putnam Nettels, *The Emergence of a National Economy, 1775–1815* (New York: Holt, Rinehart, and Winston, 1962), 53; Samuel Flagg Bemis, *Jay's Treaty: A Study in Commerce and Diplomacy* (New York: Macmillan Co., 1923), 6; Alfred LeRoy Burt, *The United States, Great Britain and British North America from the Revolution to the Establishment of Peace After the War of 1812* (New Haven: Yale University Press, 1940), Chap. 6. For a well-balanced discussion, see Ritcheson, *Aftermath of Revolution*, 167.

Detroit were secured. Young Lieutenant Colonel Josiah Harmar, commander-in-chief of the army, was of the same opinion. He spoke of "villainous emissaries" sent by the British from their forts in order to "poison the minds of the savages," and thought that one treaty negotiated at Detroit would have been worth a dozen signed elsewhere.[6] New York State, with five out of nine of the posts on its soil, was particularly anxious for Congress to find a way of dislodging the British. Governor George Clinton, who normally pursued an independent course, promised to support any action which Congress might deem advisable.[7]

Clinton had reason for concern. Of the eighty thousand Tories who had fled the United States during the war, six to seven thousand were reported to be grouped at various posts along the border, well supplied with arms and food. Who could guess their ultimate purpose? Twenty-seven-year-old Virginia congressman James Monroe, after two hazardous journeys into Canada, noted that the exiles were watching the United States for signs of civil disorder and the eventual overthrow of the government so they could return to their former positions of influence. By 1787, Sir Guy Carleton, who was now Lord Dorchester and governor of Canada, had ordered the Quebec militia to be on the alert and was expecting six relief regiments from England.

6. Report of Secretary at War Knox to Congress, March 31, 1788, Worthington Chauncey Ford *et al.* (eds.), *Journals of the Continental Congress, 1774–1789* (34 vols.; Washington, D.C.: U.S. Government Printing Office, 1904–37), XXXIV, 139, hereinafter cited as W. C. Ford *et al.* (eds.), *Journals*; Richard Warner Van Alstyne, *The Rising American Empire* (New York: Oxford University Press, 1960), 72–73. Knox's official title during the Confederation years was "Secretary at War," and Colonel Harmar was generally referred to as General Harmar although he was not promoted to the rank of brigadier general until 1787.

7. McLaughlin, "Western Posts"; New York State, *Senate Journal,* 9th Sess., January to May, 1786, pp. 4, 7; *Pennsylvania Gazette* (Philadelphia), January 25, 1786; W. C. Ford *et al.* (eds.), *Journals,* XXVI, 248.

There had also been signs of British naval activity on Lake Champlain. Sunken ships were being retrieved and restored to active duty; a small gunboat and the twenty-gun warship, *Maria*, had been fitted out; and the frontier posts were being enlarged and supplied with extra ammunition.[8]

The sense of impending hostility was further heightened by a number of border confrontations. The St. Croix River, which was supposed to mark the northeast boundary of Massachusetts (present-day Maine), was frequently confused with other rivers in the vicinity, and the true boundary was unclear. Tempers flared when a federal Indian agent notified the governor of Massachusetts in 1783 that Canadian settlers in the area were seizing disputed territory by order of their government. At the same time, Secretary for Foreign Affairs John Jay expressed concern over an attempt by New Brunswick settlers to take over American-claimed Moose Island. Jay, a man of judicious temperament and former chief justice of New York, president of Congress, envoy to Spain, and peace commissioner, felt that something should be done, but he feared that action might lead to war.[9] Perhaps the situation was well described by

8. Jay's Report to Congress, September 5, 1785, in W. C. Ford *et al.* (eds.), *Journals*, XXIX, 680; James Monroe, "Hints," September–December, 1785, in Monroe Papers, Library of Congress, Ser. 1, Vol. I. According to Professor Bradford Perkins, the British government considered Canada a valuable "base for attacks upon the United States" until 1812; Bradford Perkins, *Castlereagh and Adams* (Berkeley: University of California Press, 1964), 198. See also, Richard Champion, *Considerations on the Present Situation of Great Britain and the United States of North America with a View to Their Future Commercial Connections* (New York: S. and J. Loudon, 1786), 138; *Gazette of the State of Georgia* (Savannah), July, 1787; *Pennsylvania Gazette*, August 3, 1785, May 2, 1787; *Virginia Independent Chronicle* (Richmond), June 18, 1787.

9. John Allen to John Hancock, December 15, 1783, in Samuel Adams Papers, New York Public Library; John Jay to Thomas Jefferson, November 2, 1785, in *Diplomatic Correspondence of the United States of America, from the Signing of the Definitive Treaty of Peace, September 10, 1783, to the Adoption of the Constitution, March 4, 1789* (3 vols.; Washington,

a Canadian friend of the United States when he warned Americans in 1787:

> Your pusillanimity in suffering Britain to retain the frontier posts—the want of energy in your federal head—the contracted state of your commerce—the British reinforcing the garrisons of Canada—the many thousands of troops which were disbanded and became settlers in this province at the end of the war, and who are ready to fly to arms at a moment's warning being tired of cutting down trees and endeavoring to cultivate unfruitful land—are circumstances which unless guarded against will rend America in pieces.[10]

The posts had considerable economic as well as military value, for they were the key to a fur-trade monopoly worth £200,000 per year. The dreams of many an enterprising American were based on the assumption that the British would withdraw their garrisons "with all convenient speed," as they had promised. Merchants, trappers, and land speculators stood ready in New York to turn the Hudson and Mohawk rivers into highways of commerce. The Virginians, too, had plans; they hoped to dredge rivers, dig canals, and build roads to the west. The Potomac would become the principal highway running from east to west, Alexandria the greatest depot, and western land values would soar. But such hopes faded rapidly in the face of the British refusal to withdraw. For those who had actually invested in various profit-making schemes, it was a rude awakening. Three Pennsylvania merchants had purchased a large quantity of goods to be used to buy furs from the Indians.

---

D.C.: Blair and Ives, 1837), I, 623; Report of John Jay to Congress, September 22, 1785, in W. C. Ford *et al.* (eds.), *Journals*, XXIX, 753. New Brunswick must have been quite an unhappy place for Americans, for a year later, its customs officers seized two United States vessels in what appeared to be a premeditated violation of the treaty of peace; *Gentleman's Magazine* (London), LVI (October, 1786), 900.

10. *Gazette of the State of Georgia*, September 6, 1787.

They planned to go to Detroit, make the purchase, and return home. After obtaining special passes from the Supreme Executive Council of Pennsylvania and the Council of New York, they traveled as far as the Mohawk River only to hear that they would not be able to pass the British-held posts. In the end they were obliged to return home with depreciated merchandise on which they had paid state customs duties no less than three times![11]

The first impulse of Congress, faced with British intransigence, was to send Henry Knox to Canada with instructions to demand immediate evacuation and, when this failed, to dispatch the redoubtable John Adams on a diplomatic mission to the Court of St. James's. Adams was an excellent choice. He had gained a reputation for his courageous defense of Captain Preston, alleged villain of the Boston Massacre, and Jefferson had dubbed him "the Atlas of Independence" for his sterling service to the Continental Congress. In the years prior to 1785, he had served as American peace commissioner, first alone and then with Franklin and Jay. Despite his cantankerous ways and a touch of vanity, few men were as painstaking, observant, and combative as this lawyer from Braintree, Massachusetts.

However, just as Knox could not back up his demands with military muscle, Adams lacked a legal basis for diplo-

11. James Monroe to Thomas Jefferson, November 1, 1784, April 12, 1785, in Stanislaus Murray Hamilton (ed.), *The Writings of James Monroe Including a Collection of His Public and Private Papers and Correspondence Now for the First Time Printed* (7 vols.; New York and London: G. P. Putnam's Sons, 1898–1903), I, 42, 72; George Washington to Thomas Jefferson, May 30, 1787, in John Clement Fitzpatrick (ed.), *The Writings of George Washington from the Original Manuscript Sources, 1745–1799* (39 vols.; Washington, D.C.: U.S. Government Printing Office, 1931–44), XXIX, 218–20; Speech of Governor George Clinton, January 16, 1786, New York State *Senate Journal*, 9th Sess., January to May, 1786, p. 4; Petition of Three Merchants, September 10, 1785, Records of the Pennsylvania Assembly MSS., Pennsylvania State Archives Collection, Harrisburg, Record Group No. 7, General Assembly File Box No. 2, Undated Petitions, 1785–88.

matic maneuver. There was no question that the United States had violated the peace treaty. Massachusetts, New York, Pennsylvania, and all states to the south were preventing British merchants from collecting prewar debts which had been guaranteed under Article IV. Adams argued gamely that Americans would be in a better position to pay their debts if they could benefit from a fur trade that was rightfully theirs. He suggested that British pressure to the south of the Great Lakes might touch off an Indian war which would draw both parties into its vortex. But this impressed no one. The answer was invariably the same: the United States had violated the treaty first, and as soon as the offending states fulfilled their treaty responsibilities the frontier posts would be vacated.[12]

At times the frustrating negotiations seemed to foreshadow a new war. There were rumors that the American army would try to seize the western posts and commit the country to war. One of the volunteer companies of light infantry in Charleston, South Carolina, actually offered its services for the occasion. In London, a paper reported that eight to nine thousand Americans were about to march on the posts, and that they were proceeding under the authority of their legislatures rather than their "feeble and ineffectual Congress." Adams blustered to one of his friends that if the posts were not evacuated, he "would not go and attack them, but declare war directly and march one army to Quebec and another to Nova Scotia." [13]

---

12. "State of the Grievances Complained of by Merchants and Other British Subjects Having Estates, Property and Debts due to Them in the Several States of America," in *Diplomatic Correspondence, 1783–89*, II, 582–91. The states also violated Article VI of the treaty which prohibited postwar confiscations or other proceedings against the Loyalists. But this was not as apparent at the time.

13. *Columbian Herald* (Charleston, S.C.), September 11 and 18, 1786; John Adams to Cotton Tufts, May 26, 1786, in Charles Francis Adams (ed.), *The Works of John Adams, Second President of the United States*

The American government was in no condition for another war, however, and thoughtful people realized that such a conflict might well bring the Republic to a premature end. Adams himself admitted that "another war with Great Britain would turn to the advantage of artful allies and a turbulent, ambitious army. . . . It would entail upon our posterity forever a system of debt and taxes." And Jay advised against any ultimatum to Britain because it "would involve the United States either in war or disgrace. They are not prepared for the former, and should if possible avoid the latter." Yet something had to be done, he insisted, for "to permit these disputes to remain unsettled will be to risk mutual acts of violence which may embroil the two nations in a war." [14]

Adams decided the only answer was to concede the truth of the British argument and prevail upon those states which were reluctant to abide by the terms of 1783. Only in this way would he gain the diplomatic leverage he needed. In numerous letters he urged the states to repeal "every law that has the least appearance of clashing with the treaty." Americans should fulfill their obligations in order to force Britain to fulfill hers, which were even greater.[15]

Many agreed with him. The backcountry inhabitants of Virginia complained to their assembly that treaty violations

---

(10 vols.; Boston: Little, Brown & Co., 1850–56), IX, 549. This must have been said in jest because Adams was no warmonger.

14. John Adams to Samuel Adams, June 2, 1786, in Samuel Adams Papers, New York Public Library. See also Thomas Jefferson to James Monroe, November 11, 1784, in Monroe Papers, Library of Congress, Ser. 1, Vol. I; Reports of John Jay to Congress, September 22, 1785, and March 30, 1786, in W. C. Ford *et al.* (eds.), *Journals*, XXIX, 753; XXX, 147.

15. John Adams to John Jay, June 16, 1786, in *Diplomatic Correspondence, 1783–89*, II, 668–69; John Adams to John Jay, May 25, 1786, to Cotton Tufts, May 26, 1786, in Adams (ed.), *Works of John Adams*, VIII, 394–96; IX, 549.

were endangering the entire country, subverting the "basis of the Confederation," and setting Virginia at odds with the union. The obligation to repay debts was, after all, an "immutable law of justice," and "any refinement in the explanation of treaties" was "unbecoming the character of Republicans," a "breach of public faith," and a "prostitution of the liberties of this country." Some took the optimistic view that American compliance with the treaty would lead to British compliance as well. Alexander Hamilton, often a cynic in such matters, predicted that the principle of reciprocity would serve the interests of New York; and Secretary Jay informed Congress that the United States had indeed been the first to violate the treaty, and that state violations should be corrected.[16]

The great question, though, was how could Congress prevail upon unwilling states since it lacked both judicial and military power under the Articles of Confederation? All it could do was to urge compliance upon the delinquent states, stressing the fact that the security of all the states hung in the balance. Many warnings of this kind were issued, and Adams was told to broadcast the fact that the government

16. Report of John Jay to Congress, October 13, 1786, in W. C. Ford *et al.* (eds.), *Journals*, XXXI, 781–874; James Madison to Edmund Pendleton, April 22, 1787, in Hunt (ed.), *Writings of Madison*, II, 355; Virginia Legislative Petitions, Amherst County, November 9, 1784, Augusta County, October 25, 1786; *New Jersey Gazette* (Trenton), June 19, August 28, 1786; *Pennsylvania Gazette*, June 7, 1786, and May 2, 1787; Alexander Hamilton, "A Letter from Phocion to the Considerate Citizens of New York," January 1–27, 1784, in Harold Coffin Syrett (ed.), *Papers of Alexander Hamilton* (13 vols.; New York: Columbia University Press, 1961–), III, 491–92. According to Professor Ritcheson, most of the southern debts owed to British merchants were in the hands of the poorer classes and backwoodsmen—such people as were represented by Patrick Henry and opposed the Constitution. Twice in 1784, the popular party in Virginia blocked Madison's efforts to enforce the peace treaty, and an attempt was later made to tie the debt issue to a return of the slaves which Britain had carried off during the war; Ritcheson, *Aftermath of Revolution*, 66–67.

was doing everything possible to ensure justice for British creditors.[17] But this was not enough. The states would not cooperate despite unremitting labor on the part of Congress and various individuals. The same constitutional weakness that thwarted the nation in its dealings with the Indians now hindered its diplomatic struggle with Great Britain.

Each of these cases pointed directly to the need for constitutional reform. Hugh Williamson, delegate to Congress from North Carolina, wrote: "Congress received a very serious complaint from the minister of France concerning the conduct of the magistracy in one of the states protecting a French pirate, another mournful proof that unless we have a federal government we shall not long escape from the depredations of some foreign nation." [18] James Madison, who was especially conscious of these problems, noted that foreign powers had been moderate and pacific thus far, but that this attitude might not continue; since a dispute with another nation would be a serious matter, it should not be up to "part" of the community to implicate "the whole." After sponsoring unsuccessful legislation in his state assembly to bring Virginia under tighter congressional control, he finally concluded that broad constitutional reform was the only way of preventing "those frauds on the subjects of foreign powers which might disturb the tranquility at home or involve the Union in foreign contests." [19] Nor were

17. Resolutions of Congress, unanimously approved, March 21, 1787, Report of John Jay, Secretary for Foreign Affairs, on Instructions to Mr. Adams, April 23, 1787, in W. C. Ford *et al.* (eds.), *Journals*, XXXII, 124–25, 177, 229.

18. Hugh Williamson to Samuel Johnston, May 30, 1788, in Edmund Cody Burnett (ed.), *Letters of Members of the Continental Congress* (8 vols.; Washington, D.C.: Carnegie Institution, 1921–36), VIII, 744. Correspondence between Virginia and Congress respecting this incident is to be found in *Diplomatic Correspondence, 1783–89*, I, 253–73.

19. James Madison, "Observations," April, 1787, in Hunt (ed.), *Writings of Madison*, II, 361–62.

Williamson and Madison the only persons to think in these terms. An article in the *New Jersey Gazette* of July 17, 1786, written by "several patriotic citizens," argued the need for a stronger central government by printing the British reply to John Adams' request for a speedy evacuation of the frontier posts. Following this, there appeared a list of all the states still violating the treaty. Surely Congress should be vested with "power adequate to the great national business." [20] And on August 7, 1786, a congressional committee proposed to amend the Articles so that Congress could institute a federal court of appeals to apply the law of nations and resolve all disputes between a state and a foreign nation.

However, while constitutional reform in the area of treaty enforcement might have improved Adams' cards, it would not have given him a winning hand. He would still have been handicapped by American military impotence which followed from two additional defects in the Articles of Confederation: Congress lacked both an independent source of revenue and an independent power to raise troops. The British, of course, might have clung to the posts even if the United States had carried out its treaty obligations. On the other hand, they might well have withdrawn *in spite of* American violations had they been confronted with substantial military power.

Because of its fiscal plight and its failure to obtain constitutional revision, Congress was limited to a token force of seven hundred men. In the years 1785 to 1787, when finances sank to their lowest ebb, Secretary Knox reduced his personal staff to three clerks and abolished the agencies of quartermaster, commissary, hospital, marine, and clothier. Such an army was hardly suitable even for police duty

20. The article also appeared in the *Maryland Journal* (Annapolis), July 4, 1786.

along a frontier stretching hundreds of miles. Knox termed it "very inadequate" and insisted on the need for at least fifteen hundred men. At the same time, Washington, Hamilton, and Von Steuben were recommending a professional army of European design, with fourteen infantry regiments and one of artillery totaling 2,631 officers and men. They also favored "a respectable navy to guard the coast against invasion." [21] In the fall of 1786, there seemed to be a ray of hope for the military when Congress voted to increase the size of the regular army from seven hundred to over two thousand; but by March of the following year the plan had to be abandoned for lack of funds.

The troops which Congress did manage to raise were poorly supplied and lacked the rudiments of warfare. It was characteristic that when Knox applied to the Treasury for a thousand dollars to buy ammunition urgently needed by troops on the Ohio River, the Treasury could not even make this "pitiful advance." The men were issued inferior guns, bayonets, and cartridge boxes. Their clothing was shoddy. Hats and coats were worthless, and some of the shirts were too sleazy to last more than a week. The shoes were so undersized that soldiers were reduced to their bare feet, and on one occasion only thirty men out of three companies had enough supplies to permit them to escort a party of surveyors. By October, 1788, veteran soldiers had not received an

21. Richard Henry Lee to George Washington, April 18, 1785, in James Curtis Ballagh (ed.), *The Letters of Richard Henry Lee* (2 vols.; New York: Macmillan Co., 1911–14), II, 349; Report of Secretary Knox to Congress, June 21, 1786, in W. C. Ford *et al.* (eds.), *Journals*, XXX, 346–47; Russell Frank Weigley, *History of the United States Army* (New York: Macmillan Co., 1967), 74, 80. In addition to the regulars, Washington wanted a common militia to enroll all between the ages of eighteen and fifty, and a volunteer militia ranging in age from eighteen to twenty-five, to receive twelve to twenty-five days of training per annum and to be officered by federal soldiers. Steuben wanted thirty days of training, and Hamilton's plans were even more ambitious; *ibid.*, 80.

Clark led a similar group as far as the Wabash. Both Clark and Logan usurped congressional prerogative, and, as expected, did little except increase the chances for a larger war. During the years 1783 to 1790, an estimated fifteen hundred Kentuckians were killed, and two thousand horses stolen; at the end of the period the Indians were more threatening than ever. By 1787, they had clearly outgrown any awe they might once have felt at the sight of Washington's victorious armies. They were now confederating and repudiating their solemn treaties with the United States.[24]

In addition to pursuing hostile tribesmen, the army was responsible for keeping land-hungry citizens off Indian territory, and it was as ill-prepared for the second assignment as it was for the first. Colonel Harmar razed hundreds of squatters' huts, but he despaired in 1785 of ever being able to expel the thousands of recalcitrant settlers and unlicensed traders who were violating federal boundaries.[25] By 1790 some fifty thousand persons had illegally entered upon Indian land along a line stretching from the upper Allegheny to Louisville and then out to Vincennes.

Still another congressional duty which suffered from the lack of funds and troops was that of Indian negotiations. Warfare could never be conclusive unless crowned by a treaty. Yet treaties were enormously expensive; they required generous gifts for the Indians, strong military support, and highly paid agents steeped in native customs and language. Thousands of dollars were spent on commissioners' fees, and the cost of supplies was also high. One Indian

24. Patrick Henry to Virginia Delegates in Congress, July 5, 1786, in William Wirt Henry, *Patrick Henry: Life, Correspondence and Speeches* (3 vols.: New York: Charles Scribner's Sons, 1891), III, 362–67; Richard Butler and Samuel Parsons to Congress, June 19, 1786, in W. C. Ford *et al.* (eds.), *Journals*, XXX, 350; Jensen, *New Nation*, 357.

25. Weigley, *History of U.S. Army*, 83; Jacobs, *Beginning of U.S. Army*, 23–24; Brown, "Role of the Army," 167–68.

issue of clothing for over a year, and they had not been paid for nearly two years. The result was a low rate of reenlistment and a high rate of mutiny and desertion. One court martial report referred to sixty-nine desertions; James Monroe was so concerned about the problem that he recommended a federal mutiny bill to provide heavy penalties for unauthorized disbanding.[22]

Considering the circumstances, Harmar did well; he managed with his midget force to protect a federal survey team and to erect a number of makeshift fortifications, but he could not begin to meet the challenges facing him. While local militia units shielded their home bases, federal troops were expected to take the offensive against Indian marauders, pursuing them across state borders and burning their villages; but the regulars were so feeble that roles had to be reversed, with state troops taking the lead.[23] In October, 1786, Colonel Benjamin Logan led Virginia troops in raids against Shawnee towns on the Miami, and George Rogers

22. John Chester Miller, *Alexander Hamilton and the Growth of the New Nation* (New York: Harper & Row, 1964), 149; James Ripley Jacobs, *The Beginning of the United States Army, 1783–1812* (Princeton: Princeton University Press, 1947), 37; W. C. Ford *et al.* (eds.), *Journals*, XXX, 119; Alan S. Brown, "The Role of the Army in Western Settlement: Josiah Harmar's Command, 1785–1790," *Pennsylvania Magazine of History and Biography*, XVIII (April, 1969), 169. Monroe also urged that two central arsenals be built, one on the Potomac, the other at West Point. These areas would be used to store arms and ammunition and as sites for military academies; James Monroe, "Hints," September–December, 1785, in Monroe Papers, Library of Congress, Ser. 1, Vol. I.

23. Joseph Jones to James Madison, June 7, 1787, in Worthington Chauncey Ford (ed.), *Letters of Joseph Jones of Virginia* (Washington, D.C.: Department of State, 1889), 152–53. Reginald Horsman asserts that the new government in 1789 inherited a complete breakdown of national Indian policy, and that a major offensive was needed to negotiate from strength. Otherwise, settlement of the Old Northwest would have been impossible; Reginald Horsman, *Matthew Elliot, British Indian Agent* (Detroit: Wayne State University Press, 1964), 59; Horsman, *The Frontier in the Formative Years, 1783–1815* (New York: Holt, Rinehart, and Winston, 1970), 39.

treaty conference held on the Wabash required, among other things, 18,000 pounds of beef, 21,000 pounds of flour and salt, and a huge supply of gunpowder. Congress could not always afford these outlays, as evidenced by the complaint of one of its agents: "In my last excursion I was obliged to procure supplies on my own credit. I wrote thereon last September and expected Congress would have granted something but I have received no answer." Sufficient troops were on hand for the conclusion of treaties at Fort Stanwix, Fort McIntosh, and Fort Finney; but in 1784, United States Indian agents were prevented from meeting with the Indians and negotiating an important treaty simply because they lacked a military escort. As a result, they failed to purchase lands across the Ohio River; settlers continued to pour into the area, and the situation finally exploded into hostilities.[26] It was unfortunate, of course, that Congress derived most of its revenue from western land sales which in turn depended on the strength of federal troop support. The fewer troops Congress maintained, the less land it sold; the less land it sold, the fewer troops it could afford to maintain.

Complicating the picture and rendering the army's task still more burdensome was the hostile presence of the British to the north and the Spanish to the south. Nearly every Indian raid in the Northwest was blamed on the British.[27] Lord

26. Patrick Henry to Virginia Delegates in Congress, May 16, 1786, in Henry, *Patrick Henry*, III, 350–52; Congressional Resolution of March 18, 1785, in W. C. Ford *et al.* (eds.), *Journals*, XXVIII, 180. See also *ibid.*, XXVII, 408; XXVIII, 330; John Allan to Elbridge Gerry, February 10, 1784, in Samuel Adams Papers, New York Public Library; Richard Spaight to Alexander Martin, July 23, 1784, and Samuel Hardy to Benjamin Harrison, August 3, 1784, in Burnett (ed.), *Letters of Continental Congress*, VII, 573, 579.

27. Jensen, *New Nation*, 170; George Washington to Jacob Read, November 3, 1784, in Fitzpatrick (ed.), *Writings of George Washington*, XXVII, 488; James Mercer to James Madison, November 12, 1784, in Burnett (ed.), *Letters of Continental Congress*, VII, 610; John Jay to

Dorchester sought to stem the tide of American expansion by encouraging the tribesmen to offer resistance wherever they could. Although he did not want to be drawn into a war with the United States, he supported Indian claims to all land north of the Ohio and hinted at British backing in case of a showdown. Sir John Johnston, the British Indian superintendent, promoted a large Indian confederation under the auspices of the Six Nations with the personal direction of the colorful Joseph Brant. Brant, a half-breed, had the remarkable distinction of being both a Mohawk chieftain and a captain in the British army. Educated under Crown patronage, he had rallied his people on the side of the Tories during the Revolution, spreading terror along the border between New York and Pennsylvania and perpetrating some of the bloodiest massacres in the Mohawk Valley. Now, in 1785, he was again organizing his tribesmen for war, and again with British backing. By the summer of 1787, Congress and the War Department had word that Brant was uniting "nearly all the Indians to the northward of the Ohio" and preparing for action.[28]

Thomas Jefferson, December 14, 1786, in Henry Phelps Johnston (ed.), *The Correspondence and Public Papers of John Jay* (4 vols.; New York: G. P. Putnam's Sons, 1890–93), III, 224; New York *Journal*, June 15, 1786; *Pennsylvania Gazette*, November 1, 1786. See also *Columbian Herald*, November 6, 1786; Samuel Parsons to William Samuel Johnson, November 26, 1785, in William Samuel Johnson Papers, Library of Congress; Report of United States Commissioners to the President of Congress, 1786, in Papers of the Continental Congress, National Archives, Microfilm #69, Item 56, pp. 283–85. Professor Ritcheson blames congressional weakness for what he calls the "Hobbesian" state of the frontier; Ritcheson, *Aftermath of Revolution*, 165, 260. See also Jerald A. Combs, *The Jay Treaty: Political Battleground of the Founding Fathers* (Berkeley: University of California Press, 1970), 86.

28. Randolph Chandler Downes, *Council Fires on the Upper Ohio* (Pittsburgh: University of Pittsburgh Press, 1940), 282–83; Report of Secretary of War Knox to Congress, July 18, 1787, in W. C. Ford *et al.* (eds.), *Journals*, XXXII, 368. This was confirmed by a congressional committee in August, 1787, *ibid.*, XXXIII, 478.

The British influenced the Indian in many ways. They showered him with presents and sent him Christian missionaries who mixed politics with religion. Samuel Adams, who was under no illusions in this regard, advised Congress to send a loyal missionary to the Six Nations "lest another should be employed by their society [the British Society for the Propagation of the Faith] under the pretext of promoting Christian knowledge among the Indians." [29] When talking to the natives, British traders flatly denied that George III had ceded the northwest territory to the United States and cited their occupation of the frontier posts as proof. They managed to convince the leaders of the French community at Vincennes that they were on British soil, that they were British subjects, and that they must give no assistance to the Americans.[30] On one occasion a baffled chief of the Seneca tribe traveled all the way to Congress in order to learn the truth about conflicting territorial claims. Congress received him graciously and showed him the actual peace treaty of 1783, signed by King George, wherein the Crown had formally conceded all land south of the Great Lakes. One can assume, however, that the initiative shown by this Seneca was unique and that British influence proved effective in most cases.[31]

The Spanish were also clever. They kept only one battered regiment of troops in the Floridas and Louisiana (Colonel Harmar was surprised to find only twenty regulars guarding St. Louis), but they were as determined as the British to thwart American westward expansion, and they

29. Report of United States Indian Commissioners Samuel Parsons and Richard Butler to the President of Congress, 1786, in Papers of the Continental Congress, National Archives, Microfilm #69, Item 56, pp. 283–85; Samuel Adams to Richard Henry Lee, March 24, 1785, in Samuel Adams Papers, New York Public Library.
30. Henry, *Patrick Henry*, II, 285; III, 369.
31. New York *Journal*, May 11, 1786.

derived great power from their management of the Indians and control of the lower Mississippi River. The Spanish empire could not be described, as Henry Adams later described it, as a whale, huge, helpless, and charming to its captors. Madrid refused to recognize the 31st parallel as the northern boundary of West Florida, claiming with some justification that under British rule the territory had extended beyond the 31st parallel as far north as the Yazoo River and that the boundary could not be arbitrarily changed simply because of a change in ownership. Moreover, by virtue of their successful campaign against the British during the Revolution, they claimed territory as far north as the Tennessee River and eastward to the Appalachians. For many years, their fort at Natchez, with its six- and twelve-pounders, along with other military outposts to the north and east, stood as symbols of their defiance.[32]

Esteban Miró, the Spanish governor with headquarters in New Orleans, did not need many regular soldiers because he could count on thousands of Indians who were as anxious as he was to stem the tide of American expansion. He had established a monopoly of trade with the red men and refused to deal with any who would not fight for him (treaties concluded in 1784 at Pensacola and Mobile stipulated that the tribes were to trade only with persons licensed by Spain).[33] Miró also had his own Joseph Brant in the person

32. British negotiators had inserted a secret clause in the preliminary peace negotiations with the United States to the effect that should Great Britain retain possession of West Florida in the general settlement, its boundary would remain the same. If, however, Spain won possession of West Florida at the peace table, the boundary would be shifted farther south to the 31st parallel. For the best accounts of Spanish-American relations during these years, see Bemis, *Jay's Treaty*, and Whitaker, *Spanish-American Frontier*.

33. John Jay to United States Commissioners, January 14, 1785, in *Diplomatic Correspondence, 1783–89*, I, 562; Hugh Williamson to Thomas Jefferson, December 11, 1784, in Burnett (ed.), *Letters of Continental*

of a quadroon Creek chieftain named Alexander McGillivray. At the age of twenty-four, McGillivray was sickly but uncannily clever at the art of diplomacy; he served the Spanish as a salaried Indian agent and longed for the day when American pioneers would be driven back across the Appalachians. His plan was to form a confederation of southern tribes and lead twenty thousand braves against the Americans. Unfortunately for him, fortunately for Congress, half the tribesmen refused to fight. Yet, in 1786, he touched off a war along the American frontier from Georgia to Cumberland which claimed the lives of two well-known pioneer leaders, Colonel William Christian and Colonel John Donelson. His tactics of falling upon small parties, murdering isolated individuals, stealing livestock, and destroying crops were so successful that he was able to force the frontiersmen to live in constant fear and desperation. By 1787, the American stations along the Cumberland had been reduced to the point of capitulation.[34]

As McGillivray and Brant forged combinations north and south that placed Americans in the jaws of a giant military vise, Britain and Spain wielded a second weapon by which they might dissolve American resistance where it could not be crushed. By granting or withholding control of the vital waterways over which settlers transported their farm products to market, western loyalty to Congress could be eroded. Spain, with her powerful fleet (third-ranked in the world) and in command of both banks of the lower Mississippi, could block the entrance to the Gulf of Mexico and deny Americans their customary access to the key port of New

---

*Congress*, VII, 623–24; New York *Packet*, September 4, 1787; *Gazette of the State of Georgia*, September 6, 1787.

34. *Dictionary of American Biography, s. v.* "McGillivray, Alexander."

Orleans. Whitehall held a similar monopoly over the Great Lakes. If external military pressure failed to drive the American farmer back, perhaps he might be induced to sever his frail connection with Congress in return for free food, farm equipment, military protection, and a guarantee of continued access to the trade routes.[35]

The Spanish struck in 1784 by closing the Mississippi to all United States shipping. Americans were informed that they could not use the river or transfer goods to oceangoing vessels at New Orleans unless they became Spanish subjects. Those who ignored the decree would be arrested. One of them, Thomas Amis, was apprehended by the Spanish garrison at Natchez on June 7, 1786, and stripped of his entire cargo, including 142 dutch ovens, 53 pots and kettles, 34 skillets, 33 cast iron boxes, and 50 barrels of flour.[36]

Westerners, faced with the loss of their only effective means of market transportation, were enraged. They spoke of raising ten thousand troops to march on New Orleans; and a group led by George Rogers Clark went so far as to retaliate against Spanish subjects at Vincennes, vowing that if Americans could not go down the river, the Dons would never come up.[37]

In the East, some spoke of the possibility of war even before they heard of the Amis incident. The *Massachusetts Centinel* warned that "the conduct of the Spaniards has long since evinced a hostile intention. By several late maneuvers we must conclude that a rupture between them and us . . . is

35. Whitaker, *Spanish-American Frontier*, 28; James Madison to George Washington, March 18, 1787, in Hunt (ed.), *Writings of Madison*, II, 323–24. See also Nettels, *Emergence of National Economy*, 58–59 for the location of western communities and their economic needs.
36. Report of John Jay Concerning Spanish Property, April 12, 1787, in *Diplomatic Correspondence, 1783–89*, III, 235.
37. Louis Guillaume Otto to Comte de Vergennes, March 5, 1787, in Bancroft, *Formation of the Constitution*, II, 415.

not far distant." Jefferson wrote from France that hostilities might be preferable to an unfavorable settlement. And even the circumspect Jay insisted on American navigation rights and asserted that the United States would be justified in going to war to vindicate them.[38]

But such talk was as hollow as Clark's threat to march on New Orleans. Spain had only to station one frigate at the mouth of the Mississippi and all efforts to vindicate American rights would be vain. Samuel Hardy, Virginia delegate to Congress, summed up the sober second thought of nearly everyone by observing that although Spanish actions were "a national outrage," the current situation seemed to "proscribe every idea of war. . . . Heaven forbid that Spain should drive us to this point." Richard Spaight, the North Carolina delegate, pointed out that Great Britain would delight in a Spanish-American war and take full advantage of it to improve her position in the Northwest.[39] Jay himself saw that a war for the Mississippi, without army or navy, would not only be futile but also distasteful to northerners who were in no hurry to encourage their already inadequate labor force to move west. Thus, when Madrid offered to send the smooth and polished envoy Don Diego de Gardoqui for a series of talks, Congress gladly accepted.

Gardoqui was well suited for his assignment. He spoke excellent English, having served as chief interpreter during negotiations with Arthur Lee, the American envoy to Spain in 1777. He had known Jay personally while Jay was in

38. *Massachusetts Centinel* [Boston], April 2, 1785; Report of John Jay Concerning Spanish Property, April 12, 1787, in *Diplomatic Correspondence, 1783–89*, III, 235.
39. Samuel Hardy to Patrick Henry, December 5, 1784, in Burnett (ed.), *Letters of Continental Congress*, VII, 620; Richard Spaight to Alexander Martin, December 6, 1784, *ibid.*, VII, 622. John Adams said the same thing in nearly the same words; John Adams to John Jay, April 13, 1785, in *Diplomatic Correspondence, 1783–89*, I, 482.

Madrid, and he was familiar with the United States since his family's trading house had served as a conduit for secret Spanish aid to the American Revolution.

Any hope that Congress held for vindicating its claims by talking rather than fighting soon died, however; for when the Spaniard arrived in New York City in the early summer of 1785, he had been absolutely forbidden to relinquish his country's claim to sole navigation of the Mississippi. This was the one issue on which the government of Torquemada refused to compromise as a result of its concern for Mexican security and the problem of contraband trade through New Orleans.

Spain's able new foreign minister, the Count of Floridablanca, hoped to take the sting out of his intransigence on the key issue by offering large commercial concessions. He may also have hoped to divide the Northeast from the South and West. The United States would be granted most-favored-nation status in trade, and Spanish naval masts would be purchased in the United States in return for gold and silver. This would guarantee new markets, a better balance of trade, and a supply of vital specie. In addition, Gardoqui was authorized to whittle down Spanish territorial claims in the Mississippi Valley as far as the 31st parallel—a virtual capitulation to the full United States claim and a cession of territory equivalent to most of present-day Alabama, Mississippi, and parts of Georgia, Tennessee, and Kentucky. To sweeten his offer still further, he was prepared to guarantee American boundaries and apply pressure on Britain to evacuate her frontier forts "by force of arms if otherwise it cannot be properly arranged"—the word "properly" would no doubt have given Spain an out if the United States continued to violate its treaty obligations. Last and not least, Madrid would pledge naval protection in the Mediterranean and continued diplomatic support for American negotiations with the pirate kings of North Africa.[40]

While he dangled this bait before the eyes of Jay and Congress, Gardoqui made a number of threatening intimations. Should Congress refuse to yield on the question of navigation, Spain stood ready to cut off her existing trade with America in fish, grain, flour, and rice. She would no longer overlook the nonpayment of American war debts, nor would she use her potent influence to promote peace between the United States and the pirate states of North Africa. She might even seek a détente with England.[41]

Gardoqui also made the most of his hidden resources and native charm. He escorted Mrs. Jay to dinner parties and took her dancing. He was lavish in his hospitality to influential members of Congress and stopped at nothing to gain their favor. Floridablanca had ordered him to use his funds liberally, and so he did. He lent five thousand dollars to Colonel Henry Lee, a key member of the Virginia congressional delegation; he made sure that Washington received a Spanish jackass for breeding mules at Mount Vernon (the animal was appreciatively named "Royal Gift"); and when Jay asked

40. Bemis, *Pinckney's Treaty*, 83. According to Vernon Setser, the offer of aid against pirate attack was the most coveted of Gardoqui's concessions; Setser, *The Commercial Reciprocity Policy of the United States, 1774–1829* (Philadelphia: University of Pennsylvania Press, 1937), 95. See also the relevant chapters in Whitaker, *Spanish-American Frontier*, and Lawrence S. Kaplan, *Colonies into Nation: American Diplomacy, 1763–1801* (New York: Macmillan Co., 1972), 169–70.

41. McMaster, *History of People of U.S.*, I, 413. One wonders if Jay did not prolong the talks and even raise a few false hopes in order to retain Spain's interim cooperation on trade and the Barbary negotiations. The successful treaty with Morocco, which was concluded in July, 1786, was not ratified by Morocco until 1788; and it was not until April 19, 1788, that Gardoqui finally dispatched to Madrid a report of the failure of his

for a license to import a Spanish stallion, he arranged for the steed to be shipped as an outright gift.

Gardoqui insisted that his position in the negotiations was eminently reasonable in light of the vast territory which he was offering and his country's naval power which would defeat any congressional attempt to engage in a test of strength. Congress would surely be wise to yield that which was beyond its grasp in return for rich diplomatic and commercial gains. Spain had been America's ally in fact if not in name during the revolutionary war, and one would hope that the present chance to promote a mutually valuable friendship would not be lost.

Circumstances made it hard for Jay to resist such an appeal. The country was faced with a postwar depression, exacerbated by British trade restrictions; there was an urgent need for new markets, hard currency, and peace with the Barbary coast. Easterners were not anxious to promote the interests of the West if this meant reducing the value of their land, encouraging their labor to move west, and shifting the political center of gravity away from the coast. No doubt there were also many who regarded the pioneers as a crude and illiterate lot of malcontents.

Jay argued that the westward flow of American pioneers would be irresistible in the long run and that Spain would be wise to come to terms with it while there was still time. His Catholic Majesty should not fall into the trap set by London. The English would be perfectly delighted to see Spain and America at loggerheads. Nothing that Jay said, however, could make the slightest dent in the basic issue. As the wearisome talks dragged on into 1786 and Gardoqui unveiled

---

talks. Even at this point, he was still hopeful that the negotiations might bear fruit under the new Constitution.

additional concessions, the New Yorker became convinced that it would be in the interest of the United States to accept the Spanish offer on one condition: that Congress agree only to *forbear the use* of the lower Mississippi for twenty-five or thirty years while reserving in principle *the right* to its use until such time as the nation would be in a position to vindicate it. Jay had never been optimistic about the negotiations and he was now firmly convinced that there was no diplomatic means of opening the river to American shipping. He therefore addressed Congress on August 3, 1786, and asked that his instructions be altered to remove navigation rights as a *sine qua non*. He also recommended that Congress appoint a select advisory committee to oversee his activities so that he might move with greater speed and secrecy.

Jay's reasoning on the navigation issue was persuasive. There could be no reliance upon France, he said, for Louis XVI would side with Charles III when the chips were down. Thus, if the United States wanted to retain the good will of France, the friendship of Spain must also be retained. Spanish influence would be most important in dealing with Algiers, Italy, and Portugal. Britain, of course, would like nothing better than to see her chief rival for the Spanish trade locked out. Moreover, American commerce could be vastly enriched by the kind of arrangements being offered by Gardoqui; there was hardly a single American product that would not find a market in Iberia. At the same time, if one were to make an enemy of Spain, she could prove to be a troublesome neighbor. Finally, "even if our right [to navigate the Mississippi] . . . was expressly declared in Holy Writ, we should be able to provide for the enjoyment of it no otherwise than by being in capacity to repel force by force." There were only three choices: "accommodation, or war, or disgrace. The last is the worst that can happen, the second we are unprepared for, and therefore our attention and endeavors should be bent to the first." [42]

The speech propelled Congress into a heated debate, with delegations dividing along geographical lines. Seven northern delegations voted to make the necessary concession, while all five of the southern contingents voted unanimously in the negative. James Monroe, ironically, was among the opponents. He had been the one who had offered the 1779 resolution calling for a sacrifice of American navigation claims in return for a Spanish-American alliance. By a vote of seven to five, Jay was thus authorized to go ahead with his plan even though it was clear that five opposing states would deny the necessary two-thirds majority (nine states) needed for final approval of a treaty. His request for a select advisory committee was denied.

Feeling somewhat encouraged, Jay fought through the fall of 1786 and on into 1787 for a clause which would *express the right* and *forbear the use* of the river by the United States. Gardoqui, however, would not yield even this inch. Jay sought words which would *imply the right* and *expressly forbear the use*. He devised a phrase which stated that the treaty neither asserted nor denied American rights and would address itself only to the question of temporary use. Again, Gardoqui refused to budge, although he did leave the door ajar. Jay supposed that he was writing to Madrid for further instructions.

One of the key problems was that Jay never knew where he stood with an ambivalent and indecisive Congress. Origi-

42. Jay never doubted this advice, but it must not have come easily. He had, after all, championed American navigation claims during the darkest days of the Revolution. Congress had ordered him to yield this point in 1779 in return for an alliance with Spain. He had made the offer reluctantly and withdrawn it the moment it was rejected.

nally, he had been ordered to keep Congress posted on every proposition that might pass between himself and Gardoqui. Seeing this as an "impossible" hindrance, he had insisted on the privilege of conducting the negotiations in private and at his own discretion; the glare of publicity would defeat any chance for useful diplomatic jousting. Congress had bowed to his wishes in this regard but had kept him in a quandary on his instructions. His nerves were now frayed, and he sounded exasperated in his report to congressional president Arthur St. Clair on April 11, 1787. Making clear that the atmosphere of the talks was more and more "unpleasant and unpromising," he pointed out that here was a golden opportunity to settle with Spain; Gardoqui seemed willing to concede all territorial issues. Yet Congress was still unable to decide on its policy. The Amis incident was now demanding some kind of action; in his report of April 12, Jay again struck a note of urgency by warning that the country must decide "either to wage war with Spain or settle all differences with her by treaty on the best terms" available. He would resign as negotiator if Congress could not accept the terms now offered. Congress might replace him or appoint two other agents to negotiate with him, but he had gone as far as he could on his own.

Six days later, Madison made a motion on the floor of Congress that Jay be relieved of his responsibility and that the talks be transferred from New York to Madrid and placed under the supervision of Jefferson. But when the motion was referred to Jay, he opposed it with crushing vehemence. Why should the United States stoop to Spain? Was it not an honor to negotiate on home soil? Was it not advantageous to have the American agent where he could be in close touch with Congress? If Madison meant only to give Jefferson the power to "confer," as stipulated in his motion,

Spain would not be interested and would likely interpret the move as an attempt to stall for time. A disgruntled Gardoqui would be sure to use his influence to defeat any good that might come of it. In a subtle but forceful plea of self-defense, Jay demanded to know why Congress was proposing such a strange alteration: "If discontented with their own [Spain's] negotiator, why this circuitous way of changing him? If with ours [himself] how has it happened that no symptoms of it have appeared?" Madison's proposal was dropped.

On May 9, 1787, Jay implored Congress for the last time. He wrote to St. Clair for express instructions regarding American differences with Spain. Three days later, he was informed that Congress could not agree and therefore could issue no instruction. With the Constitutional Convention getting under way, attention was shifting to Philadelphia and the talks with Gardoqui only continued *pro forma*. Jay became quite ill in the fall and he seems to have made no more serious efforts on behalf of the treaty. He plunged instead into the ratification contest, content to postpone the Spanish question until he could see the shape of things to come at home. As Congress died out of the picture, so did hopes for a diplomatic solution, at least temporarily.[43]

In the meantime, Jay's actions were castigated by the majority of southern and western leaders—so much so, in fact, that his reputation never recovered.[44] He had planted seeds

43. Report of John Jay to Arthur St. Clair, April 11, 1787, in John Jay Papers, Columbia University Special Collections; John Jay's Reports to Congress, April 18 and April 20, 1787, in Papers of the Continental Congress, Item 81, National Archives; John Jay to Arthur St. Clair, May 9, 1787, *ibid.*, Item 125.

44. Interestingly enough, he was supported by such southern leaders as Edward Rutledge of South Carolina, Richard Henry Lee of Virginia (uncle of the colonel to whom Gardoqui had made his loan of five thousand dollars) and Washington, whose knowledge of frontier problems was

for a political alliance between the South and the West which would later help carry the Jeffersonians to victory over their Federalist opponents. Furthermore, his decision provoked widespread fear of federal power and aroused sentiment for a clause in the new Constitution retaining the two-thirds majority required for senatorial approval of treaties.

The most immediate effect of Jay's strategy was to accelerate the movement toward a dissolution of the union. Ever since 1783, the idea of breaking the nation into two or three separate confederations had been fashionable in some circles, with nationalist leaders steadfastly opposing the idea on the grounds that any division would invite foreign intervention, which in turn would cause the downfall of the republican experiment. Hamilton had fought the idea in the New York assembly, reminding his colleagues that Rome conquered the members of the Achaian League by "sowing dissensions among them." David Ramsay, chairman of Congress in 1786, insisted that the union must not collapse, because "intestine wars would follow till some Caesar seized our liberties, or we would be the sport of European politics and perhaps parcelled out as appendages to their several governments." [45] But these were voices crying in the wilderness. Little by little, the Confederation government was proving to be fatally deficient. The Treasury reported on June 27, 1786, that only the adoption of a federal impost could "pre-

---

outstanding. Washington had long held that the allegiance of the West was vital for the union and that the best way to secure it was to link it with the East by a system of canals and roads. He also agreed with Jay that the United States was too weak to challenge Spain in a military contest and should therefore take advantage of Gardoqui's inviting offer. For Rutledge's support, see Rutledge's letter to Jay, November 12, 1786, in John Jay Papers, Columbia University Special Collections.

45. Edmund Cody Burnett, *The Continental Congress* (New York: W. W. Norton & Co., 1964), 641; Syrett (ed.), *Hamilton*, IV, 92. Hamilton's example of the Achaian League was only one of many historical

serve the Union of the several states from dissolution." By 1787, Congress was witnessing the failure not only of the impost amendment, but also of its efforts to gain control over foreign commerce. It remained for the Jay-Gardoqui issue to bring the union to the breaking point, with Monroe charging that Jay was deliberately forcing the issue with the South in order to split the country into separate nations. Jay himself was concerned that talk of an alleged incompatability between western and eastern interests (with which he disagreed) might reach the ears of the British who would use it to weaken the union.[46]

As it was, when news of the seven-to-five vote reached Kentucky and Tennessee in December, 1786, it ignited a bonfire of consternation in the breasts of those who regarded the use of the Mississippi as vital. Congressional military impotence, combined now with this threatened loss of livelihood, was too much for the already-weakened bonds of patriotism to withstand. James Robertson, leader of four thousand settlers along the Cumberland River, beset by five or six hundred Indian warriors, desperately in need of military reinforcement and unable to turn to North Carolina or Congress, offered to join McGillivray in a raid on Spanish garrisons. When this failed, he offered to accept the protec-

---

examples used by the nationalists to illustrate the perils of a weak Confederation. Madison's writings and the *Federalist* contain many analogies drawn from classical antiquity. A recent study of the use of historical analogy by the founding fathers is Peter C. Hoffer, "The Constitutional Crisis and the Rise of a Nationalistic View of History in America, 1786–1788," *New York History*, LII (July, 1971), 305–23. For other references to the advocacy of dissolution, see Burnett, *Continental Congress*, 595–96, 689; Main, *Antifederalists*, 283–84. According to Charles Warren, dissolution was the principal fear of the nationalists; Warren, *Making of the Constitution*, 9.

46. Burnett, *Continental Congress*, 659; John Jay to Thomas Jefferson, December 14, 1786, in John Jay Papers, Columbia University Special Collections.

tive influence of Spain. John Sevier, *beau-ideal* of the people of the Holston and governor of the self-proclaimed state of Franklin, was also ready to follow the Spanish flag. And the calumnious James Wilkinson, bright star of Kentucky politics, spent three months of the summer of 1787 conferring with Governor Miró in New Orleans. At the end of his visit, he pledged allegiance to the king of Spain and promised to deliver his area into Spanish hands.

Not that the secessionist spirit was something new. Men like Wilkinson had long felt that their loyalty to Congress could not outweigh the prospect of military and commercial gain offered by Spain; others had been flirting with the government of George III which offered the use of the Great Lakes and even military aid against Spain.[47] As early as 1784, Washington asserted that "the western settlers, (I speak now from my own observation), stand as it were upon a pivot; the touch of a feather would turn them any way;" and in the following year, Secretary Jay expressed the fear that "a considerable number of persons" had already succumbed to British wiles.[48] But by 1787, the situation had reached a critical stage. Joseph Brant, just back from London after conferring with the highest British officials, had held

47. There is mention of a British Act of Parliament designed along these lines in a letter from James Carrington to James Madison, May 31, 1788, in Burnett (ed.), *Letters of Continental Congress*, VIII, 744–45. It should be noted that neither Floridablanca nor Pitt were openly encouraging secession at this juncture; but their covert offers were so attractive that westerners had no feasible alternative in the quest for trade and security.

48. Report of John Jay to Congress, September 5, 1785, in W. C. Ford *et al.* (eds.), XXIX, 680; George Washington to Benjamin Harrison, October 10, 1784, in Fitzpatrick (ed.), *Writings of George Washington*, XXVII, 475. Recently, Edmund Morgan has written that "the most immediate threat to the American Union" was the possible "secession of the lower Mississippi and Ohio Valleys from the United States"; "The Puritan Ethic and the American Revolution," *William and Mary Quarterly*, XXIV, Ser. 3 (January, 1967), 20.

a meeting in Detroit for the purpose of achieving an Indian confederation to block any further American expansion and wipe out all settlements north of the Ohio. Brant had held similar conferences in the past only to see tribal unity undermined by congressional Indian agents; but this time his chances seemed good. The Detroit gathering angrily denounced the treaties of Forts Stanwix, McIntosh, and Finney; it repudiated all prior agreements with the United States; and it drafted a formal address to Congress from the United Indian Nations which was signed on December 18, 1786. Meanwhile, McGillivray was creating havoc in the Southwest; the Mississippi and Great Lakes trade routes were closed; and Congress had shown its willingness to acquiesce in the status quo. In short, the leaders of the frontier were looking to the future, and the future did not appear to lie with the United States. A letter which Congress received in the spring of 1787 appraised the situation in somber but accurate terms: "Preparations are now making here (if necessary) to drive the Spaniards from their settlements at the mouth of the Mississippi. In case we are not countenanced and succored by the United States (if we need it) our allegiance will be thrown off and some other power applied to. Great Britain stands ready with open arms to receive and support us. . . . You are as ignorant of this country as Great Britain was of America."[49]

Two final problems relating to national security and resulting from a lack of funds should be noted. The first of these was a series of raids on American shipping by the Barbary pirates of North Africa. These marauders from Algiers, Tunis, Tripoli, and Morocco regarded the Mediterranean as their private lake and roamed it in swift corsairs, en-

49. Copy of a letter from a gentleman at the Falls of the Ohio, December 4, 1786, in *Diplomatic Correspondence, 1783–89*, III, 248.

couraged by their rulers to prey on the vessels of any nation which refused to pay the price of "protection." The powerful Dey of Algiers was so dependent upon piracy that confiscation of ships and cargoes and the holding of crewmen for high ransom provided the main source of income for his state treasury.[50] The Mediterranean trade had traditionally been of major importance to nearly every state as well as the trans-Appalachian settlements. Jefferson estimated that in colonial days it had provided Americans with a market for one sixth of their wheat and flour, and one fourth of their dried and pickled fish. In the process, they had employed eighty to one hundred ships of twenty thousand tons apiece, manned by twelve hundred seamen annually. The United States Consul General at Paris, Thomas Barclay, wrote in 1786 that it was "absolutely essential to the commerce of our country" to be at peace with Morocco.[51]

Given the importance of this trade, there was naturally a strong desire to prevent its disruption after 1776 when the protective cover of the British flag was withdrawn. Thus, as early as 1778, Congress tried to adjust to new circumstances by securing aid from its European allies. One of the notable clauses of the Franco-American treaty of amity and commerce (1778) was a promise by Louis XVI that his government would employ its "good offices" in protecting American commerce from the pirates. A treaty with the Netherlands (1782) contained a similar provision. And dur-

50. Milton Cantor, "Joel Barlowe's Mission to Algiers," *The Historian*, XXIV (1963), 176. According to Cantor, commercial seizures were so important to the Dey of Algiers that cessation of customary practices would quite possibly "cost him his head." He could not afford to be at peace with too many nations at one time.
51. Raymond Bixler, *The Open Door on the Old Barbary Coast* (New York: Pageant Press, 1959), 10; Ray Watkins Irwin, *The Diplomatic Relations of the United States with the Barbary Powers, 1776–1816* (Chapel Hill: University of North Carolina Press, 1931), 34.

ing the peace negotiations of 1782–1783, the American team tried unsuccessfully to obtain the same pledge from Great Britain.[52]

A series of unfortunate events then followed in quick succession. On October 1, 1783, the American ship *Betsey* was seized by Moroccan pirates and held hostage at Tangier. Congress responded by designating Adams, Franklin, and Jefferson as a commission of three to treat with each of the Barbary powers; but before anything further could be done, Algiers concluded a peace with Spain and gained full freedom to attack American shipping beyond Gibraltar. On July 27, 1785, the Yankee ship *Maria* was captured just as it was about to enter Cadiz. All its merchandise was seized, and its crewmen were stripped, taken to Algiers, and enslaved. Three days later, the Philadelphia brig *Dauphin* was seized. And on October 13, 1785, when news of the capture of the two ships reached Congress, a letter from John Paul Jones arrived at the same time informing all the delegates that Algiers had formally declared war on the United States.[53]

American shipowners dependent upon the Mediterranean trade faced ruinous consequences. Congress was in no position to provide naval protection since it had just been forced to sell the few armed vessels owned by the United States

52. See Irwin, *Diplomatic Relations*, 20–24.
53. John Adams to John Jay, December 15, 1784, in *Diplomatic Correspondence, 1783–89*, I, 471; North Carolina delegates to Congress to Alexander Martin, March 1, 1785, in Burnett (ed.), *Letters of Continental Congress*, VIII, 50; W. C. Ford *et al.* (eds.), *Journals*, XXX, 11–12; Luella J. Hall, *The United States and Morocco, 1776–1956* (Metuchen, N. J.: Scarecrow Press, 1971), 49. The American ships which ventured into the Mediterranean depended on convoy protection by Dutch or Spanish cruisers, and there was always the fear of a sudden Algerian-Portuguese peace. Such a peace was arranged by the British in 1793 and it resulted, as expected, in the immediate capture of eleven American vessels and a hundred seamen; James A. Field, Jr., *America and the Mediterranean World, 1776–1882* (Princeton: Princeton University Press, 1967), 34–38.

at the end of the Revolution. Insurance rates rose from 2 to 5 or 6 percent, and it became difficult to find sailors willing to navigate where Barbary activity had been reported. Rufus King, a promising young Massachusetts delegate to Congress, observed that "even our merchants charter foreign vessels which are protected from the Barbary cruisers to carry our produce to market." King's assessment must have been accurate, because Jefferson reported as late as 1790 that American trade to Mediterranean ports had "not been resumed at all since the peace." [54]

Aside from any consideration of economic loss, serious in itself, public opinion in the United States was "deeply shocked by the taking of American citizens into Moslem captivity." On December 28, 1785, a letter was read on the floor of Congress in which some of the prisoners described the details of their capture and imprisonment. "The severities we endure," wrote three American ship captains, "are beyond comprehension; we are stript of our wearing apparel, and brought to a state of bondage and misery." Many captives were forced to carry heavy stone and lumber on long hauls over mountainous roads. Some retained a degree of freedom; and at least one, James Cathcart, rose through the ranks of Moslem officialdom to become the Dey's chief Christian clerk. But even Cathcart was subjected to insult

54. Thomas Fitzsimmons to James Searle, April 4, 1785, in Emmet Collection, #9465, New York Public Library; Rufus King to John Adams, May 5, 1786, in Charles R. King, *The Life and Correspondence of Rufus King* (6 vols.; New York: G. P. Putnam's Sons, 1894–1900), I, 173; John Adams to John Jay, December 15, 1784, in *Diplomatic Correspondence, 1783–89*, I, 471; *Massachusetts Centinel*, April 27, 1785; New York *Gazette*, January 2, 1786; St. George Tucker, *Reflections on the Policy and Necessity of Encouraging the Commerce of the Citizens of the United States of America and of Granting Them Exclusive Privileges of Trade* (Richmond and New York: Sam and John Loudon, 1786), 12; Nettels, *Emergence of National Economy*, 57.

and nearly to execution. Others, less fortunate, were mistreated to the point of physical injury. Some went blind, and thirty eventually died of the plague. Congressional delegates received petitions urging them to deal speedily with the Barbary pirates, and the president of Congress, Richard Henry Lee, warned that "if we are not lucky enough to purchase a peace from these barbarians before they taste the sweets of plundering our commerce, it may be long before we can quiet them and be most difficult to accomplish." [55]

Congress gave the Adams-Franklin-Jefferson team a portfolio of eighty thousand dollars and authorized them to hire special agents, if necessary, for the purpose of buying peace with Morocco, Algiers, Tunis, and Tripoli. But the money that Congress was able to raise proved insufficient. Only Morocco, whose sultan happened to be a person of just and liberal disposition, would settle for reasonable terms. Sidi Muhammad ordered the release of the *Betsey* in July, 1785, and in 1786 agreed to a milestone treaty which incorporated the principles of most-favored-nation and neutral rights. This was the first treaty between a Barbary and a Christian power ever to exclude provision for tribute. The other three states demanded exorbitant sums. Adams, who preferred tribute to a costly war, held several conferences with the Tripolitan ambassador, Abdrahaman. It is hard to imagine a straitlaced New Englander inhaling perfumed smoke and imploring the favor of a turbaned Mussulman, but there he was. Abdrahaman talked on and on, assuring Adams that he desired peace from the depths of his soul; his entire life was dedicated to doing good, and nothing would delight him more than

55. Henry G. Barnby, *The Prisoners of Algiers: An Account of the Forgotten American-Algerian War, 1785–1797* (New York: Oxford University Press, 1966), 215; *Gentleman's Magazine*, LVI (February, 1786), 172; Richard Henry Lee to Samuel Adams, October 17, 1785, in Samuel Adams Papers, New York Public Library.

friendship between his country and the United States; war would be ghastly to contemplate, especially between Christian and Turk. All that Adams need do to ensure peace was to make an offering of $200,000! Adams was not surprised, for he knew the Dutch were paying Algiers an annual tribute of $100,000. The British were said to have spent $90,000 between 1759 and 1789 on gifts for the Dey of Algiers alone, and Spain was estimated to have purchased five years of peace with Algiers for four and a half million dollars.[56] Even so, Abdrahaman's price was impossibly steep, and the same held true for Algiers and Tunis.

The very act of maintaining diplomatic relations with the Barbary powers was costly. American envoys were pressed for exotic gifts such as jeweled weapons, fine garments, and modern warships. Every time a ruler died or another came to power, every time a marriage or birth occurred in the royal family, every time a holy day was celebrated, the American agent was expected to furnish a suitable present. Every time the United States sent a new consul, he had to bring some form of largess—and the Barbary rulers seem to have insisted on frequent changes of consuls! [57]

Attempts to ransom the captives proved no more successful than the peace negotiations. In March, 1786, Congress sent John Lamb, a brigadier general and customs collector for the port of New York, on a mission to Algiers with

56. Irwin, *Diplomatic Relations*, 12; John Adams to John Jay, December 15, 1784; *Diplomatic Correspondence, 1783–89*, I, 471; Gilbert Chinard, *Honest John Adams* (Boston: Little, Brown & Co., 1933), 201; Page Smith, *John Adams* (2 vols.; Garden City, N. Y.: Doubleday and Co., 1962), II, 618. The Moroccan treaty was approved by Congress on July 18, 1787; news of its ratification by Morocco was received in Madrid on November 2, 1788; and Thomas Barclay, who had represented the United States, was commended by Congress for his outstanding efforts. The total cost to the United States was about thirty thousand dollars.

57. Irwin, *Diplomatic Relations*, 199.

authorization to secure the release of twenty-one American prisoners at a price of two hundred dollars each. The Dey, however, wanted six times this much, and Lamb advised Congress to save its money.[58] Jefferson sought the aid of a religious order known as the Mathurins or "Order of the Holy Trinity and Redemption of Captives" which, for centuries, had made a specialty of negotiating the ransom of Barbary prisoners. But Jefferson was no more successful than Adams or Lamb, although he embarrassed Congress by agreeing to pay the Mathurins ten thousand dollars more than the Treasury could afford.[59]

Some leaders opposed the payment of any tribute at all on general principles. Jay, as mentioned before, had hoped to obtain Spanish naval aid against the pirates and, in his negotiations with Gardoqui, had won a promise of such aid in return for abandoning American navigation claims on the Mississippi. When his treaty was rejected, he felt Congress should urge American merchants to arm their vessels and, if necessary, provide subsidies for this purpose. He also wanted to build a naval squadron of five forty-gun ships for the express purpose of patrolling the Mediterranean. If the arming of merchantmen led to war, Jay would not flinch. "The

58. Nettels, *Emergence of National Economy*, 67; Report of the Treasury Board, July 31, 1787, in W. C. Ford *et al.* (eds.), *Journals*, XXXIII, 442. The Pennsylvania Society for Promoting Abolition of Slavery appealed to the Constitutional Convention in Philadelphia to abolish the slave trade in America and argued that "the captivity and sufferings of our American brethren in Algiers seems to be intended by Divine Providence to awaken us to a sense of the injustice and cruelty of dooming our African brethren to perpetual slavery and misery"; *Gentleman's Magazine*, LVII (October, 1787), 925.

59. Irwin, *Diplomatic Relations*, 44–45. Only in May of 1789 did Jefferson receive even slight encouragement from Congress in the form of a promise that funds would eventually be forthcoming. The promised funds did not materialize, however, before the Mathurin Order collapsed under the impact of the French Revolution; *ibid.*, 45–46.

great question," he wrote, "is whether we shall wage war or pay tribute. I, for my part, prefer . . . war." The only problem with Jay's solution was that armaments and warships were expensive, and the funds were nowhere in sight. Jefferson was so angered by the refusal of Britain and France to protect Americans against Barbary depredations that he suggested in January of 1786 that Congress should be empowered to levy a special tariff on European commerce so as to compensate for the expense incurred in obtaining "freedom of navigation in European seas." Basically, however, he believed there should be one answer to Barbary rulers if they refused to negotiate a reasonable peace:

> If they refuse why not go to war with them? Spain, Portugal, Naples, and Venice are now at war with them; every part of the Mediterranean therefore would offer us friendly ports. We ought to begin a naval power if we are to carry on our own commerce. Can we begin it on a more honorable occasion or with a weaker foe? I am of opinion Paul Jones with half a dozen frigates would totally destroy their commerce, not by attempting bombardments, but by constant cruising and cutting them to pieces by piecemeal.[60]

This course of action, he felt, was recommended by justice, honor, and self-respect. "I ask a fleet of one hundred and fifty guns," he said, "the one half of which shall be in constant cruise." He hoped, however, that the United States would not have to fight alone, and he proposed a plan for

60. Report of the Secretary for Foreign Affairs to Congress, October 20, 1785, in W. C. Ford *et al.* (eds.), *Journals*, XXIX, 843; Louis Guillaume Otto to Comte de Vergennes, October 8, 1785, in Bancroft, *Formation of the Constitution*, I, 460; John Jay to Marquis de Lafayette, February 16, 1787, in *Diplomatic Correspondence, 1783–89*, I, 321; Irwin, *Diplomatic Relations*, 51; Thomas Jefferson to James Monroe, November 11, 1784, in Monroe Papers, Library of Congress, Ser. 1, Vol. I. Jones was at this time unemployed and a strong advocate of such action.

collective security which won the endorsement of Portugal, Naples, the two Sicilies, Venice, Malta, Denmark, and Sweden.[61]

Many persons besides Jefferson hoped to see American naval power strengthened. The Barbary outrages were a painful reminder that the wartime navy had been sold and dismantled. What would happen if the nation should be involved in another war, this time without French aid? Perhaps Congress would not be as fortunate as it had been in 1781. As one author put it, "We have fatally experienced the want of a naval force heretofore: we may at a future day deplore the want of an ally to supply the deficiency as formerly." Pierse Long, delegate to Congress from New Hampshire, asked simply, "Is there no way that can be found out to begin a navy?" The influential Virginia politician, William Grayson, proposed a plan which also called for naval power. His idea was to form an alliance with European powers to maintain a permanent naval force that would guard the Mediterranean for peaceful shipping. Each participating country would furnish one naval squadron. A similar possibility would be to invite the Order of Malta to assume responsibility for protecting all ships belonging to the contracting parties. Each country would furnish a quota of money to enable the Order to maintain a constant force at sea.[62]

The problem with Grayson's plan, as with Jefferson's and all others, was a lack of funds. Secretary Jay pointed out

61. Thomas Jefferson to John Adams, July 11, 1786, in *Diplomatic Correspondence, 1783–89*, I, 792; Irwin, *Diplomatic Relations*, 50.

62. Tucker, *Reflections*, 9; Pierse Long to John Langdon, August 6, 1786, in Burnett (ed.), *Letters of Continental Congress*, VIII, 414; motion made in Congress by William Grayson and seconded by John Kean, July 27, 1787, in W. C. Ford *et al.* (eds.), *Journals*, XXXIII, 419; *Pennsylvania Gazette*, September 27, 1786.

that the United States could not enter such an alliance because it could not supply its quota of the money or ships. Such measures could only be undertaken if Congress could, in Jay's words, "draw forth the resources of the country." [63] But Congress found it so difficult under the Articles of Confederation to raise money that it could no more embark on a naval construction program than it could protect its frontier or pay its debts.

One other source of danger stemming from insufficient federal taxing power was the foreign debt. National credit would be an obvious and invaluable asset in time of war. As Washington put it, "Were we without credit, we might be crushed by a nation of much inferior resources but possessing higher credit." [64] Moreover, the international law of this time regarded consistent failure to pay debts as a just cause for armed intervention by the creditor nation. Arrears of interest and capital on the American foreign debt mounted steadily during the years 1783–1788, and Congress was forced to resort to the dangerous expedient of borrowing capital from one source to pay interest on another.[65] John

63. Report of John Jay to Congress, August 2, 1787, in W. C. Ford *et al.* (eds.), *Journals*, XXXIII, 452; John Jay to Thomas Jefferson, December 14, 1786, in Johnston (ed.), *Papers of John Jay*, III, 223.

64. George Washington to Thomas Jefferson, May 2, 1788, in Washington Papers, Library of Congress, Ser. 4, Vol. 240. See also Isaac Lee to William Lee, July 18, 1785, in Perkins Papers, Clements Library, Ann Arbor, Michigan; Samuel Otis to James Warren, February 6, 1788, in Burnett (ed.), *Letters of Continental Congress* VIII, 696; Miller, *Alexander Hamilton*, 150; Burnett, *Continental Congress*, 642; John Adams to Arthur Lee, September 6, 1785, in Adams (ed.), *Works of John Adams*, IX, 537; Thomas Jefferson to Commissioners of the Treasury, February 7, 1788, in *Diplomatic Correspondence, 1783–89*, II, 143; *Pennsylvania Gazette*, June 21, 1786, Richard Henry Lee to Patrick Henry, January 21, 1785, in Ballagh (ed.), *Letters of Lee*, II, 325; W. C. Ford *et al.* (eds.), *Journals*, XXX, 56–57; XXXI, 753–58.

65. In the period 1784–1789 the principal of the foreign debt increased from $7,830,517 to over $10,000,000 while the arrears of foreign interest grew from $67,137 to $1,640,071; quoted from Charles J. Bullock, "The

Adams warned that if the United States did not satisfy its creditors, "it will be but a few years . . . before we are involved in another war." Copies of his numerous letters were sent to all the state governors by the president of Congress, who remarked that "the precarious state of our public credit abroad is so powerfully expressed in these letters as to render a comment unnecessary. They prove incontestably the necessity of immediate vigorous measures for supplying the treasury of the United States. . . . Your enlightened legislature, Sir, will see the close connection that subsists between national safety and national faith—that the loss of the latter will have the most malignant effects upon the former." [66] No one knew how France would react to American forestallment. "I wish to God," exclaimed one writer, "we had paid our debts to our good ally and were well rid of her— for there's danger in remaining the connection of a power whose character it is to destroy her friends—not her enemies." French treatment of Poland, Geneva, Holland, and now the Turks should be a warning. Nor could Dutch loans be taken for granted. The New York *Packet* printed an article on April 13, 1786, to emphasize the danger of not

---

Finances of the United States from 1775 to 1789, with Especial Reference to the Budget," *Bulletin of the University of Wisconsin* (Economics, Political Science, and History Series), Vol. I, No. 2 (June, 1895), 117–273, in Channing, *History of U. S.*, III, 463. See also Treasury Board Report, February 8, 1786, in W. C. Ford *et al.* (eds.), *Journals*, XXX, 54–59. At the beginning of 1786 the national debt stood at $42,000,000. Of this nearly $8,000,000 was owed to foreign countries, and the interest on the foreign debt amounted to $2,415,956; McMaster, *History of People of U.S.*, I, 356.

66. John Adams to Robert R. Livingston, July 18, 1783, in Francis Wharton (ed.), *The Revolutionary Diplomatic Correspondence of the United States* (6 vols.; Washington, D.C.: Government Printing Office, 1889), VI, 562; John Adams to Arthur Lee, September 6, 1785, in Adams (ed.), *Works of John Adams* IX, 537; President Richard Henry Lee to the Governors of all the States, January 24, 1785, in Papers of the Continental Congress, National Archives, Microfilm Roll #24, p. 319.

paying debts owed in Holland: "Can it be supposed that our creditors will not avail themselves of those means of payment to which our weakness invites. . . . Defeating the British army was not more necessary to the establishment of this empire, than providing for the foreign debt is to its preservation." One week later, the *Packet* again sounded the alarm: "The European powers will be paid, right or wrong, or occupy some part of the territory of a fraudulent, faithless nation, as a security and a pledge. What part is fit and deserving of French fleets and Spanish garrisons as capital towns in the most faithless part of the thirteen states: New York and Albany." [67]

In summary, Congress lacked two prerequisites for a satisfactory national defense under the Articles. The first was exclusive control of foreign relations; and the second, an independent source of revenue. In the case of the former, Congress had been vested with the all-important treaty power but could not exercise it effectively. Individual states violated the Anglo-American accords with impunity, they hamstrung federal Indian policy, and were capable of antagonizing foreign nations to the point of jeopardizing the security of the entire union. In the case of congressional inability to tax, there were unfortunate implications for every aspect of national defense including troop strength, troop supply, Indian relations, naval power, payments of ransom, tribute, and the national debt.

Such a prospect and such weakness contributed substantially to the mounting demand for constitutional reform which reached a climax in the years 1786 and 1787.

We have seen how the maverick record of individual

67. John Armstrong to Horatio Gates, May 30, 1788, in Burnett (ed.), *Letters of Continental Congress*, VIII, 743; New York *Packet*, April 13, 1786.

states in the area of foreign relations caused congressman Hugh Williamson to prefer a stronger central government to the danger of unwanted war; how the same problem caused James Madison to sponsor legislation in the Virginia assembly which would prevent his state from further encroachment on federal authority; and how a congressional committee in the summer of 1786 proposed a constitutional amendment providing for a federal court of appeals to resolve all disputes arising between a state and a foreign nation.

More important, however, than the problem of treaty enforcement as an issue in the nationalist movement, was the weakness of the armed forces. Benjamin Hawkins was aware of this when he depicted Spain as a force which "strengthens our bonds of union," and so was John Jay when he termed the Barbary threat a blessing in disguise, for "the more we are ill-treated abroad the more we shall unite and consolidate at home." Jay's role in the nationalist movement can hardly be overestimated. As secretary for foreign affairs, he was in a uniquely favorable position to promote nationalism by corresponding not only with the state governors but with the various legislatures as well. And his zeal was remarkable. His advocacy of a stronger government was surpassed by no one with the possible exception of George Washington, and it was reiterated in innumerable letters. He even campaigned for intermarriage between persons of different states because "they tend to assimilate the states and to promote one of the first wishes of my heart, viz. to see the people of America become one nation in every respect." [68]

68. Benjamin Hawkins to Thomas Jefferson, March 8, 1787, in Burnett (ed.), *Letters of Continental Congress*, VIII, 552; John Jay to the president of Congress, October 13, 1785, and to John Adams, May 4, 1786, in Johnston (ed.), *Papers of John Jay*, III, 171, 195. For samples of Jay's enthusiasm in this vein see his letters dated July 19, 20, 24, 28, 1783; April 7,

It is significant that all forty-four officers of the Continental army from the state of Pennsylvania who were alive in 1787, and whose views are known, were in favor of the new Constitution.[69] Many felt that with a stronger army, Britain might be more easily persuaded to abandon the frontier posts. Likewise, Spain's decision to deprive American farmers of vital access to the Mississippi River was viewed as a direct consequence of America's military impotence. The Spanish, who were by no means military giants, might be frightened into an equitable settlement if Congress could only bolster its military potential. The North Carolina delegation to Congress wrote: "We can say, in general, the conduct of Spain on this subject is not liberal, and we presume it would be very different if they thought us a more formidable neighbor." Rhode Island's delegation expressed alarm at both the pirate raids, which threatened to choke off Mediterranean markets, and the fact that "an enemy on our frontiers stands prepared to take every advantage of our prostrate situation. . . . Our federal government is but a name; a mere shadow without any substance; and we think it our duty to inform the state that it is totally inefficient for the purpose of the Union." [70]

Jay didn't believe that the country could develop sufficient national spirit under the Articles of Confederation to defend itself from eventual European intervention, and John Adams warned that unless a better revenue system

---

December 13, 1784; May 31, July 15, October 13, 14, 1785; January 9, February 22, May 29, and July 14, 1786, *ibid.* Similar remarks by Rufus King and Stephen Higginson with regard to military weakness are given in Jensen, *New Nation*, 256.

69. Weigley, *History of U.S. Army*, 84–85.

70. North Carolina Delegates to North Carolina Assembly, December 15, 1787, in Burnett (ed.), *Letters of Continental Congress*, VIII, 690; Rhode Island Delegates to Congress to Governor John Collins, September 28, 1786, *ibid.*, VIII, 471–72.

was devised, "every servant of the United States in Europe ought to go home, give up all points, and let our exports be done in foreign bottoms." James Monroe considered it strange, in light of hostile European designs, that "we sho'd be disputing whether we shall . . . strengthen the Union." Another congressman noted that Savannah was threatened by seven or eight thousand Indian warriors, and warned, "if we are to be much longer unblessed [sic] with an efficient, national government, destitute of funds . . . I fear we shall become contemptible even in the eyes of the savages themselves." In line with this sentiment was an amendment to the Articles offered by South Carolina congressman Charles Pinckney in May of 1786 which would have given Congress the power to raise troops independently of the state legislatures. Finally, Washington observed that "the importance assumed by Great Britain" and "other powers on the continent are strong . . . motives for us to establish a well-toned government." [71]

One American historian has said that "in an indirect sense, the brutal Dey of Algiers was a Founding Father of the Constitution." [72] Perhaps the European monarchs and the American Indians also deserve membership in the society of founding fathers. In any case, the sense of national insecurity and of impending danger was a major drive wheel in the movement for constitutional reform which culminated in the Philadelphia convention of 1787. Together with other

71. Frank Monaghan, *John Jay* (New York: Bobbs-Merrill Co., 1935), 279; Irwin, *Diplomatic Relations*, 52–53; James Monroe to James Madison, December 26, 1785, in Hamilton (ed.), *Writings of Monroe*, I, 111–12; Nicholas Gilman to John Sullivan, November 7, 1787, in Burnett (ed.), *Letters of Continental Congress*, VIII, 676; George Washington to Henry Knox, March 3, 1788, in Fitzpatrick (ed.), *Writings of George Washington*, XXIX, 435.

72. Thomas Andrew Bailey, *A Diplomatic History of the American People* (New York: Appleton-Century-Crofts, 1955), 65.

forces it not only gave rise to the convention but also determined the kind of document which emerged and ensured its ultimate acceptance. Throughout the ratification campaign, Federalists would refer continually to the hostility of Europe and the insecurity of the Confederation.

# II

# The Challenge
of Foreign Trade
Restrictions

*It may be doubted whether any of the evils proceeding from
the feebleness of the Federal Government contributed more
to that Great revolution which introduced the present system, than the deep and general conviction that commerce
ought to be regulated by Congress.*

CHIEF JUSTICE JOHN MARSHALL[1]

Urgent as military matters might have seemed at the time,
no problem concerned more people or evoked a greater demand for constitutional reform than that of foreign trade
restrictions. It was a problem which led first to Annapolis
and later to Philadelphia where in 1787 the doors opened
upon a range of reform which far transcended the problem
itself.

For a century and a half the American economy had
functioned within the protective folds of the British Empire. Sources of credit were established and markets secured
in order to suit the special needs of the colonists. Prior to
the Revolution, American vessels carried a major share of

1. Brown v. Maryland (1827), quoted in Warren, *Making of the Constitution,* 568.

52

imperial commerce. The shipbuilding and whaling industries flourished. Moreover, although Americans could not market much of their agricultural produce in Britain, they were able to purchase British manufactures by selling food and wood products to the British West Indies in return for specie.[2] A Yankee ship might sail from Boston to Jamaica to exchange dairy products for specie, then to London for tools and textiles, and finally home to New England. Another "triangular" voyage might involve the exchange of New England rum for African slaves, slaves for Caribbean molasses, and molasses for more rum. In each case, access to the British West Indies was the key to a favorable balance of trade.

Once the United States gained independence, there was no assurance that such an arrangement would continue. In fact, its continuance would have constituted an unprecedented privilege never before granted by Parliament to a foreign country. However, because the established commer-

2. Benjamin Franklin stated before a committee of the House of Commons, with reference to the proposed Stamp Act, that the colonies imported £500,000 of British goods while exporting only £40,000. The balance, he said, was made up by selling goods to the West Indies in exchange for money; Franklin's Testimony Before a Committee of the House of Commons in 1766 in Albert Bushnell Hart (ed.), *American History Told by Contemporaries* (5 vols.; New York: Macmillan Co., 1897–1929), II, 407–11. According to one pamphleteer, three fourths of American provisions and nearly the entire grain trade had found its market in the British West Indies; Tucker, *Reflections*, 8. For further evidence that the United States had served traditionally as the granary of the British West Indies and for the best account of the incredible variety and purpose of other items traded to the British islands see William Bingham, *Letter from an American Now Resident in London to a Member of Parliament on the Subject of the Restraining Proclamation and Containing Strictures on Lord Sheffield's Pamphlet on the Commerce of the American States* (Philadelphia: Robert Bell, 1784) and Sir Philip Gibbes, bart., *Reflections on the Proclamation of the Second of July 1783, Relative to the Trade Between the United States of America and the West-India Islands* (London: n.p., 1783), 14.

cial pattern had benefited all concerned, and in view of the fact that the United States had opened its ports to British ships, it was hoped that American vessels would be accorded easy access to the British West Indies. Indeed, there was even hope that the imperial navigation laws would be relaxed to permit an American carrying trade between the British West Indies and other parts of the world.[3]

Several indications pointed in this direction. First, the principle of commercial reciprocity had been included in the preliminary peace treaty. Second, the British minister in charge of negotiations, the earl of Shelburne, believed strongly in Adam Smith's theory of free trade. Finally, the West Indian planters were firmly committed to the traditional pattern of trade, and their views were given powerful expression by Edmund Burke and by Shelburne's successor, William Pitt. Pitt, who was Chancellor of the Exchequer, master of Parliament, and a financial wizard at the age of twenty-six, introduced an astounding bill on March 3, 1783, which would have restored to Americans almost all of their former trade privileges. Among other things, it would have admitted to the ports of Great Britain and her possessions in the New World American goods in American bottoms on the same terms as British goods in British bottoms. It would thus have allowed Americans to reap all the advantages of their former colonial status without any of the restrictions.[4]

John Adams wrote in his diary that "time and the natural course of things will produce a good treaty of commerce.

3. John Francis Mercer to George Weedon, March 11, 1783; James Madison to Thomas Jefferson, May 13, 1783, in Burnett (ed.), *Letters of Continental Congress*, VII, 70, 163.
4. Bancroft, *Formation of the Constitution*, I, 55–56. For a good account of the British attitude, see Vincent Todd Harlow, *The Founding of the Second British Empire, 1763–1793* (2 vols.; New York: Longman's Green and Co., 1952), Vol. I, Chap. 9, and Burt, *United States*, 55–59.

Great Britain will soon see and feel the necessity of alluring American commerce to her ports by facilities and encouragements of every kind." [5] Adams reasoned that since Britain did not want her American trade siphoned off to the Continent, she would bid high to retain the lion's share—even granting reciprocity if necessary. This was a fair assumption, but it faded quickly.

Pitt's bill met staunch opposition from shippers and red-blooded nationalists. Powerful voices in Parliament such as William Eden (later Lord Auckland) pleaded for the maintenance of imperial traditions and warned that by ruining the British carrying trade, the bill would eventually sap the lifeblood of the Royal Navy. In addition, Lord Sheffield, not content to speak out in Parliament, published his celebrated *Observations on the Commerce of the American States with Europe and the West Indies* (London, 1783) in which he argued that since Congress was powerless to regulate commerce under Article IX of the Articles of Confederation it could not restrict British trade. Britain could therefore retain all former advantages without making a single concession. He also observed shrewdly that "no treaty can be made with the American states that can be binding on all of them. . . . When treaties are necessary, they must be made with the states separately. Each state has reserved every power relative to imports, exports, prohibitions, duties etc. to itself." In conclusion, he urged heavy restrictions on American trade with the British West Indies in order to aid British merchants and upset the American economy.[6]

5. Entry for April 28, 1783, in Lyman Henry Butterfield (ed.), *Diary and Autobiography of John Adams* (4 vols.; New York: Atheneum, 1962), III, 113.

6. John Baker Holroyd, First Earl of Sheffield, *Observations on the Commerce of the American States with Europe and the West Indies* (London: J. Debrett, 1783), 69–70. The pamphlet evoked a blast of criticism from America including: *The Commercial Conduct of the United States*

Sheffield's pamphlet created a sensation and made its mark on the new Fox-North ministry. A debate in the House of Lords revealed a widespread consensus that American trade should indeed be taken for granted, and that Congress was too weak to retaliate against British discriminatory restrictions. Many felt that the United States had no government at all. Lord Walsingham thought that laws applying to the United States should be applied to the ships of each state separately; and he was seconded by Lord Thurlow. In the end, the offer of commercial reciprocity was withdrawn, and regulation of commerce with the United States was shifted to the Privy Council.[7]

The Council acted quickly. On July 2, 1783, it issued a decree closing the British West Indies to American ships and sailors; the decree barred the entry of all American goods into the British West Indies except for an enumerated list which did not include such important items as dairy products, fish, and cured meats.[8]

In recent years, questions have been raised regarding the

---

*of America Considered by a Citizen of New York* (New York: S. and J. Loudon, 1786); *A Few Salutary Hints, Pointing Out the Policy and Consequences of Admitting British Subjects to Engross Our Trade and Become Our Citizens* (New York: S. Kollock, 1786); Tench Coxe, *A Brief Examination of Lord Sheffield's Observations on the Commerce of the United States* (Philadelphia: M. Carey, 1791); Bingham, *Letter from an American.*

7. Sheffield's pamphlet ran through two editions in 1783 and reached a sixth in 1784. See Bancroft, *Formation of the Constitution,* I, 62–63.

8. W. L. Grant, James Munro, and A. W. Fitzroy (eds.), *Acts of the Privy Council of England, Colonial Series* (6 vols.; Hereford and London, 1908–12), V, 530. There is irony in the fact that these Orders in Council were issued on precisely the same day the Continental Congress had chosen to declare independence in 1776. Both days were weighted with momentous implications. Just as July 2, 1776, can be regarded as the beginning of a new era in American history, July 2, 1783, can been seen as the first link in a chain of events which terminated in the formation of a new and lasting political order.

effectiveness of these restrictions. It has been shown, for example, that smuggling occurred immediately after the war and was welcomed by island officials. However, there is also evidence that after a brief period the restrictions were enforced with some success and that they curtailed American trade substantially. Much of the smuggling from this time on seems to have gravitated toward the Dutch West Indies, Surinam in particular, rather than either the British or French possessions.[9]

When senior officer Horatio Nelson was sent to patrol the West Indies in November, 1784, he found Americans conducting business as usual with the connivance of the local naval commander, Sir Richard Hughes, and the local governors. However, he "promptly suppressed" the illicit trade, seizing five of the ships engaged in it, to the great consternation of the local merchants whose wrath dogged him for years in the form of law suits. Furthermore, although Hughes did not support Nelson's conduct, he took credit for it when the officers of the Royal Treasury thanked him in March of 1786 for his zeal in promoting British commerce. Americans credited Nelson's patrol with unusual vigilance

9. Merrill Jensen has argued that due to smuggling and local connivance, "the British order in council remained for the most part ineffective" and "trade with the West Indies went on after the war as it had done before"; *New Nation*, 198. For a similar view, see Alice B. Keith, "Relaxations in the British Restrictions on the American Trade with the British West Indies, 1783–1802," *Journal of Modern History*, Vol. XX, No. 1 (March, 1948), 1–18. But see also Lowell Joseph Ragatz, *The Fall of the Planter Class in the British Caribbean, 1763–1833* (New York and London: Century Co., 1928), 184–94. Ragatz maintains that the Orders in Council caused a major trade realignment and much distress *despite* widescale smuggling. Curtis P. Nettels, whose specialty is the economic history of this period, maintains that American trade "suffered severe losses" as a result of the Orders in Council; Nettels, *Emergence of National Economy*, 55. See also *Gazette of the State of Georgia*, April 12, 1787; McDonald, *E Pluribus Unum*, 203–204; Combs, *Jay Treaty*, 84, 87–88.

in preventing anything that resembled an American ship from passing within three leagues of any British island. One American smuggler was reported to have wangled permission to land on one of the British islands in order to repair an alleged leak. But he also had his four hundred barrels of flour confiscated in the process. Other reports testified in more general terms to the "danger of sending the produce of America to the West Indies in any other than British bottoms, navigated according to law." [10]

Professor Curtis P. Nettels cites impressive statistics to document a sharp decline in the United States-West Indian trade both in exports and imports during the postwar period. Ships which came from the British West Indies and registered at American ports in 1788 had declined 46 percent as compared with those registered in 1766. Or, to take another example, New England fish exports to *all* the West Indies dropped in annual value from $448,000 for the prewar years to $284,000 for the period 1786–1790. And such evidence is reinforced by L. J. Ragatz' statistics on the British West Indian economy. Ragatz shows that the British islands suffered a serious depression in the period 1783 to 1793 due to severance of trade with the United States despite a large increase in imports from Canada, Nova Scotia, and Newfoundland. [11] The dislocation of West Indian trade seems, therefore, to have been substantial.

The West Indian problem, however, was only one aspect of a more general disruption of Anglo-American trade. Ad-

10. *Dictionary of National Biography s.v.* "Nelson, Horatio." New York *Packet,* April 27, 1786. The captain who lost his flour, interestingly, was in command of a ship owned by Robert Morris of Philadelphia. See also *New Jersey Gazette,* April 24, 1786; *Gazette of the State of Georgia,* April 12, 1787; *State Gazette of South Carolina* (Charleston), October 11, 1787.

11. Nettels, *Emergence of National Economy,* 55–56; Ragatz, *Fall of the Planter Class,* 184–86, 190–94.

ditional Orders in Council barred the ships of one state or nation from carrying goods of another state or nation to any port in the British Empire. This meant that if the British should decide to treat the United States as sovereign agents in matters of commerce (and Americans fully expected them to do so), then a Massachusetts ship would not be able to carry Virginia tobacco to London.[12]

Still other Orders in Council impeded American traffic to Newfoundland, Nova Scotia, and the British home islands. Newfoundland and Nova Scotia had formerly provided markets for rum, lumber, and other American products in return for corn and bills of exchange. They were now closed to American ships. Moreover, American vessels carrying goods to the British Isles had to pay higher fees than British ships and encountered heavy duties on rice, tobacco, pitch, tar, turpentine, ships, oil, and other goods. American fish, whale oil, and salted meats could not be imported into Great Britain at all. And American grain was usually excluded by prohibitive duties.

Even though the United States maintained a favored position *vis-à-vis* the rest of the world in trade with Britain, the net impact of the various restrictions on her economy was heavy and swift. Atlantic trade and commerce was so vital that its fate was inextricably tied up with the fate of nearly every branch of American enterprise.[13]

12. Setser, *Commercial Reciprocity*, 64; Bancroft, *Formation of the Constitution*, I, 62–63, 67. Southerners would not, however, have been at the complete mercy of British shipping interests. Forrest McDonald credits local shipping with carrying one fourth of South Carolina's exports and one third of Georgia's after the war; McDonald, *We the People: The Economic Origins of the Constitution* (Chicago: University of Chicago Press, 1958), 131–32, 213–14.

13. For the various restrictions and their effect, see "Extract from the Secret Journal of Foreign Affairs," September 29, 1783, *Diplomatic Correspondence, 1783–89*, I, 38; McDonald, *We the People*, 381–82; Jensen, *New Nation*, 163; McLaughlin, *The Confederation*, 73; Smith, *John*

Loss of the rich triangular trade and the sudden inaccessibility of important British colonial ports ruined many a shipowner. Up and down the seaboard, the absence of American-owned ships was striking. The Pennsylvania judge, George Bryan, wrote from Philadelphia in 1786, "Our navigation was wholly in the hands of foreigners." The situation in New York City was no better. One delegate to Congress expressed astonishment at seeing "the quantity of vessels in this city from all parts of England . . . carrying our goods to market." The ports of Boston and Charleston, similarly, were dominated by British ships.[14]

Farmers also suffered. Not all of them, of course, could produce a surplus for export, nor did all of them live in an area with access to transportation; but a great many did raise surplus commodities and were in a position to ship their produce to foreign markets.[15] These individuals were

*Adams*, II, 635; Nettels, *Emergence of National Economy*, Chap. 3. It should be noted that some American exports to Great Britain did retain their duty-free, prerevolutionary status. These included potash, pearl ash, bar iron, and timber. Moreover, the duties paid on American pitch, tar, and tobacco were less than those laid upon similar commodities from other countries; Victor Selden Clark, *History of Manufactures in the United States* (3 vols.; New York: McGraw Hill, 1929), I, 228.

14. George Bryan to [?], undated, in George Bryan Papers, Historical Society of Pennsylvania, Philadelphia. For the same opinion see the New York *Journal*, February 23, 1783; Petition of the Inhabitants of Portsmouth, Virginia, November 5, 1785, in Virginia Legislative Petition Collection, Virginia State Library, Richmond; Pierse Long to John Langdon, January 31, 1785, in Burnett (ed.), *Letters of Continental Congress*, VIII, 18. James Monroe was told that all the New Yorkers together owned no more than two ships; James Monroe to Thomas Jefferson, August 15, 1785, in Bancroft, *Formation of the Constitution*, I, 450. John Jay remarked that "the commerce of America is so reduced that extraordinary efforts are necessary to extricate it from its present embarrassments"; quoted by Louis Guillaume Otto in a letter to Comte de Vergennes, August 13, 1786, *ibid.*, II, 378. See also Smith, *John Adams*, II, 633–34; Paul L. Varg, *Foreign Policies of the Founding Fathers* (East Lansing: Michigan State University Press, 1963), 52–53, 57.

15. This point is central to the thesis expounded in Main, *Antifederalists*. Main contends that the great majority of surplus or commercial farm-

pinched in two ways. First, they lost the British West Indian market for their salted meat, fish, and dairy produce, and they found their wheat virtually excluded from the British home market by the Corn Laws. Second, they were forced to transport their produce in British bottoms at higher, possibly prohibitive, rates. Chancellor Robert R. Livingston of New York expressed a common opinion when he remarked that a trade "in our staple commodities *in our own vessels*" [italics inserted] to the British West Indies is essential. Otherwise "our wheat and our flour must lay on our hands and sell for 4/- a *bush*, and 12/- a *cwt*. and under. . . . Much, nay even our well being, depends upon it." [16]

Injuries suffered by farmers and shipowners were felt

---

ers supported the Constitution as opposed to subsistence farmers, whose political opinions were less predictable. G. de Brassine, in a treatise addressed to the Pennsylvania Assembly dated November 28, 1786, states simply that "agriculture languishes because exportation decreases"; Records of the Pennsylvania Assembly, State Archives, Record Group #7, General Assembly File, Box #2, Undated Petitions, 1785–1788. See also Samuel Eliot Morison, *The Maritime History of Massachusettts, 1783–1860* (Boston and New York: Houghton Mifflin Co., 1921), 41. A general town meeting of Philadelphia citizens and the residents from two other districts resolved that since agriculture was the principal occupation, and since it was dependent on the export trade, "it becomes necessary to extend the latter"; *Pennsylvania Gazette*, June 22, 1785. In a recent study of New York politics in this period, Alfred F. Young has indicated that the percentage of farmers growing surplus produce for foreign export was greater than has been realized. "Farmers in the entire Hudson Valley engaged in commercial agriculture for the export market"; Alfred Fabion Young, *The Democratic Republicans of New York* (Chapel Hill: University of North Carolina Press, 1967), 91.

16. Dumas Malone and Basil Rauch, *Empire for Liberty: The Genesis and Growth of the United States of America* (6 vols.; New York: Appleton-Century-Crofts, 1960), I, 221. The quotation is from George Dangerfield, *Chancellor Robert R. Livingston of New York, 1746–1813* (New York: Harcourt, Brace, 1960), 221. For the same view see an article in the *Independent Gazetteer* by "A Pennsylvania Farmer," September 27, 1787, quoted in John Bach McMaster and Frederick Dawson Stone (eds.), *Pennsylvania and the Federal Constitution* (Lancaster, Pa.: Inquirer Printing and Publishing Co., 1888), 128.

by merchants as well. The ascendancy of British shipping meant that British goods not only traveled on British ships but were sold by British retailers. Slowly but steadily after 1783 people began to notice an increase in the number of British merchants selling British goods on British account. The newspapers carried accounts of the distress of American trade and the way in which British commercial agents seemed to be snooping around and checking up on American businessmen, always ready to grab property in the absence of credit. One paper announced: "The appearance of a British agent formerly was rare; some extraordinary emergency brought him to America; the credit of the American merchant was then held sacred; his character was not esteemed so trifling as to need an overseer. His honor was considered as ample security; but now . . . our business is inspected, and scarsely [sic] a house in London but has one among us whose whole employ is to trace us through every labyrinth of our business." Native American merchants, resenting the increased competition, thundered in a manner reminiscent of the days when the British East India Company decided to establish its own retail agencies in America for the sale of tea. Wrote Samuel Adams to his cousin John, "Our merchants are complaining bitterly that Great Britain is ruining their trade and there is good reason to complain." [17]

There was also good reason for complaint on the part of another group—the shipbuilders, whose trade was closely dependent upon the success of American merchants. Since shipping provided the principal means of mass transporta-

17. Bancroft, *Formation of the Constitution*, I, 185; *Pennsylvania Gazette*, June 29, 1785; *Masssachusetts Centinel*, May 7, 1785; *Pennsylvania Gazette*, September 20, 1785; Samuel Adams to John Adams, July [?], 1785, in Samuel Adams Papers, New York Public Library.

tion, the construction of heavy vessels was "a great business." Prior to the Revolution, hundreds of ships were produced annually in New England alone; and even during the war shipbuilders continued to thrive by replacing vessels destroyed by the enemy. In 1783 the shipyards were filled with vessels under construction. After the war, however, demand decreased as the United States Navy cancelled its orders and disposed of its fleet for lack of funds; and, most important of all, the British Privy Council issued its trade and navigation decrees.[18]

In addition, British citizens were forbidden to purchase any ships which had been built or repaired in the United States after 1776. Since American-built ships had always constituted a major portion of the imperial marine, this restriction had serious effects. In the year 1776, the British had employed 2,342 American-built ships and only 1,260 foreign-built ships. By 1784, however, the number of American ships had fallen to 1,126 as compared to 2,892 foreign-built. One newspaper reported, "On the 18th of June last (1787) was sold at Lloyd's Coffeehouse, the ship Thompson, of 400 tons burden, Philadelphia-built, not four years old for no more than 850! This ship before the American war would have sold for 3,000!—so much for the encouragement of shipbuilding in America." [19]

The sudden drop in demand for American ships was especially depressing in Massachusetts. Before the war, the Bay State had launched about a hundred and twenty-five

18. Champion, *Considerations*, 36; James Madison to Thomas Jefferson, September 20, 1783, in Hunt (ed.), *Writings of Madison*, II, 21.

19. Varg, *Foreign Policies*, 51; Miller, *Alexander Hamilton*, 134; New York *Packet*, April 24, 1786; *Gazette of the State of Georgia*, October 25, 1787; Champion, *Considerations*, 14–17. American ships were 30 percent cheaper than ships built in Scotland or Ireland even though American manufacturers had to import various components such as cordage and sails.

vessels annually. In 1784, the number declined to forty-five, and in the following two years to fifteen or twenty. By 1789, the combined production of all the shipyards of New England totaled eleven vessels. This, however, was only symbolic of a general distress covering the length of the eastern seaboard. Since the Northeast had built only about three fifths of all American ships, other parts of the country with thriving centers of marine construction were similarly affected. These included New York, Philadelphia, Chesapeake Bay, and South Carolina.[20]

Allied trades suffered as well. The *Massachusetts Centinel* warned in May of 1785 that not only was shipbuilding about to be ruined but also "every article of rigging; sails; blocks; also cordage ready fitted by the rigger, together with all the variety of ship chandlery. . . . The consequence must be an entire ruin of our ship-builders, blacksmiths, rope-makers; riggers, block-makers, sailmakers; with every other branch of business connected in the equipment of vessels." A Virginia legislative petition complained of the blow to "that most valuable branch of business, ship-building, with all those branches of trade dependent on it, and a nursery of seamen." [21]

One additional cause of the decline in shipbuilding stemmed from the fact that another group of persons, ordinarily good customers for ships, had been severely injured by British restrictions. These were the fishermen and

20. Morison, *Maritime History*, 34; Nettels, *Emergence of National Economy*, 52; McLaughlin, *The Confederation*, 75; Ritcheson, *Aftermath of Revolution*, 367.

21. *Massachusetts Centinel*, May 7, 1785; Virginia Legislative Petitions, Nansemond County, November 4, 1785. Alexandria, in particular, was noted for its shipbuilding industry. See also *ibid.*, Norfolk County, Town of Portsmouth, November 5, 1785, which expressed concern for mechanics, seamen, and shipbuilders.

whalers. Before the war, their business had employed 1,450 ships, as well as 12,000 fishermen and seamen, and they had been able to market large quantities of fish, whale oil, and whalebone outside the country. The British postwar regulations, however, deprived them of their greatest cod market, the British West Indies, as well as their only foreign market for whale oil and whalebone, England. So serious was the damage done to the industry that by 1789 New England's whaling tonnage stood at one third of the prewar level, and entire seaport towns were faced with ruin.[22]

Aside from the damage done to various groups, British policy seriously upset the American balance of trade. British exports to the United States in 1784 totaled £3,679,467 as compared to imports from the United States totaling £749,345. In 1786, the respective totals were still far out of balance at £2,308,023 compared to £893,594.[23] There was no way to pay for all the British manufactured goods which crowded American harbors. Some American sea captains, thwarted by Nelson's vigilance, tried loading their dried cod and pickled beef for substitute markets. There was some trade with France and Holland, and many looked hopefully to a new commerce with China and East India. But any increase in these directions must be weighed against the decline in trade with Spain, southern Europe, and the Mediterranean as a result of the Barbary threat. Moreover, new trade routes could not be developed in a day, nor could

22. McLaughlin, *The Confederation*, 73; Champion, *Considerations*, 50–51; Morison, *Maritime History*, 30–31. This, as Morison explains, was true even though the Treaty of Paris had guaranteed fishing rights for Americans on the banks of Newfoundland and Nova Scotia. See also Smith, *John Adams*, II, 633; Varg, *Foreign Policies*, 53.

23. Richard B. Morris (ed.), *The Encyclopedia of American History* (New York: Harper and Row, 1961), 112, 114. See also Young, *Democratic Republicans*, 79, for a clear confirmation of this condition in New York.

the distant Orient and pirate-infested Mediterranean replace the Caribbean as a trade outlet.[24] Thus, millions of Spanish-milled dollars were transferred from the United States to Great Britain until the supply of available specie ran dry. Secretary Jay noted starkly that the British continued to flood the American market while they "take pains to cut off every source within their reach by which we may make remittances." And James Madison warned, "the Revolution has robbed us of our trade with the West Indies, the only one which yielded us a favorable balance, without opening any other channels to compensate for it. . . . In every point of view, indeed, the trade of this country is in a deplorable condition." [25]

Congress' initial response to the commercial distress was a diplomatic appeal to the Court of St. James's. The crusty and indomitable John Adams was instructed to obtain a favorable commercial treaty as well as speedy evacuation of the frontier posts. His mission was handicapped, of course, because Congress lacked the power to regulate national commerce and therefore to retaliate against England, but he was nonetheless optimistic that a satisfactory settlement could be arranged.

The cold reception which he received upon arrival in London in June, 1785, dampened his spirits somewhat. George III greeted him pleasantly. Indeed, the King assured him that although he had been the last to sanction independence, he would also be "the last to infringe it." But here

24. Barnby, *Prisoners of Algiers*, 67; Setser, *Commercial Reciprocity*, 54; Clark, *History of Manufactures*, I, 228.
25. Sir John Temple to Lord Carmarthen, July 7, 1786, in Bancroft, *Formation of the Constitution*, II, 371; John Jay to John Adams, September 16, 1785, in Johnston (ed.), *Papers of John Jay*, III, 165; James Madison to Richard Henry Lee, July 7, 1785, in Hunt (ed.), *Writings of Madison*, II, 151.

the warmth ended. Adams was snubbed by the court generally, and the disdainful attitude of Lord Sheffield seeped into newspaper editorials and was reflected above all in the policy of the prime minister, William Pitt.[26] A man of sensitivity and bristling patriotism, Adams imagined that the people of London were afraid to look him in the face out of guilt for their recent bad behavior.

Not one to admit defeat, however, he endeavored to put his best foot forward. He discussed the subject of a commercial treaty several times with the foreign minister, Lord Carmarthen, and he conferred with Pitt.[27] He tried to convince the British that Congress could be expected to strike back effectively in the absence of reciprocal commercial arrangements. He pointed out that since Americans could no longer pay for British imports with shipments of rice, tobacco, and oil, they were forced back upon specie and credit, and that when the specie was exhausted, the trade would end. But he always met with the same attitude. Neither Pitt nor Carmarthen feared American reprisals, and they simply reminded him that Congress had no more authority to negotiate a commercial treaty than it did to regulate state commerce.[28] After the initial interviews, Adams was ignored as much as possible and his questions elicited a mortifying silence. In 1787, when Lord Grenville spoke in

26. John Adams to John Jay, July 19, 1785, in *Diplomatic Correspondence, 1783–89*, II, 398.

27. Chinard, *Honest John Adams*, 199–200; Smith, *John Adams*, II, 649.

28. Smith, *John Adams*, II, 636. Adams had encountered the same attitude on the part of the duke of Dorset, British ambassador to France. Dorset had written that "the apparent determination of the respective states to regulate their own separate interests renders it absolutely necessary . . . that my court should be informed how far the commissioners can be duly authorized to enter into any engagements with Great Britain which it may not be in the power of any one of the states to render totally fruitless and ineffectual"; duke of Dorset to commissioners, March 26, 1785, in *Diplomatic Correspondence, 1783–89*, I, 575.

Parliament on the subject of trade, he defended the ministry's policy with respect to the United States on the grounds that "we do not know whether they are under one head, directed by many, or whether they have any head at all." [29]

To all outward appearances, Adams' three-year mission to the Court of St. James's might have been considered a failure. The prospect for a *rapprochement* between the two countries seemed as remote in 1787 as it had in 1785. Only when the new Constitution was on the verge of adoption did Grenville and Carmarthen indicate a willingness to negotiate. All of which merely confirmed Adams' feeling that there was not as yet in America "any national government, but that as soon as there shall be one, the British court will vouchsafe to treat with it." [30]

But Adams had been shrewd enough to realize that his frustration in the field of diplomacy might not be for naught. The British Orders in Council would prove to be "a blessing" in disguise if only they exposed the weaknesses of the Confederation and sparked a movement at home to create more energy in Congress. They might, in the words of Gouverneur Morris, do "more political good than commercial mischief." [31]

With this idea in mind, Adams took it upon himself to demonstrate to his countrymen three things: first, that diplomacy unsupported by military power could do nothing for American commerce unless Americans could demonstrate that they were both willing and able to impose retali-

29. William Smith to John Jay, April 1, 1787, in *Diplomatic Correspondence, 1783–89*, III, 67.

30. Chinard, *Honest John Adams*, 217; John Adams to John Jay, February 14, 1788, in *Diplomatic Correspondence, 1783–89*, II, 826.

31. John Adams to John Jay, May 4, 1785, in Adams (ed.), *Works of John Adams*, VIII, 240; Gouverneur Morris to John Jay, September 24, 1783, in Bancroft, *Formation of the Constitution*, I, 65.

atory restrictions on British trade; second, that this would require concerted action on the part of all the states; and third, that such action could best be accomplished by granting Congress the power to regulate commerce.[32]

Adams was the first person to urge retaliatory action by the states, and he was the most persistent. From his prolific pen came warning after warning, plea after plea, to spur American leaders to action.[33] Two weeks after the Order in Council of July 2, 1783, Adams wrote to Robert R. Livingston that the Privy Council was acting on the assumption that Americans "had no common legislature for the government of commerce." Consequently, "the United States will have occasion to brace up their confederation and act as one body with one spirit. If they do not it is now very obvious that Great Britain will take advantage of it in such manner as will endanger our peace, our safety, and even our existence." He urged that Congress be given power to regulate the trade of the entire nation "for if the union of the states is not preserved. . . . we shall find our foreign affairs the most difficult to manage of any of our interests." [34] Thereafter, he kept up a steady stream of letters in similar vein to the

32. John Adams to John Jay, May 5, 1785, in Adams (ed.), *Works of John Adams*, VIII, 242.

33. Setser, *Commercial Reciprocity*, 55, 81. Especially relevant are his letters of May 3, May 8, July 29, August 6, 10, 25, 28, 30, 31, October 15, 17, 21, 25, November 4, December 6, 1785; January 4, and February 27, 1786.

34. John Adams to Robert R. Livingston, July 16, 18, 1783, in Wharton (ed.), *Diplomatic Correspondence*, VI, 554, 561. One should note that Adams was not yet committed to the idea of constitutional reform, although he would be soon. He wrote in August, 1784: "Many gentlemen in Europe think the powers in the Confederation are not adequate. The Abbé de Mably and Dr. Price have taken the pains to publish their advice. They may be right but I am not yet of their opinion"; John Adams to James Warren, August 27, 1784; Adams (ed.), *Works of John Adams*, IX, 526.

secretary for foreign affairs and to members of Congress. In 1788, a congressional report on the Department of Foreign Affairs noted that the clerk "had recorded five volumes of Adams' letters and was working on the sixth." [35]

Although Adams was quick to suggest the need for a constitutional amendment which would give Congress the power to regulate commerce, he also encouraged efforts by individual states until these proved useless. Initially, he suggested that states should either bar British ships and goods from their harbors or tax them heavily. The important thing was that some kind of pressure be brought to bear on the British, for there would be no commercial treaty until Albion was made to feel the need for it.[36]

When meetings were held in Massachusetts and Rhode Island to agree on a system of retaliating against the Orders in Council, Adams dashed back enthusiastic reports of their beneficial effect on British opinion. In one letter he told about the time when Commodore Hood of the Royal Navy had expressed the hope that such meetings would not obstruct the return of Anglo-American friendship, and he had replied proudly that, in his judgment, Bostonians and other Americans would not be satisfied with anything less than a commercial treaty based on the principle of reciprocity. The commodore hoped such a treaty could be arranged. Again and again Englishmen would ask Adams what America could offer in return for access to their West Indies, and he hoped he would soon be able to reply: "repeal of our navigation acts." [37]

When Adams saw that the separate states were unable to

35. Graham Henry Stuart, *The Department of State* (New York: Macmillan Co., 1949), 8.

36. John Adams to John Jay, June 26, 1785, in *Diplomatic Correspondence, 1783–89*, II, 386–87.

37. *Ibid.*; John Adams to John Jay, August 30, October 21, 1785, quoted in McMaster, *History of People of U.S.*, I, 245. See also Adams' letter to Jay, May 4, 1785, in Adams (ed.), *Works of John Adams*, VIII, 240.

agree on a uniform policy, he urged Congress to gather data from the different localities so that it could recommend a regulatory system acceptable to all the states. But more important, he repeatedly urged the states to yield their regulatory power to Congress. When New York voted to vest Congress with such power, he implored: "It cannot . . . be too earnestly recommended to all the states to concur with the state of New York in giving to Congress full power to make treaties of commerce, and in short to govern all our external commerce; for I really believe it must come to that." [38]

His opinions reached a wide and influential audience including congressmen, officials on both the state and national level, and private citizens. One of his letters was specifically cited in a congressional report as evidence that "an additional cement to the Union is necessary . . . by having a well-formed federal government." Various state delegations to Congress enclosed copies of Adams' letters in messages to their governors.[39] And many American newspapers of the period reflected a real awareness of the type of problems he faced. A typical excerpt read: "It has long been wished that Congress were vested with powers to regulate our commerce. . . . Our ambassadors would no longer be reflected upon as acting for a body without a head; our negotiations abroad would be more decisive; and our character as an independent nation be established." [40]

38. John Adams to John Jay, July 19, 1785, in Adams (ed.), *Works of John Adams*, VIII, 279–83.

39. Report of the Committee on Dispatches from Foreign Ministers, September 25, 1783, in Burnett (ed.), *Letters of Continental Congress*, VII, 305; for example, in the case of Virginia, see *ibid.*, VII, 366–67. In New England, especially, Adams was highly respected and his letters widely distributed. Robert Morris forwarded one to the governor of Massachusetts, and Abiel Foster sent one to the president of New Hampshire; *ibid.*, VII, 334, 336.

40. *Pennsylvania Packet and Daily Advertiser* (Philadelphia), September 20, 1785. Similar remarks also appeared in the *New Jersey Gazette*,

Adams' exhortations fell on fertile soil. People in every geographical area had begun to experience the effects of British trade restrictions, and to many it was a matter of pride as well as purse. A large grass roots reaction was building up throughout the country.[41]

The response in New England was most vigorous. Here, along the seaboard, ships lay at anchor, shipbuilders and allied craftsmen idled their time away, merchants bowed to foreign competition, fishermen stayed home, and commercial farmers suffered severely. More than other areas, it relied on the West Indies trade not only for its dealings with Britain, but also for its purchase of tobacco and southern produce. Boston had long been known as "the mart town of the West Indies." [42]

Town meetings aired the problem of trade and urged their state legislatures to invest Congress with full power to regulate commerce. The merchants and traders of New Haven petitioned for an act of Congress "prohibiting the subjects of any foreign nation whose ports are shut against the citizens of these states, from trading in any of the United States." The merchants of Portsmouth, New Hampshire, resolved to join those of Philadelphia in securing equal rights for American shipping. Recognizing the need for recipro-

---

May 22, 1786; New York *Journal*, May 11, 1786; *Columbian Herald*, June 26, June 29, 1786. The same awareness is reflected in private communications, such as one addressed to the Pennsylvania judge, George Bryan, expressing Adams' fear of not being accepted in London as a valid representative for all the states; David Jackson to George Bryan, July 27, 1785, in George Bryan Papers, Historical Society of Pennsylvania.

41. The Massachusetts congressman, Rufus King, reported in December, 1785, that "the merchants throughout the states are agreed; they urge the necessity of commercial regulations; and the sessions of the several legislatures during the winter will be employed on this subject"; Rufus King to John Adams, December 4, 1785, in Burnett (ed.), *Letters of Continental Congress*, VIII, 268.

42. Morison, *Maritime History*, 17, 32.

cal commercial treaties, they pointed out that "if the citizens of America are not allowed to be carriers for any other nation, neither ought any other nation to be carriers for them." Newburyport instructed its congressional delegates to work for commercial regulations and complained about "the discouraging embarrassments of our commerce." In Boston a very large and respectable body of merchants and shopkeepers drew up two petitions, one addressed to the Massachusetts General Court, the other to Congress. They complained that British ships and cargoes entered American ports on a par with American; that American exports such as rice, oil, and tobacco were handicapped by enormous British duties; that the great increase of British merchants in America threatened a monopoly of all trade; that there was an alarming decrease in the circulation medium; and that the carrying trade was almost annihilated by English navigation acts. Pledging to discontinue their patronage of British merchants, they established a committee of correspondence to enlist the cooperation and support of merchants in other seaport towns.[43]

In New York and Philadelphia the response was much the same. When Congress moved to New York City on January 11, 1785, local tradesmen made it clear that they wanted their representatives to concur with those of other states in augmenting congressional power to meet every exigency of the union. The Chamber of Commerce urged

43. John Habersham to Joseph Clay, June 24, 1785, in Burnett (ed.), *Letters of Continental Congress*, VIII, 151–52; Setser, *Commercial Reciprocity*, 54; Roger Sherman to Elias Shipman *et al.*, May 7, 1784, in Burnett (ed.), *Letters of Continental Congress*, VII, 516; John Langdon to [?], February 12, 1784, in John Langdon Papers, Historical Society of Pennsylvania, Philadelphia; *New Jersey Gazette*, July 10, 1786; New York *Journal*, June 15, 1786; *Pennsylvania Herald* (Philadelphia), June 3, 1786; *Gentleman's Magazine*, LV (October, 1785), 824; *Massachusetts Centinel*, April 16, 20, 1785.

Congress to retaliate against painful British restrictions and dispatched a circular letter deploring economic conditions. On June 20, 1785, an assembly of prominent New York merchants resolved that congressional regulation of trade was absolutely essential.[44] Meanwhile, popular meetings in Philadelphia came to the same conclusion.[45] A memorial to the Pennsylvania General Assembly signed by such notables as Tench Coxe, George Clymer, and Thomas Fitzsimons indicated that the "fundamental defect in the Constitution" was lack of congressional control over commerce, and that state control "cannot be longer retained but at the expense of the general welfare." [46] The same opinion was expressed in the reply of Philadelphia merchants to the circular letter from Boston in which it was stated that nations would continue to benefit from American trade without any mutual concessions "until we shall be able to meet their restrictions and exclusions with some effectual system adopted to our new situation. But however necessary or desirable this might be, a great difficulty lies in the way:—the defect in the con-

44. Bancroft, *Formation of the Constitution*, I, 186; *Gentleman's Magazine*, LVI (March, 1785), 259; Clarence Eugene Miner, *The Ratification of the Federal Constitution by the State of New York* (New York: Columbia University Press, 1921), 25. Backing the resolution were such names as Livingston, Schuyler, Troup, Malcolm, Duer, and Hamilton.

45. Bancroft, *Formation of the Constitution*, I, 187; *Pennsylvania Gazette*, June 22, 1785. George Bryan wrote to William Augustus Atlee, June 23, 1785, "We have had a town meeting concerning the ill state of trade and the British regulations. . . . Mr. Ingersoll has acquired great popularity by presiding at the event. Mr. Morris' friends, fearing something they might not like would issue, opposed it and have rather suffered thereby with the people"; William Augustus Atlee Papers, Library of Congress. Samuel Bryan had written in May of "a general disposition in people to vest Congress with efficient powers for the regulation of commerce"; Samuel Bryan to George Bryan, May, 1785, in George Bryan Papers, Historical Society of Pennsylvania.

46. Memorial of a Committee of Merchants, April 6, 1785, in Records of the Pennsylvania Assembly, State Archives, Record Group #7, General Assembly File, Box #2, Undated Petitions, 1785–1788.

stitutional powers of Congress, made the harder to supply from the jealousy of some of the states of the authority of that body." During the last session of assembly, continued the letter, "a resolution was passed at our instance requesting Congress to devise a system of commercial powers for itself to be recommended to the concurrence of the states—and it is not improbable, if Congress should think fit to act upon it, but that in this instance a regard *to national interest* may get the better of that jealous spirit which on other occasions has hitherto defeated the wisest plan of redeeming our national credit and character." If Congress failed, the states would have to act independently, but "nothing would give a more violent shock to the first principles of our union than such independent acts in a matter of such common interest and concern." [47]

While the merchants of the northern states formulated petitions and drafted letters of protest, southern leaders also spoke in favor of government retaliation against Britain.[48] George Mason of Virginia warned of the depressing effect of British restrictions, and in Georgia a grand jury lamented that Congress had not yet been given power "sufficient to carry into effect the regulations of our trade." The planters of South Carolina were as angry as the merchants of Boston because the British trade monopoly forced them to pay high prices for imported articles while receiving a bare minimum

47. Committee of Philadelphia Merchants to the Committee of Merchants and Traders of Boston, May 19, 1785, in Emmet Collection, New York Public Library, Item #9328. The Philadelphians included Richard Wells, John Nesbitt, John Nixon, Thomas Fitzsimons, Mordecai Leurs, George Clymer, Charles Pettit, John Wilcocks, Isaac Hazlehurst, Clement Biddle, Samuel Howell, James Ross, and Tench Coxe.

48. Nathan Dane, on returning to Congress in 1786, wrote that "the disposition for vesting commercial powers in Congress appears to me to be more general particularly in the Southern states than I expected it to be"; Nathan Dane to James Bowdoin, January 10, 1786, in Burnett (ed.), *Letters of Continental Congress*, VIII, 283.

for their staple crops. Jefferson realized this and pointed out that the charges imposed by the British for the use of their ships were in fact a tax on American agriculture. Madison predicted that southern planters would be furious if they ever realized the full extent to which foreigners were exploiting them. Virginia tobacco which sold for one price on the James River was being bought up by British merchants and then hawked in Philadelphia for a quick profit of nearly 50 percent. These same merchants then turned around and sold English manufactured goods in Virginia at exorbitant prices. Thus, the South, too, suffered from an unfavorable balance of trade and a shortage of specie.[49]

Southern merchants, seamen, and shipbuilders did not wield as much influence as those of the North, but they did not hesitate to raise their voices in complaint. At Norfolk, Portsmouth, Suffolk, and Alexandria they held meetings and drafted petitions similar to those of New York and Boston. They lamented the loss of the West Indian market, the decline in shipbuilding, the dark future for native seamen, and the difficulty of competing with British carriers for even a share in the coasting trade.[50] Foreign ships were carrying goods on inland routes which had always been the exclusive preserve of native merchants. A petition of citi-

49. *Pennsylvania Gazette*, January 25, 1786; McMaster, *History of People of U.S.*, I, 272; Nathan Schachner, *Thomas Jefferson* (2 vols.; New York: Appleton-Century-Crofts, 1951), I, 364; James Madison to James Monroe, June 21, 1785, to Jefferson, August 20, 1785, in Hunt (ed.), *Writings of Madison*, II, 147–48, 161.

50. McMaster, *History of People of U.S.*, I, 273; Channing, *History of U.S.*, III, 471; Combs, *Jay Treaty*, 84; Keith, "Relaxations," 1, 4. See petitions drafted by the merchants, traders, and other inhabitants of the towns of Suffolk and Portsmouth, November 4 and 5, 1785, one from Petersburg, November 24, 1785, signed by ninety-nine persons and complaining that "foreigners are our manufacturers, our merchants, and our carriers," one from Norfolk, November 4, 1785, signed by ninety-four persons, one from Fredericksburg, signed by forty-nine, and one from Alexandria, November 5, 1785, signed by seventy-six; Virginia Legislative Petitions.

zens from Petersburg, Virginia, noted the declining state of commerce and looked with favor upon "the early and repeated efforts of the general assembly to effectuate a national remedy for this evil with pleasure." The petition went on to assert that, "it is with unspeakable regret they have observed that either from a want of energy in the Constitution or unanimity in the councils of the Confederacy, every expedient has hitherto proved ineffectual. . . . The increase of our shipping we humbly conceive of immense moment to the interests of this country; and while the British are exerting their utmost influence to engross the whole carrying trade to themselves, it is surely of high consequence to counteract their ruinous machinations." [51]

It should be noted at this point that shipping and commercial interests were not alone in demanding that Congress be authorized by amendment to regulate commerce. Another group also joined the chorus for different reasons. These were the native manufacturers struggling to build their enterprise in the face of stiff British competition.

This was a period of remarkable industrial development. Factories were thriving in cities such as Boston, Philadelphia, Providence, and New Haven. In Kentucky men were building a greater variety of things in 1790 than even the people of New York had manufactured twenty-five years earlier. Cotton and woolen mills were going up in New England and Pennsylvania. Entrepreneurs were turning out large quantities of paper, sailcloth, nails, iron bars, buttons, hats, hard soap, candles, loaf sugar, brown sugar, and gun-

51. Memorial of Petersburg citizens including William Davies and St. George Tucker, November 3, 1786, in Virginia Legislative Petitions, Dinwiddie County. The Virginia House of Delegates had voted on December 4, 1783, to enable Congress to prohibit British ships from carrying American goods to the West Indies; *Pennsylvania Gazette*, December 17, 1783.

powder. Private associations were organizing to obtain protective legislation from the state houses, and women were taking their stand along with the men. The ladies of Hartford, Connecticut, were joining forces, as were the ladies of Halifax, South Carolina; and like-minded groups were to be found in Richmond, Boston, and Germantown, Pennsylvania, to name a few.[52]

The protectionist cause had a general appeal because it promised an industrial base for the military in case of another war with Britain. It would help to restore the balance of trade by lessening the demand for imports, it would halt the lethal leakage of specie to England; and, by undercutting traditional reliance upon Great Britain, it would invigorate the nation's pride. In the words of one widely circulated essay, "a people who have recourse to foreign markets for almost every article of their consumption can be independent in name only." [53]

The year 1785 was studded with meetings and resolutions demanding passage of protective tariff laws. In Massachusetts, New Hampshire, Rhode Island, New York, and Pennsylvania such laws passed. However, as in the case of similar attempts to retaliate against foreign commercial restrictions, the individual states found that only a uniform policy adopted by all states could be truly effective, since the most successful manufacturers were selling or planning to sell their products out of state. Northern manufacturers wanted to sell to the southern market, but without tariff

52. Bancroft, *Formation of the Constitution*, I, 187, 495; New York *Packet*, September 1, 1785, November 17, 1785; *Pennsylvania Gazette*, June 22, 1785, August 31, 1785, October 5, 1785; *Massachusetts Centinel*, April 20, 1785, April 23, 1785, April 27, 1785, May 7, 1785; Boston *Gazette*, August 22, 1785; *New Jersey Gazette*, July 10, 1786; *Virginia Gazette* (Richmond), November 30, 1786. See also Clark, *History of Manufactures*, I, 229–30; Richard Wigginton Thompson, *The History of Protective Tariff Laws* (Chicago: R. S. Peale and Co., 1888), 32–36.
53. Thompson, *History*, 36.

cover they ran into ruinous British competition. Only a federal tariff could provide the kind of protection they needed. And because Congress, under the Articles, had no more power to enact tariff laws than other kinds of commercial legislation, the manufacturers joined the chorus of exporters, importers, shippers, and merchants.[54]

But regardless of which groups wanted to vest Congress with the power to regulate commerce—whether manufacturers, merchants, shipowners, or planters—the ensuing protest meetings and expressions of distress testified to the fact that British restrictions were forging "a new bond of union" among citizens of the various states. They reflected a growing belief that the basic frame of government needed revision. And this, of course, is what John Adams had anticipated when he said his failure to lift British restrictions might prove "a blessing" in disguise.[55]

It is interesting to observe that Adams was not alone in regarding British injuries as a likely blessing. Secretary Jay, an outspoken advocate of congressional control over commerce had foreseen this too. He was sure that if Americans ever realized their full danger they would surely augment the power of Congress.[56] Rufus King shrewdly suggested that "if this well-founded uneasiness is attended to by wise and moderate men in the several states, it may be improved to purposes the most beneficial to our national government." And Gouverneur Morris, a brilliant young assistant superintendent of finance, agreed that "nothing can do us so much good as to convince the eastern and southern states how necessary it is to give force to the federal government; and

54. Nettels, *Emergence of National Economy*, 69–71. See Jensen, *New Nation*, Chap. 14, for an account of what the individual states were doing by way of protection.

55. Jensen, *New Nation*, 255–56.

56. Monaghan, *Jay*, 279. George Washington felt the same way; Fitzpatrick (ed.), *Writings of George Washington*, XXVIII, 161.

nothing will so soon operate that conviction as foreign efforts to restrain the navigation of the one and the commerce
of the other." [57] James Monroe, who led the fight in Congress for federal control of commerce, also believed that
"the restrictions . . . have a good effect. They will operate
more powerfully than the utmost force of argument could
do for strengthening our government." [58]

Although such predictions were borne out in the long
run and people focused increasingly on the lack of any provision in the Articles for congressional regulation of commerce, there were certain attitudes and traditions which
temporarily hindered the nationalists from achieving their
goals. Most people emerged from the Revolution convinced
that the separate states could and should regulate their own
affairs. This was particularly true in the realm of commerce
because of Britain's attempts to wrest political power from
the colonial assemblies in the name of trade regulation. Now
that independence had been won, many people were as reluctant to entrust their affairs to a national congress as they
had been to acquiesce in parliamentary authority. Moreover, there did not seem to be any need for national control
as long as the states themselves acted promptly to retaliate
against the Orders in Council.

They did, indeed, act promptly. One by one, every state
but Connecticut passed some kind of legislation.[59] Many
states levied special tonnage duties on incoming British ships.
New Hampshire, Massachusetts, Maryland, Virginia, and

57. Rufus King to Elbridge Gerry, May 1, 1785, in King, *Rufus King*,
I, 93; Gouverneur Morris to John Jay, September 25, 1783, January 10,
1784, both in Johnston (ed.), *Papers of John Jay*, III, 86, 104–105.
58. James Monroe to Thomas Jefferson, April 12, 1785, in Hamilton
(ed.), *Writings of Monroe*, I, 69.
59. Setser, *Commercial Reciprocity*, 63. For a good summary of commercial laws passed by various states between 1783 and 1789, see Bemis,
*Jay's Treaty*, 33.

North Carolina all chose to subject British vessels to a special tax of 5s. per ton. Pennsylvania fixed the rate at 7s6d. New York, Delaware, and even Georgia (with its relatively light commercial traffic) adopted similar provisions.

A second means of retaliation was to levy a special tax on *goods* imported in British ships. Six states chose this policy. In New York, Massachusetts, and New Hampshire, goods imported by British ships were taxed twice as heavily as goods landed by American vessels. In Rhode Island the discriminatory differential soared as high as 300 percent.

Still another scheme was for a state to prohibit British vessels from loading American produce in its ports. The Massachusetts General Court, which reacted with unusual vigor to the British Orders, became the first state legislature to resort to this third alternative, doing so on June 23, 1785. Shortly thereafter, Governor Bowdoin was asked to gather information on all foreign commercial regulations which might affect Massachusetts. He was instructed to compile an abstract of all customs and duties levied upon American vessels in foreign ports, and "in conformity to the spirit of Confederation," to communicate his findings to the executives of the other states in an effort to arrive at a uniform policy.[60]

Massachusetts, leading the way for her sisters, was followed by New Hampshire and Rhode Island, then by New York, Pennsylvania, and South Carolina—and in such fast succession that the chances of forcing open the British sugar island by unanimous retaliation seemed excellent.[61] Rufus King wrote in December, "The states are more and more

60. Massachusetts delegates to James Bowdoin, August 18, 1785, in Burnett (ed.), *Letters of Continental Congress*, VIII, 188–90.
61. The *Pennsylvania Gazette* had stated confidently on July 27 (1785) that if a uniform policy were "adopted by all the states, as sound policy dictates, the West India islands will be speedily and gladly opened to the thirteen stripes."

embracing the notion that they must rely upon themselves rather than upon alliances or treaties with foreign nations." [62]

Contrary to expectation, however, the state efforts collapsed in the absence of a uniform policy. There was always some state which refused to discriminate against the British and chose to profit at the expense of its neighbors.[63] Connecticut, for one, refused steadfastly to sacrifice her local interest for the general welfare; thus, British ships, after being denied access to the ports of Massachusetts, New Hampshire, and Rhode Island steered a steady course for New Haven. Massachusetts, unable to endure the consequences of a disadvantaged position, reluctantly suspended her navigation act in July of 1786. In the same way, Pennsylvania was forced to repeal most of the high duties which neighboring states refused to match.[64] While New York passed discriminatory laws against British ships and goods, New Jersey elected to conduct business as usual in the hope of nourishing infant commercial centers at Perth Amboy and Burlington. New York countered by levying an exorbitant tax on all foreign goods crossing its border, but an angry New Jersey lashed back with a heavy tax on Sandy Hook Lighthouse.[65]

In the face of such conflict, other states hesitated to take the lead against Britain. Virginia's House of Burgesses reached an impasse over the issue of discriminatory legislation when James Madison recalled the bitterness existing

62. Rufus King to John Adams, December 4, 1785, in Burnett (ed.), *Letters of Continental Congress*, VIII, 268.

63. Edmund Morgan has compared the fruitless efforts of the individual states to the non-importation agreements directed against the Townshend duties which foundered when the merchants of one colony gave way; Morgan, "The Puritan Ethic."

64. Samuel Adams to Elbridge Gerry, September 19, 1785, in Bancroft, *Formation of the Constitution*, I, 457; Jensen, *New Nation*, 298–99.

65. Jensen, *New Nation*, 338–39.

between Massachusetts and Connecticut, New York and New Jersey, Pennsylvania and Delaware. There was no answer to the argument that whatever goods might be barred from Norfolk and Alexandria would be admitted to Maryland and North Carolina and smuggled from there into Virginia.[66]

The unhappy situation was well summarized in a British magazine which was pleased to report: "By the latest letters from the American States, the restraint laid upon their trade with the British West India islands has thrown them into the utmost perplexity; and by way of retaliation they are passing laws inimical to their own interest; and what is still worse, inconsistent with each other. . . . Hence the dissentions that universally prevail throughout what may be called the thirteen Dis-United States." [67]

And yet, the situation was not without promise, for, as Jay had remarked, good would come out of evil; "these discontents nourish federal ideas." As the futility of separate action became evident, and as individuals such as John Adams and George Washington increasingly stressed the need to rely on Congress, newspapers began to lend their support, and the result was a remarkable shift in public opinion.[68]

66. McMaster, *History of People of U.S.*, I, 276.
67. *Gentleman's Magazine*, LV (September, 1785), 740.
68. John Jay to Marquis de Lafayette, July 15, 1785, in *Diplomatic Correspondence, 1783–89*, I, 304; John Adams to John Jay, July 19, 1785, in Adams (ed.), *Works of John Adams*, VIII, 282; George Washington to the president of Congress, June 22, 1785, to George William Fairfax, June 30, 1785, to Marquis de Lafayette, May 10, 1786, to Chevalier de la Luzerne, August 1, 1786, all in Fitzpatrick (ed.), *Writings of George Washington*, XXVIII, 174, 183–84, 421–22, 500; John Francis Mercer to Benjamin Harrison, December 10, 1783, Thomas Stone to James Monroe, December 15, 1784, John Habersham to Joseph Clay, June 24, 1785, Pierse Long to John Langdon, September 18, 1785, William Grayson to James Madison, November 14, 1785, Nathan Dane to James Bowdoin, January 10, 1786, to Samuel Phillips, January 20, 1786, to Samuel Adams, February 11, 1786, Henry Lee to George Washington, April 21, 1786, all in Burnett

By May of 1785, there was talk of "a general disposition in people to vest Congress with efficient powers for the regulation of commerce." And by August of the following year, according to one newspaper, the need for federal regulation of commerce "has been so often enforced and descanted on that the whole subject appears to be worn threadbare." [69]

Not surprisingly, the movement to vest Congress with the power to regulate foreign commerce received the greatest encouragement from Congress itself. Here, at the helm of central government, the gnawing problems of the Confederation were experienced firsthand, and there was a sense

(ed.), *Letters of Continental Congress*, VII, 390, 628; VIII, 151–52, 219, 255, 283, 305, 343; George Washington to William Carmichael, June 10, 1785, to George W. Fairfax, June 30, 1785, to David Humphreys, September 1, 1785, in Bancroft, *Formation of the Constitution*, I, 439, 444, 453; Thomas Stone to James Monroe, December 15, 1784, in Monroe Papers, Library of Congress, Ser. 1, Vol. I; Rufus King to John Adams, November 2, 1785, December 4, 1785, May 4, 1786, in King, *Rufus King*, I, 113, 115, 171; Benjamin Rush to Richard Price, May 25, 1786, in Lyman Henry Butterfield (ed.), *Letters of Benjamin Rush* (2 vols.; Princeton: Princeton University Press, 1951), I, 388; John Jay to Benjamin Franklin, December 13, 1784, to Marquis de Lafayette, January 19, 1785, in Johnston (ed.), *Papers of John Jay*, III, 136, 138; Marquis de Lafayette to John Jay, March 19, 1785, John Adams to John Jay, May 3, 1785, John Jay to John Adams, October 14, 1785, in *Diplomatic Correspondence, 1783–89*, I, 302, 487; II, 420. For Robert R. Livingston, see Dangerfield, *Livingston*, 221–22; *Massachusetts Centinel*, April 20, 1785; Boston *Gazette*, August 29, 1785; *New Jersey Gazette*, January 2 and April 24, 1786; New York *Packet*, May 4, June 9, and August 14, 1786; New York *Journal*, July 6, 1786. For other indicators of a rapid change in opinion, see Virginia Legislative Petitions, Essex County, May 25, 1784, Fredericksburg County, December 2, 1784, Nansemond County, November 4, 1785, towns of Norfolk, November 4, 1785, Portsmouth, November 5, 1785, Alexandria, November 5, 1785, and Petersburg, November 24, 1785; Champion, *Considerations*, 142; Tucker, *Reflections*, 16. Some states, of course, notably Maryland and Virginia, had instructed their congressional delegations as early as the fall of 1783 to work for an amendment to the Articles of Confederation which would give Congress the power to regulate commerce; Jensen, *New Nation*, 401–402.

69. Samuel Bryan to George Bryan, May, 1785, in George Bryan Papers, Historical Society of Pennsylvania; New York *Packet*, August 14, 1786.

for the potential greatness of a stronger union. Those who acted as spokesmen for all the states in foreign affairs could best appreciate the need for congressional control of commerce and for uniform policies in general. Congress served as a national nerve center into which flowed the stimuli of world affairs. To Congress, also, came reports from other capitals and the official correspondence of all American agents abroad.

Before any of the state legislatures were even aware that a problem existed, Congress had swung into action to meet the threat posed by British commercial restrictions. A report issued on September 25, 1783, by the Congressional Committee on Dispatches of Foreign Ministers echoed Adams' previous warning (July 18) of the need for a stronger federal government, asserting that "not only a continuation but an additional cement to the Union is necessary . . . by having a well-informed federal government." The reasoning is worth noting:

> Should we be deprived of a direct trade with the British and French West India Islands, and of carrying the produce of those islands to Europe, great sources of wealth and convenience to the United States will be lost. Should the other restriction take place, and the vessels of each of the American states be confined to the importation into Great Britain of the exports from that state only, a great part of the carrying trade which arises from the exportation of American produce to Europe will be engrossed by Europeans, the great nursery of seamen will be a good degree lost and a very important and profitable branch of commerce be transferred from the citizens of these United States to foreigners. It is therefore of the highest importance in the opinion of your committee, especially as these restrictions are probably only a part of a system which if carried into effect must prove completely ruinous to the American commerce, that a General Power be somewhere lodged for regulating the concerns of the

United States; for should those restraining systems be pursued by Britain and France and other states which will probably be drawn into the same system, some regulations to exclude them for our carrying trade will be absolutely necessary, or they may eventually become the sole carriers even of our own produce.[70]

The report aroused considerable concern among members of Congress over the foreign trade issue. A new committee was appointed in the spring of 1784 to investigate the problem, and its report won unanimous approval on April 30. The report asserted that since, under the Articles of Confederation, Congress lacked the power to regulate foreign commerce, this power should be granted by all the states for a term of fifteen years. "Unless the United States can act as a nation and be regarded as such by foreign powers," it argued, "and unless Congress for this purpose shall be vested with powers competent for the protection of commerce, they can never command reciprocal advantages in trade; and without such reciprocity, our foreign commerce must decline and virtually be annihilated." [71]

While the April 30 recommendation was being considered by the states, Congress began to contemplate more radical steps. The nationalist leader, James Monroe, who had taken Madison's place in Congress, proposed that a special committee be appointed to reconsider the April 30 recommendation and reappraise the situation in general. His pro-

70. Report of the Committee on Dispatches from Foreign Ministers, September 25, 1783, in Burnett (ed.), *Letters of Continental Congress*, VII, 304–305.

71. W. C. Ford *et al.* (eds.), *Journals*, XXVI, 269–70. There were two points to the recommendation: Congress was to be granted the power to close American ports to ships of countries with whom the United States had no commercial treaty (aimed directly at Britain); secondly, with respect to ships from countries which did have a commercial treaty, to require that these ships bring goods only from their own countries (in order to reserve all other import trade for American shipowners); Setser, *Commercial Reciprocity*, 60.

posal was accepted and he became chairman of the new committee.[72] He and his colleagues went to work immediately and in less than one month proposed a major alteration in government: the ninth article of the Articles of Confederation should be amended to enable Congress to exercise control over national commerce.[73] Like most congressmen, Monroe no longer hoped that Britain would agree to a mutually advantageous treaty without an impressive increase in congressional power. Moreover, he thought the amendment would create an iron bond of union in an otherwise weak confederation.

The opponents of Monroe's plan were led by the able and zealous guardian of states' rights, Richard Henry Lee, who opposed any increase in congressional power for fear that a seemingly minor change might usher in radical reforms. Lee, a Virginian, urged that a navigation act be recommended to the states to "continue in force for a limited time." Behind him were a number of other southerners who feared a northern monopoly of the carrying trade, especially if the northern states were joined by Maryland, with its large commercial port at Annapolis, and Delaware, which excelled in naval architecture. There was even a possibility that Virginia might ally herself with northern interests in abolishing the slave trade.[74]

72. The other committee members were Richard Spaight of North Carolina, John Houston of Georgia, William S. Johnson of Connecticut, and Rufus King of Massachusetts. Significantly, every one of these men participated in the Constitutional Convention of 1787 and became ardent Federalists.

73. Monroe Committee Report, March 28, 1785, in W. C. Ford *et al.* (eds.), *Journals*, XXVIII, 201–205; Pierse Long to John Langdon, January 31, 1785, in Burnett (ed.), *Letters of Continental Congress*, VIII, 18. The report of Monroe's committee was issued on February 16 and read in Congress on March 28, 1785. It included an excellent review of the commercial situation.

74. James Monroe to Thomas Jefferson, July 15, 1785, Richard Henry Lee to James Madison, August 11, 1785, in Burnett (ed.), *Letters of Con-*

Monroe admitted that his amendment would work "a deep and radical change in the bond of Union." But contrary to Lee he felt that the urgency of the commercial crisis outweighed the risks involved in constitutional reform. To satisfy some of his critics, he required the approval of eleven states for the passage of commercial legislation. He also tried to dispel fears of tyrannical central control by stipulating that all revenue from trade duties would go into the state treasuries.[75]

Such safeguards were not sufficient, however, to win majority support, and Monroe's proposal was postponed indefinitely. As Madison had pointed out, the state legislatures were still too much afraid of losing their prerogative. The argument for a stronger central government would be least persuasive to "minds unaccustomed to consider the interests of the State as they are interwoven with those of the Confederacy, much less as they might be affected by foreign politics." [76] The time was not ripe for change. Some states had not yet decided for or against the April 30 recommendation; the possibility that all states might be able to agree on a temporary grant of commercial power to Congress forestalled the movement toward constitutional reform.

Congress itself dropped the idea of reform for the moment and decided instead to evaluate progress on the April 30 recommendation. A grand committee reported on March 3, 1786, that ten states had endorsed the recommendation in principle, while the remaining three, Delaware, Georgia, and South Carolina, were hesitant only because they con-

*tinental Congress*, VIII, 166, 181. These arguments foreshadowed the debates which were to take place at the Philadelphia Convention in 1787.

75. Bancroft, *Formation of the Constitution*, I, 192–94.

76. W. C. Ford *et al.* (eds.), *Journals*, XXIX, 533, 539; James Madison to James Monroe, August 7, 1785, in Hunt (ed.), *Writings of Madison*, II, 160.

sidered the proposed grant too weak. How remarkable in light of previous hostility to congressional power! Few people in 1783 would have given serious consideration to congressional resolutions on the subject of commerce. On the other hand, serious complications were also reported. Individual states, it was found, could not agree on how Congress should exercise control. South Carolina was the only state to exceed the April 30 recommendation by requesting that Congress be given power to regulate *all* commerce, domestic as well as foreign. Maverick North Carolina insisted that congressional control of commerce become an article of confederation with the approval of twelve states. At the same time, Connecticut, Pennsylvania, and Maryland set divergent dates upon which their grants were to take effect. And, to complicate matters further, Rhode Island limited her grant by fixing a terminal date of twenty-five years.[77]

The congressional report was therefore pessimistic. It stressed the fact that, as things stood, there could be little hope for commercial treaties other than those already concluded, and no prospect of one with Great Britain "on terms reciprocally advantageous." Nevertheless, it advised Congress to urge the states once again to harmonize their responses to the April 30 recommendation.[78] In a last futile

77. Francis Dana to the Massachusetts Assembly, July 22, 1784, Nathan Dane to James Bowdoin, January 10, 1786, to Samuel Phillips, January 20, 1786, to John Choate, January 31, 1786, in Burnett (ed.), *Letters of Continental Congress*, VII, 570–71; VIII, 283, 288, 294; Report on the Committee on Commercial Treaties, March 3, 1786, in W. C. Ford *et al.* (eds.), *Journals*, XXX, 93–94; McMaster, *History of People of U.S.*, I, 361.

78. Report of the Committee on Commercial Treaties, February 28, 1786, in W. C. Ford et al. (eds.), *Journals*, XXX, 87–88. Madison noted that the necessity for harmonizing state commercial policies was becoming more obvious with every day that passed; James Madison to Thomas Jefferson, January 22, 1786, in Hunt (ed.), *Writings of Madison*, II, 218. American commissioners had tried but failed to conclude treaties with Denmark, Austria, Sardinia, the Papal States, Naples, Tuscany, Russia, Saxony, and Portugal.

plea to the state legislatures, Congress alluded to the commercial distress besetting the country and reaffirmed its conviction that the commerce of the entire nation must be brought under control because "reason and experience demonstrate that this power cannot be exercised by the government of any state." [79]

By this time, the nationalist movement was gathering momentum, quickened by the evident failure of the states to arrive at a common understanding, and by the fact that for seven months national government had virtually ceased to exist. Newspapers warned that time was running out.[80] The New York *Packet* emphasized the immediate need for congressional power "to regulate commerce and fulfill national engagements." Many members of Congress were now willing to take a second look at Monroe's amendment and consider seriously for the first time the idea of a general convention "for adjusting commercial affairs," and revising the Articles of Confederation.[81]

79. An Address from the United States in Congress Assembled to the Legislatures of the Several States, August 31, 1786, in W. C. Ford *et al.* (eds.), *Journals*, XXXI, 613, 618. Nothing came of the plea, although all states had indicated some form of approval for the April 30 recommendation by 1787. Connecticut, Pennsylvania, Maryland, and South Carolina could not agree on when their grants should begin to take effect. New Hampshire and North Carolina also remained unsettled; Committee Report, October 23, 1786, *ibid.*, XXXI, 908–909.

80. New York *Packet*, May 4, June 19, 1786; *New Jersey Gazette*, May 8, 1786; *Pennsylvania Gazette*, August 31, 1785. Congress failed to muster a quorum on all but three days out of seven months; Rufus King to Elbridge Gerry, April 30, 1786, in Burnett (ed.), *Letters of Continental Congress*, VIII, 346; Smith, *John Adams*, II, 651. According to Bancroft, difficulties in obtaining a quorum had led to the consideration of a constitutional convention as early as 1784; Bancroft, *Formation of the Constitution*, I, 166.

81. New York *Packet*, June 15, 1786; John Jay to George Washington, March 16, 1786, in Johnston (ed.), *Papers of John Jay*, III, 186–87. See also, Benjamin Franklin to Thomas Jefferson, March 20, 1786, in Albert Henry

The nationalists in Congress, led by energetic Charles Pinckney of South Carolina, took advantage of the change in sentiment by persuading their colleagues to deliberate on the state of the nation. They then succeeded in securing the appointment of a grand committee to consider the question of constitutional reform. Much to the dismay of Richard Henry Lee and his followers, the committee broadened its discussion to include a wide range of topics. In the end, it recommended the addition of executive and judicial branches to the federal government, a bicameral legislature, direct federal sovereignty over the people, and federal power to coerce the states. On August 7, 1786, the committee proposed seven additional articles of confederation, the first being a provision for congressional control of commerce.[82] However, the recommendations were never submitted for approval to the seperate states. Congress became absorbed in a controversy over pending negotiations with Spain and gave its immediate attention to fiscal and Indian affairs.

At the same time, events taking place in Annapolis, Maryland, were establishing a rival focal point in the movement for constitutional reform. The Annapolis Convention which met in September of 1786 was intended to provide a forum in which delegations from every state might agree on a common commercial policy. Nationalist leaders, however, were well aware that it could also lead to serious constitutional re-

---

Smyth (ed.), *The Writings of Benjamin Franklin* (10 vols.; New York and London: Macmillan Co., 1905–1907), IX, 499; William Grayson to James Madison, March 22, 1786, in Burnett (ed.), *Letters of Continental Congress*, VIII, 333; Nathan Dane to Samuel Phillips, January 20, 1786, in Nathan Dane Papers, Library of Congress.

82. Thomas Rodney, "Diary," May 3, 1786, in Burnett (ed.), *Letters of Continental Congress*, VIII, 350; Committee Report, August 4, 1786, in W. C. Ford *et al.* (eds.) *Journals*, XXXI, 494–97.

form. The chief architect of the meeting, for example, saw an opportunity to give "additional powers to Congress." [83] Reforms in taxation, military establishment, or treaty power would not create totally new powers for the national government; rather, as Madison later indicated, they were a substitution of more effective modes of administering old powers. But congressional control of commerce *would* be a totally new power. As such, it would bear important implications. When, in 1785, Monroe had proposed to give Congress the power to regulate foreign commerce, he recognized the "deep and radical change" it would create in the "bonds of union." If adopted, he wrote, it would "certainly form the most permanent and powerful principle in the Confederation." According to Rufus King, the federal commerce power would run so "deep into the authorities of the individual states," that it could never be exercised without a federal judiciary.[84] According to Madison, regulation of *foreign* commerce would be "incomplete and ineffectual" without *interstate* regulations as well.[85] These ideas were later used by various pamphleteers to defend the Constitution during the ratification debate, and they must have been a factor in deciding the Constitutional Convention to opt for a more radical reformation than that embodied in the New Jersey Plan.[86]

83. James Madison to James Monroe, January 22, 1786, in Hunt (ed.), *Writings of Madison*, II, 223. John Jay felt that in order to achieve any permanent good, the Annapolis Conference would have to lead to the establishment of three separate branches of government: legislative, judicial, and executive; Monaghan, *John Jay*, 283.

84. Clinton Rossiter (ed.), *The Federalist Papers* (New York: New American Library, 1961), No. 45, p. 293; James Monroe to Thomas Jefferson, June 16, 1785, and Rufus King to Jonathan Jackson, September 3, 1786, both in Burnett (ed.), *Letters of Continental Congress*, VIII, 143, 460. See also Jay's opinion in a similar vein, cited in footnote 83.

85. Rossiter (ed.), *Federalist Papers*, No. 42, p. 267.

86. For example, Edmund Randolph, "Letter on the Federal Conven-

As is well known, only five state delegations arrived to participate in the Annapolis sessions, causing all decisions to be postponed. However, the sparse representation was not indicative of the degree of public support. Four states, Massachusetts, New Hampshire, Rhode Island, and North Carolina, appointed delegations which failed to arrive on time. Others, according to Madison, were favorably disposed. Maryland hesitated, ironically, for fear of undermining the authority of Congress; Connecticut was restrained by a delicate twist of politics; and South Carolina felt satisfied that she had agreed to grant Congress temporary power over her commerce.[87] Nor did the disappointing show of delegates prevent those in attendance from recommending a full-scale constitutional convention to be held the following summer in Philadelphia. In a report drafted by Hamilton, it was suggested that delegates to the next convention should not be restricted to a discussion of commercial matters alone, since "the power of regulating trade is of such comprehensive extent that to give it efficacy . . . may require a correspondent adjustment in other parts of the federal system." [88] The delegates, therefore, should be free to deliberate on any issue whatever.

This Annapolis Report was a milestone along the way to Philadelphia and a signal victory for the nationalists. But it was also an indication of the decisive importance of British trade laws as a stimulant to constitutional reform. Its origi-

tion," October 16, 1787, in Paul Leicester Ford (ed.), *Pamphlets on the Constitution of the United States, Published During Its Discussion by the People, 1787–1788* (Brooklyn: n.p., 1888), 267; Roger Sherman, "A Citizen of New Haven," No. 2, December 25, 1788, in Paul Leicester Ford (ed.), *Essays on the Constitution of the United States, Published During Its Discussion by the People, 1787–1788* (Brooklyn: n.p., 1892), 238.

87. W. C. Ford *et al.* (eds.), *Journals*, XXXI, 678; James Madison to Thomas Jefferson, August 12, 1786, in Hunt (ed.), *Writings of Madison*, II, 262.

88. W. C. Ford *et al.* (eds.), *Journals*, XXXI, 679.

nal cause and immediate appeal flowed from the Orders in Council, and its ultimate success can be traced in large part to the apparent failure of John Adams' mission and to the effect of this on local, state, and congressional politics.

The report was laid before Congress on September 20, then referred to a grand committee, and ignored for several months. Reports of civil disorder in Vermont, New Hampshire, and Massachusetts demanded immediate attention. Southern delegates became incensed over Jay's negotiations with Gardoqui, and there was serious talk of dissolving the union.

When Congress finally reconvened on February 2, it turned again to the Annapolis scheme. Certain northern delegates such as Rufus King and Nathan Dane suspected a southern plot to restrict congressional power because of Virginia's supposed opposition to general commercial regulations. Accordingly, they questioned the legality of a constitutional convention called by any authority other than Congress. Some argued that any association of Congress with the Philadelphia Convention might impart to it an undesirable flavor of nationalism. Such arguments, however, soon subsided before a series of fortuitous events.

On February 3, Congress learned that Virginia had endorsed the Philadelphia Convention and was sending George Washington as one of its delegates. Two weeks later the New York legislature defeated a proposed federal impost, killing a long-cherished hope that Congress might obtain a steady source of revenue. On February 20, New York followed the lead of Virginia and instructed its delegation in Congress to endorse the idea of a constitutional convention, and on the same day a grand committee, formed to consider the Annapolis Report, submitted a favorable recommendation. By this time, Delaware, New Jersey, Pennsylvania, and North Carolina had also appointed delegates. The pressure of these events, coupled with the growing anxiety over Shays's Rebellion and the general sense of national insecurity, may have prompted suspicious northerners to change their minds, for on February 21 Rufus King moved on behalf of the Bay State that Congress formally endorse the idea of a constitutional convention. His motion was adopted.[89]

The convening of the Philadelphia Convention in the spring of 1787 confirmed Madison's prediction that the Annapolis meeting would "probably miscarry" but "lead to better consequences." [90] Nationalists, who had long seen that British trade restrictions might stimulate demands for a stronger central government, now had their chance. The door was open for constitutional reform far transcending the immediate issue of commercial control. To Antifederalists, this door resembled the lid of Pandora's box. But to ardent nationalists such as Hamilton and Madison, the open door invited a remedy for every ill that beset the Confederation.

89. For congressional action on the Annapolis Report, see Burnett, *Continental Congress*, 676–77. Robert A. Feer, in his recent article, claims that there is no evidence to show that Shays had any decisive impact on the decision of the various states to appoint delegates to Philadelphia; Feer, "Shays's Rebellion," 393.

90. James Madison to James Monroe, January 22, 1786, in Hunt (ed.), *Writings of Madison*, II, 223.

# III

# The National
# Mood

*To the man who shall say, "It is of no consequence to consult national honor," I only answer thus,—"If thy soul be so narrow and depraved as to believe this, it were a needless attempt to cure thee of thy error."* [1]

The two previous chapters have dealt with tangible problems. This one is devoted to the discussion of something equally important: a mood. Military and commercial problems helped to produce a sense of national insecurity which coincided with a fierce patriotic pride. The combination of fear and hope in turn heightened the impact of each individual problem on the demand for constitutional reform. The psychic factor is hard to describe and virtually impossible to measure, but it is a natural and necessary background for any study of the reform movement. It should be noted at the outset that the American perception of reality was not always accurate. Certain fears and hopes may

1. Alexander Hanson, "Remarks on the Proposed Plan of a Federal Government," in P. L. Ford (ed.), *Pamphlets on the Constitution*, 244.

have been exaggerated, but they nonetheless moved men to action.

We turn first to the element of apprehension. Americans after 1783 became increasingly aware of their country's position as a fledgling republic in the midst of hostile monarchs. They looked about and could not be sure of a single ally among the world powers. Indeed it appeared that the European nations, though divided on most issues, might find a cause for unity in their opposition to the United States.

Britain's abiding hostility loomed before Americans as an object of special concern. It seemed too much to expect that a world power as mighty as Britain would ever accept defeat at the hands of as weak and unstable a nation as the United States. As soon as King George could shake the European jackals from his back, he would turn again for a final showdown. Richard Henry Lee could see no difference between a North and a Pitt: "The same men still rule in secret, the same measures are wished to be practiced upon. . . . The nation too like a strong, proud, and sullen man, angry from unexpected defeat, and imputing misfortunes to casualties, would seem not averse to a second trial." [2] John Adams, observing Whitehall at close range, warned repeatedly that the United States would have to defeat her former enemy

2. Richard Henry Lee to Samuel Adams, November 18, 1784, in Samuel Adams Papers, New York Public Library. For similar opinions see Nathan Dane to Samuel Phillips, January 20, 1786, in Nathan Dane Papers, Library of Congress; John Francis Mercer to James Madison, November 12, 1784, in Burnett (ed.), *Letters of Continental Congress,* VII, 609; John Jay to Marquis de Lafayette, July 15, 1785, to Thomas Jefferson, July 13, 1785, to John Adams, September 6, 1785, all in *Diplomatic Correspondence, 1783–89,* I, 303, 615; II, 389; George Washington to Jacob Reed, August 11, 1784, to Henry Knox, December 26, 1784, both in Fitzpatrick (ed.), *Writings of George Washington,* XXVII, 455–56; XXIX, 124; James Monroe to James Madison, March 6, 1785, in Hamilton (ed.), *Writings of Monroe,* I, 65.

a second time. "Everything is calculated," he said, "to involve us in a war with England." Only poverty, strained relations with Ireland, and European involvement, according to Adams, held Britain back from venting her full wrath against America. Jefferson's opinion of England was unequivocal: "That nation hates us." [3]

In a variety of ways, the former mother country seemed to indicate a desire to reverse the outcome of the revolutionary war. She began by striking what appeared to be an unnecessarily harsh blow at the American shipping industry and export trade. It has been noted that the British could justly claim that they were only applying the principles of their age-old navigation laws. But since a commercial policy of reciprocity would have benefited the British as much as the Americans in the short run, British actions were generally regarded as evidence of a desire "to crush the commerce and navigation of America." [4] Americans felt helpless. They relied on British credit; they admitted a decided preference for British goods as compared with other foreign imports, and their every effort to pass retaliatory legislation ended in frustration. They had freed themselves from British territorial imperialism but could find no defense against this more subtle kind of domination.

Two other British actions regarded by Americans as hostile were the holding of fortifications on American soil in violation of the spirit of the peace treaty and an embargo

3. John Adams to John Jay, April 13, 1785, to Arthur Lee, September 6, 1785, both in Adams (ed.), *Works of John Adams*, VIII, 235; IX, 536–37; John Adams to John Jay, July 19, 1785, November 15, 1787, in *Diplomatic Correspondence, 1783–89*, II, 399, 817; Ritcheson, *Aftermath of Revolution*, 44.

4. Tucker, *Reflections*, 6–7, 14–15; Donald Lewis Smith, *John Jay* (New York: Columbia University Press, 1968), 99; Ritcheson, *Aftermath of Revolution*, 16–17.

on the export of machine tools to the United States. The posts, as we have seen, were deemed vitally important for a satisfactory defense against Indian raids and outright invasion from the North, to say nothing of their value in terms of the fur trade. With regard to the embargo, it was clear that American infant industries stood in need of punches, presses, hammers, lathes, and the like. By blocking the sale of such items, the Court of St. James's seemed to be offering another proof of its general attitude. John Adams observed in his report to John Jay on the industrial ban, "It shows the spirit of this country towards the United States and summarily comprehends a volume of politics for us." [5]

More notorious than Britain's embargo on machine tools was her supposed cooperation with the Barbary pirates. English merchants, including Lloyd's of London, were accused of deliberately exaggerating the damage done to American shipping by pirate corsairs in order to boost the insurance premiums Americans would have to pay. And Benjamin Franklin claimed there was a maxim among British merchants that "if there were no Algiers, it would be worth England's while to build one." [6] There was, too, an element of truth in these suspicions, for after 1783 the British consul at Algiers, Charles Logie, took pains to inform Algerian pirate captains that they were now at liberty to seize all ships sailing out of North American ports unless they carried British passports. Later, when the American ship *Maria* was captured by pirates in July, 1785, its crew members were told that they would not be released until they made peace

5. John Adams to John Jay, August 28, 1785, in *Diplomatic Correspondence, 1783–89*, II, 463.
6. Tucker, *Reflections*, 12; Elbridge Gerry to Rufus King, May 30, 1785, in King, *Rufus King*, I, 102. Franklin is quoted in Irwin, *Diplomatic Relations*, 17.

with their Father, the King of England! Logie, who inter-
viewed them in Algiers during their captivity, pointed out
that they would not be prisoners if they had not rebelled
against Great Britain. He also offered to aid anyone who
wished to become a British citizen. And so much under
Logie's influence was the Dey personally that he not only
rebuked the *Maria* crew for its disloyalty to King George
but refused to recognize the United States and would not
receive an agent sent by Congress to negotiate a treaty of
peace.[7]

Running parallel to British actions which imperiled the
country from without was the threat of subversion from
within. From the earliest days of independence, there was
always the fear that the United States government might
be overthrown by forces inside its borders. In a celebrated
letter to Thomas Jefferson, John Adams wrote, "You are
apprehensive of foreign interference, intrigue, influence. So
am I." His cousin Samuel, warned of the need to guard
against British "emissaries under the guise of merchants, re-
penting refugees, schoolmasters, and other characters" who
"unless care is taken may effect another and fatal revolution." He recalled that the commonwealth of England had
lasted only twelve years before the exiled king was restored
with all the rage and madness of royalty. And, fearful of factions forming in the United States which would be partial
to one foreign nation or another, he deprecated "the most
favored nations predominating in the councils of America."
Of similar mind was a faction of Congress which opposed
any exchange of ministers with the outside world because
it might establish inroads of subversion for America's enemies. James Monroe expected to encounter the hidden influence of British agents at the Annapolis Convention in

7. Barnby, *Prisoners of Algiers*, 34, 37, 74, 81.

1786, and George Washington later heard that spies were arriving by the half dozens on every foreign ship.[8]

The most likely agents of British influence in America were thought to be the Tories who had refused to take up arms against their king or had actively opposed the patriot cause. As losers, bereft of property and honor, they were now suspected of biding their time in the hope of undermining republican government and delivering their country back into the rapacious hands of Great Britain. Surely they should be expelled. One writer predicted that, with the war for independence over, revolutionary fervor would die down, patriots would soon be preoccupied with making a living, and Tory influence would reassert itself: "The number of those who are in reality malcontents in America, are not so small as may be imagined; nor are their views and hopes so humble as many suppose.... The Tory principle contains in it a mortal and irreconcilable hatred to our government. That this principle will be communicated, is too probable when we consider the wealth, the art, and perseverance and fashion of many of its present possessors.... In a little time the last spasm of republican spirit will be over." [9]

8. Chinard, *Honest John Adams*, 213; Samuel Adams to Richard Henry Lee, December 23, 1784, to John Adams, November 4, 1783, both in Samuel Adams Papers, New York Public Library; Smith, *John Adams*, II, 617; Max Farrand (ed.), *The Records of the Federal Convention of 1787* (4 vols.; New Haven: Yale University Press, 1911), II, 285; Marquis de Lottiniere to George Washington, January 27, 1788, in George Washington Papers, Library of Congress, Ser. 4, Vol. CCXL; James Monroe to James Madison, September 3, 1786, in Burnett (ed.), *Letters of Continental Congress*, VIII, 461. No good study of subversive forces in the United States during the years 1783–1800 has been done. The degree to which popular fears conformed to reality is therefore unknown.

9. "A Letter from Phocion to the Considerate Citizens of New York," January 1–27, 1784, in Syrett (ed.), *Papers of Hamilton*, III, 494; Bingham, *Letter from An American*, 7–21. It should also be noted that the return of Loyalists was a political issue which would later divide Federalists from Antifederalists.

One Tory who had taken refuge in England during the Revolution bravely returned to Virginia only to be tarred and feathered by his neighbors for having "the effrontery" to come home to his native land. When the state governor tried to uphold law and order, he received a petition from one hundred and eighty persons defending their right to tar and feather and asserting that the governor's action could only "give a dangerous damp to that spirit of opposition to British violence, British influence, and British intrigue which hath once saved the state and may again be necessary for its defense." [10]

The fear of subversive activity was especially prevalent in New England. The *Massachusetts Centinel* asserted: "Our internal foes are still at work; they are making use of every method in their power, to interrupt our tranquility and sow the seeds of discord and dissention." When the Bay State began to have difficulty maintaining control over her independent-minded northern and western counties, political opposition to the party in power was often regarded as British-inspired. When Boston heard about Shays's Rebellion, it dispatched a circular letter to other Massachusetts towns declaring, "We are convinced that the present disturbances arose from British emissaries residing amongst us, whose every wish is for our overthrow and ruin." Jefferson, who observed events from afar, blamed England for Shays's Rebellion. Washington was of the same opinion, and Madison felt sure that the Shaysites had "opened a communication with the Viceroy of Canada." The New York *Journal* exclaimed: "The country is in an uproar; and who has done it? British agents." The *Pennsylvania Gazette* carried a similar message, and from British Grenada came word that was

10. Virginia Legislative Petitions, Essex County, May 25, 1784, in Virginia Legislative Petition Collection, Virginia State Library, Richmond.

hardly calculated to quiet suspicions: "The inhabitants of this place are in great spirits and highly elated, owing to a report that an insurrection has taken place in New England, and that 15,000 men had already taken arms, and 20,000 more in readiness to join them against the Congress and in support of the British flag." [11]

Many congressmen were concerned about the separatist leanings of the self-proclaimed state of Vermont whose loyalty to Congress was doubtful and whose leaders were said to be flirting with Canada in the hope of promoting their foreign trade. William Grayson, congressman from Virginia, warned that Vermont and Great Britain were "on close and secret terms," and Alexander Hamilton made the same point in his celebrated speech of March 23, 1787, in which he assured the members of the New York State Assembly that Ethan and Ira Allen had established a close connection with the Canadian government. Reminding his colleagues of the imminent danger of disunion, he suggested that a British policy of "divide and conquer" would "lay hold of Vermont as a link in the chain of events." Subsequently, the example of Vermont, happy under British rule and free from taxes, would be a powerful example for the other states to follow.[12]

11. *Massachusetts Centinel*, April 2, 1785. On May 21, 1785, the *Centinel* again expressed concern over "the danger of British influence being introduced among us"; *New Jersey Gazette*, October 9, 1786; George Washington to David Humphreys, December 26, 1786, in Fitzpatrick (ed.), *Writings of George Washington*, XXIX, 126; James Madison to Edmund Pendleton, January 9, 1787, in Hunt (ed.), *Writings of Madison*, II, 307; New York *Journal*, September 28, 1786; Ritcheson, *Aftermath of Revolution*, 422. The *Pennsylvania Gazette*, September 27, 1786, was convinced that "the present disturbances arise from British emissaries." See also *ibid.*, December 20, 1786. Although the Grenada report was exaggerated, it did indicate which way the wind was blowing.

12. Bancroft, *Formation of the Constitution*, II, 419; Syrett (ed.), *Papers of Hamilton*, IV, 135–36.

The Vermonters were indeed making private overtures to the British government.[13] And well they might. Embroiled in border disputes with New Hampshire and New York, they could not count on the Hudson or Connecticut Rivers as outlets for their timber, grain, and pork products. The only alternative was the lake-and-river route northward to Quebec. Reunion with Great Britain would not only provide them with access to the Atlantic, it would be a guarantee of protection against hostile neighbors. Fortunately for Congress, the British showed little interest in a political union. They were anxious to promote an economic connection and prolong Vermont's separatist influence on the rest of New England. But they were not anxious to assume the burden of defending Allen from a possible three-front attack. The only advantage of political union would have been some added protection for their Champlain forts, and the United States did not seem to be in any position to threaten these.[14]

Congress feared the spread of separatist spirit to the surrounding countryside. Elbridge Gerry, congressman from Massachusetts, reported in November, 1786, that there had been and would be meetings "for the purpose of reuniting the American States to the government of Great Britain." And when Daniel Shays entered the picture in the fall of 1786, a connection was quickly drawn between the Shaysites and the Green Mountain Boys. Both appeared to favor a union with Canada, and the people of Vermont seemed to be encouraging their neighbors to the south.[15]

13. *Pennsylvania Gazette*, May 17, 1786, quoting the *Halifax* (Nova Scotia) *Morning Post*; Committee of the Council of Commerce to Lord Dorchester, 1787, in Washington Papers, Library of Congress, Ser. 4, Vol. CCXXXIX, Item #106.

14. Richard Warner Van Alstyne, *American Diplomacy in Action* (Stanford, Calif.: Stanford University Press, 1947), 60.

15. Elbridge Gerry to Rufus King, November 29, 1786, in King, *Rufus*

The degree to which Shays's Rebellion may have been instigated by Ethan Allen's followers or by British agents remains to be seen. But the fact that contemporary leaders were thinking along these lines is a further illustration of the American image of Great Britain, an image neatly summarized in a newspaper account of the year 1786: "The expenditure of secret service money since the year 1782 has been great beyond all conception . . . large sums are granted to the Barbary pirates; and . . . the different tribes of Indians to the West are furnished with supplies to incite them to acts of perfidy and inhumanity against us. . . . Thus we see the destruction of this country is still the darling object of the hopeful rulers of Britain." [16]

Had the British actions and attitudes been viewed in isolation, they would have given some cause for concern; but they assumed an even darker aspect when viewed in the context of anti-Americanism prevalent throughout Europe. From the start of the postwar period, it seemed clear that the United States would attract few friends and that its position in a world of national giants would be lonely. The austere Charles III of Spain had not relished his part in the creation of a republic adjacent to his New World possessions. It was no secret that his aim in succoring the Revolution had been purely selfish and that the government of

---

*King*, I, 197. There was even a rumor that a certain group in the New York legislature, "the seditious party," had opened communications with the Viceroy of Canada; Catherine Drinker Bowen, *Miracle at Philadelphia* (Boston: Little, Brown & Co., 1966), 31. See also John Jay to Thomas Jefferson, December 14, 1786, in *Diplomatic Correspondence, 1783–89*, I, 809; *Virginia Gazette*, November 30, 1786; William Grayson to James Monroe, November 22, 1786, in James Monroe Papers, Library of Congress, Ser. 1, Vol. I; Edward Carrington to Edmund Randolph, December 8, 1786, and William Grayson to James Madison, November 22, 1786, both in Burnett (ed.), *Letters of Continental Congress*, VIII, 511, 516.

16. New York *Journal*, June 15, 1786, quoting the *Pennsylvania Herald* of June 3.

Torquemada had determined to contain American westward expansion, first by influencing the terms of peace,
then by applying military pressure along the southwest and
closing the Mississippi River to American shipping. Many
Americans felt that London and Madrid had formed some
kind of mutual understanding in 1785 and might even join
forces to check American growth. Britain supported Spain's
closure of the Mississippi, and Spain had granted British
merchants a share in the sale of arms, ammunition, and other
goods to the southern tribes of Indians. Should the English
and Spaniards ever decide to take the field together, it was
expected that their combined strength and geographical position would be formidable.[17]

And what of America's other wartime ally? With France
there had been a sense of genuine friendship during the
Revolution and a feeling that this spirit would continue. The
illusion was rapidly dispelled, however, when Paris lined up
with Madrid on a number of Spanish-American disputes.
When Spain closed the Mississippi, the French approved.
During the peace talks of 1782 when doubt arose over the
proper extent of America's western boundary, Paris and
Madrid were as one in favoring the Alleghenies rather than
the mighty river beyond. Some of France's actions were
understandable in light of her Family Compact with Spain,
but not all. The French government appeared to harbor an
antagonism uniquely its own. When Americans called upon
Louis XVI to aid them against the Barbary pirates (he had
promised to employ his "good offices" in the treaty of 1778),
his minister offered only advice and empty expressions of

17. James Monroe to Thomas Jefferson, June 16, 1786, in Hamilton
(ed.), *Writings of Monroe*, I, 137; George Washington to Thomas Jefferson, August 23, 1792, in Fitzpatrick (ed.), *Writings of George Washington*, XXXII, 128–30; *Pennsylvania Gazette*, January 10, 1787.

good will. Indeed, there were reports that the French were encouraging raids against American commerce in order to enrich their own.[18]

France was also suspected of subverting the American government. According to one source, "she spared neither art, influence, or money to effect her purposes. She has consuls, vice-consuls, agents both public and private distributed and pensioned in every part of America."[19] Secretary Jay opposed the Franco-American consular convention of 1782 because it would permit French agents to serve anywhere in the country and facilitate a spy network. A substitute convention which was finally signed in 1788 omitted the objectionable clauses.

It is interesting to note that Leonore F. Moustier, the French minister to the United States in 1787, regarded the American government as a "phantom of democracy" which would end in tyranny. Moustier wanted to block American efforts to secure control of the lower Mississippi and suggested that France reestablish her North American empire in the region between the Alleghenies and Mississippi with headquarters at New Orleans. It would be easy to under-

18. Comte de Vergennes to Louis Guillaume Otto, August 23, 1786; Otto to John Jay, October 23, 1786, in *Diplomatic Correspondence, 1783–89*, I, 241–42. Even in August, 1778, when French aid had been requested to expedite the voyage of American ships which were being held up in Italian ports for fear of Barbary raids, the "cooperation of French officials proved to be lukewarm and their pretended aid of little consequence"; Bixler, *Open Door*, 12. This contrasted with Spain's willingness to aid in treaty negotiations, Portugal's cooperation, Sweden's helpful services, Danish aid, and Sardinia's loan to the United States of a number of gunboats. The Dutch, also, promised to protect American Mediterranean interests; Irwin, *Diplomatic Relations*, 30, 197–98. None of the nations was offering aid out of disinterested benevolence, of course. Spain, for example, was primarily interested in concluding the Jay-Gardoqui talks on a winning note.

19. Champion, *Considerations*, 153.

mine frontier loyalty to Congress, and Spain would be glad to yield New Orleans since her object, which was to contain the United States, could only be accomplished by France.[20]

Later, in 1793, when the impetuous Edmund Genêt arrived in America to represent the new French republic, he submitted official documents to the State Department which showed that the Bourbon statesmen had indeed been unfriendly, that France had been entirely on the side of Spain in the dispute over navigation of the Mississippi, and that France and Spain had been equally jealous of the growing power and ambition of the United States. Most remarkable of all, the documents showed that France had tried to prevent the ratification of the Constitution in 1788. Instructions given to Genêt by the French government included the following: "The Executive Council ... has seen ... that at the very time the good people of America expressed their gratitude to us in the most feeling manner ... Vergennes and Montmorin thought that it was right for France to hinder the United States from taking that political stability of which they are capable; because they would soon acquire a strength which it was probable they would be eager to abuse." [21] Genêt's information was correct, for Montmorin had indeed written to his American *chargé d'affaires* in August, 1787, with regard to the Constitutional Convention: "His Majesty thinks, on the one hand, that the deliberations will have little chance of success ... on the other hand that

20. Moustier's ideas are contained in an exhaustive three-hundred-page report on the Mississippi Valley, its economics, geography, and politics; Van Alstyne, *Rising American Empire*, 73–74.

21. Walter Lowrie and Matthew St. Clair Clarke (eds.), *American State Papers: Documents, Legislative and Executive, of the Congress of the United States, From the First Session of the First to the Third Session of the Thirteenth Congress, Inclusive: Commencing March 3, 1789, and Ending March 3, 1815* (38 vols.; Washington, D. C.: Gales and Seaton, 1832–61), I, 572.

it suits France to have the United States remain in their present state, because if they should assume the consistence of which they are susceptible they would soon acquire a force and power which they would probably be very eager to abuse." [22]

As one pamphleteer put it, France had aided America's revolution out of sheer self-interest and had begun to regard the United States as a rival the moment peace was concluded.[23]

French commercial policy was equally discouraging. Immediately after the war, Americans had assumed that France would favor them with a degree of disinterested benevolence. John Adams was certain in July, 1783, that France and England would not join forces to "make a common cause against us, even in relation to the carrying trade to and from the West Indies . . . rivals and enemies at heart

22. Quoted in Samuel Flagg Bemis, *John Jay, Secretary for Foreign Affairs for the Continental Congress, September 21, 1784, to September 15, 1789*, Vol. I of Samuel Flagg Bemis, *The American Secretaries of State and Their Diplomacy, 1776–1925* (10 vols.; New York: Alfred A. Knopf, 1927–29), I, 262. Armand-Marc, Comte de Montmorin-Saint-Hérem, succeeded Vergennes as French foreign minister when the latter died in 1787. His American chargé d'affaires was Louis Guillaume Otto who had followed the Marquis de La Luzerne as France's chief envoy to the United States.

23. *The Political Establishments of the United States of America in a Candid Review of Their Deficiencies, Together With a Proposal of Reformation, Humbly Addressed to the Citizens of America, By a Fellow Citizen* (Philadelphia: Robert Bell, 1784), 17. Felix Gilbert has asserted that Americans began their struggle for independence confident that when they defeated the British they would assume their rightful place in the family of nations. Their dealings with other countries would be based on the enlightened principle of free trade which, when established throughout the world, would usher in an era of continual peace. According to Gilbert, a gradual change occurred in the American outlook on the rest of the world in the days after the Declaration of Independence and the Model Treaty of 1776. With the war over and the peace concluded, American statesmen became more aware of power factors; Felix Gilbert, *To the Farewell Address* (Princeton: Princeton University Press, 1961), 16–18, 43, 51, 56–57, 63, 69–72, 88–89.

they eternally will be." ²⁴ He predicted that his countrymen would receive generous access to the French West Indian trade. But the hope soon died.

It is true that four French ports were declared free in 1784: Dunkirk, L'Orient, Bayonne, and Marseilles; a few West Indian ports were also opened to small American ships for a limited number of items. It is likewise true that when Jefferson became minister to France in 1785 he obtained, with the help of Lafayette, a radical reduction of duties on American whale oil and permission for Americans to ship fish to the West Indies. But such concessions were minor; free ports were not equivalent to a free market, and it was the latter that mattered most. Furthermore, several royal decrees of 1784 and 1785 cut severely into American trade with the French Caribbean (Martinique, Guadeloupe, and Haiti). One *arrêt* of August 30, 1784, barred Americans from importing wheat and flour or exporting sugar, coffee, cotton, and cocoa. This was especially discouraging to the middle states such as New York and Pennsylvania, whose principal exports were wheat and flour. Another *arrêt* of 1785 granted a bounty of ten livres per quintal on all dried cod if caught and shipped by French subjects in French ships into the French West Indies, and a second bounty of five livres per quintal for cod shipped by Frenchmen in French ships to Portuguese, Spanish, or Italian ports. Still another *arrêt* achieved a similar effect in reverse. It imposed a duty of five livres per quintal on all dried cod imported into the islands by any stranger or in any foreign bottom.²⁵

24. John Adams to Robert R. Livingston, July 18, 1783, in Wharton (ed.), *Diplomatic Correspondence*, VI, 560–61.

25. Bancroft, *Formation of the Constitution*, I, 206–208; Setser, *Commercial Reciprocity*, 88–89. New England was particularly injured in this case. Massachusetts and New Hamphire shortly afterward enacted navigation laws which applied to French shipping as well as British. These

French and British policy bore a striking resemblance in the eyes of many. Some suspected England and France of conspiring to throttle American commerce. Seventy-six inhabitants of Alexandria, Virginia, blamed France as much as Great Britain for their current state of commercial distress. John Adams spoke of a French design "of ruining, if they can, our carrying trade, and annihilating all our navigation and seamen." Urging Congress to retaliate against foreign trade restrictions, he asserted, "The French deserve it as much as the English, for they are as much enemies to our ships and mariners. Their Navigation Acts are not quite so severe as those of Spain, Portugal and England (as they relate to their colonies, I mean) but they are not much less so; and they discover as strong a lust to annihilate our navigation as anybody." [26] Charles Pinckney of South Carolina also lumped France and England together and thought both nations were "pushing their fisheries with astonishing exertions and endeavoring to depress ours." And congressman Elbridge Gerry enclosed one of the French edicts in a letter to his colleague, Rufus King, in which he remarked bitterly that, "their object, it appears to me, is to pursue their prospect of a powerful navy by increasing their nursery for seamen and destroying ours. France has been evidently averse to our being powerful by land or sea, and this edict strikes at the foundation of our naval establishment." [27]

---

laws, however, were never enforced due to complaints voiced by French merchants to Vergennes, who relayed them to Congress through Jefferson, *ibid.*, 89.

26. *Ibid.*, 54; John Jay to Marquis de Lafayette, January 19, 1785, in Johnston (ed.), *Papers of John Jay*, III, 138; Virginia Legislative Petitions, Alexandria, November 5, 1785; John Adams to Thomas Jefferson, July 18, August 7, 1785, in Adams (ed.), *Works of John Adams*, VIII, 279, 292.

27. Charles Pinckney's speech of August 16, 1786, in W. C. Ford *et al.* (eds.), *Journals*, XXXI, 941; Elbridge Gerry to Rufus King, March, 1785, in King, *Rufus King*, I, 74. Gerry's suspicions seemed to be confirmed in

Nor did France and Britain seem to be the only adversaries of a nation committed to the revolutionary principle of free trade, a nation which saw the reduction of trade barriers as indispensable for achieving world peace; all of Europe was wedded to the idea of mercantilism. Holland, one of the first nations to sign a trade agreement with the United States, was accused of being "jealous of our commerce." She had joined the rest of the powers in refusing Congress a loan for the purchase of peace with Algiers, and Jay noted that the Dutch minister would not give American shipowners the customary letters of introduction to the island of Batavia. Spain was excluding American ships and goods from her West Indian possessions, and her policy on direct trade with the United States left so much to be desired that many Americans were willing to yield navigation rights on the Mississippi in order to open up a more profitable trans-Atlantic business. Even the Holy Roman Emperor was reported to have "imbibed British prejudices" against American commerce.[28] Perhaps a statement issued

1786 when the French and British monarchs overcame their traditional enmity to sign a joint commercial treaty in which Britain made certain concessions to France with regard to the fisheries. King reacted violently, seeing in the pact evidence of insidious designs on the part of France and recommending that little dependence be put on her in the future. See Monroe's letter to Madison, May 31, 1786, in Hamilton (ed.), *Writings of Monroe*, I, 133; also, Louis Guillaume Otto to Comte de Vergennes, May 20, 1786, in Bancroft, *Formation of the Constitution*, I, 504. A copy of the treaty appears in the New York *Packet*, January 16, 1787. There followed a commercial convention in January, 1787, an agreement settling disputes of the French and English India Companies in August, 1787, and a treaty settling the attitudes of France and England toward Holland in November, 1787.

28. John Jay to Robert R. Livingston, July 19, 1783, in Johnston (ed.), *Papers of John Jay*, III, 55; Report of John Jay to Congress on a Joint Letter from Adams and Jefferson, May 29, 1786, *ibid.*, III, 198; John Jay to John Adams, February 3, 1786, to Thomas Jefferson, July 14, 1786, in *Diplomatic Correspondence, 1783–89*, I, 727–28; II, 511. Virginia merchants complained of discrimination by "many of the commercial powers" and

by the New York Chamber of Commerce best sums up the way Americans in 1786 viewed their economic relationship with the outside world: "All Europe did indeed desire to see us independent; but now that we are become so, each separate power is desirous of rendering our interests subservient to their commercial policy." [29] One foreign country was no different from another. All were enemies.

Still another apparent index of anti-Americanism was the tone of the foreign press. From his post in London, John Adams found the English newspapers bitterly hostile as well as inaccurate on American affairs, and he added that such distortions were "encouraged by every court and government in Europe." Continental accounts of the United States were often copied verbatim from the English press. From this polluted source, foreigners learned that the American population had decreased by a million during the war, that slaves were being imported in ever larger numbers, that indentured servants in America were treated as badly as slaves, and that Americans were unwilling and unable to pay their debts to British creditors (which was true). Especially damning was a letter allegedly written by Dr. Richard Price, one of Britain's few outspoken friends of America, in which Price regretted some of his former enthusiasm for the United States and doubted its prospects for survival. John Jay claimed he had met only six foreigners in the course of his entire life who really understood American affairs. He lamented the fact that there were so few states

---

found that "the politics of Europe" was "opposed to their just expectations"; Virginia Legislative Petitions, City of Fredericksburg, December 2, 1784. John Adams, who concurred in this opinion, asserted that "all nations are contriving to take advantage of us"; John Adams to Rufus King, June 14, 1786, in King, *Rufus King*, I, 181–83. See also Marquis de Lafayette to John Jay, February 11, 1787, in *Diplomatic Correspondence, 1783–89*, I, 316.

29. *Boston Gazette*, January 9, 1786.

and ministers "who think it convenient to magnify Americans whether by word or deed." Benjamin Franklin reported from France that it was obvious from "the general turn of the ministerial newspapers . . . and by the malignant [accounts?] their ministers make . . . of every little accident or dissension among us . . . that they bear us no good will." Even in the Hague, efforts were made to discredit the American government.[30]

Some of the most unfriendly tracts came from the pen of French writers. Abbé Mably's *Observations sur le gouvernment et les lois des États-Unis*, published in 1784, disparaged America's faith in the common man, criticized the freedom of press and religion, and suggested that Americans would eventually succumb to commercialization. François Soulès wrote, in his *Histoire des troubles de l'Amerique Anglaise* (1787), that "in America the wise are few indeed." Mallet du Pan, admittedly a dyed-in-the-wool monarchist, pointed out that the colonists had prospered before the Revolution, that many Americans had opposed the war, and that the Revolution was illegitimate. And the French newspaper, *Mercure de France*, recalled scornfully that in a country where all men were said to be equal, there were still 700,000 slaves.[31]

Admittedly, there were European intellectuals who hailed the American experiment, but they were few and far between. Prussian liberals composed odes to American free-

30. John Adams to John Jay, December 15, 1785, in *Diplomatic Correspondence, 1783–89*, II, 549; Price's letter was printed in England and reprinted in France circa 1784–85; Durand Echevarria, *Mirage in the West* (Princeton: Princeton University Press, 1957), 126; John Jay to Marquis de Lafayette, June 16, 1786, in Johnston (ed.), *Papers of John Jay*, III, 200–201; Report of Benjamin Franklin to Congress, December 25, 1783, C. W. F. Dumas to John Jay, October 26, 1787, both in *Diplomatic Correspondence, 1783–89*, I, 61; III, 596.

31. Quoted in Echevarria, *Mirage*, 128–29.

dom and eagerly awaited the downfall of hereditary nobil-
ity. Men like Lafayette, La Rochefoucauld-Liancourt, and
Abbé le Pradt regarded the New World with unreserved
approval. However, their sentiments were not those of the
leading journals of the time.

Americans thus perceived a spirit of anti-Americanism
well beyond the confines of Great Britain. They were apt to
generalize and explain European hostility in terms of a natural antagonism between royalist and republican ideals. They
assumed that the mere existence of the United States threatened the throne of every king and foreshadowed the con-
version of the world to democracy. William Smith, secretary to the American legation in London, wrote to John Jay
that monarchs would "always watch us with a jealous eye
while we adhere to and flourish under systems diametrically
opposite to those which support their governments and enable them to keep mankind in subjection." And Richard
Henry Lee, president of Congress, was convinced that there
existed "a general jealousy beyond the water of the powerful effects to be derived from republican virtue here." [32]

32. William S. Smith to John Jay, December 6, 1785, in *Diplomatic
Correspondence, 1783–89*, III, 12; Richard Henry Lee to Samuel Adams,
March 14, 1785, in Ballagh (ed.), *Letters of Lee*, II, 343. Fifty years later,
John Quincy Adams used graphic language to describe the view of Europe
which prevailed during the Confederation period. He recalled that,

With Britain and Spain, controversies involving the deepest interests
and very existence of the nation, were fermenting, and negociations
of the most humiliating character were pending . . . . With the other
European states there was scarcely any intercourse. The Baltic was an
unknown sea to our navigators . . . Scarcely had the peace of our
independence been concluded, when three of our merchant vessels
had been captured by the corsairs of Algiers, and their crews . . .
appealing to their country for redemption, in vain. Nor was this all. . . .
all the shores of the Black sea, of the whole Mediterranean, of the
islands of the African coast, of the southern ports of France, of all
Spain, and Portugal, were closed against our commerce, as if they had
been hermetically sealed; while Britain, everywhere our rival and com-

This feeling of suspicion toward the outside world, para-
noiac at times but nevertheless real, existed alongside a
second and perhaps more dominant aspect of the national
mood: the feeling of patriotic pride. As newcomers in the
field of international politics, Americans naturally resented
any injuries or slights which might place their country in an
inferior light. Moreover, they hoped to impress the world
with the advantages of the republican system, Thus, while
suspicion heightened their awareness of military and commercial challenges, pride stimulated their urge to reform.

Many felt that they were engaged in nothing less than
the task of remaking the earth. They were undertaking a
great experiment in kingless government and were anxious
to prove to Europe that nations as well as individuals could
live by moral standards. As continental philosophers such as
Condorcet looked across the Atlantic, they thought they
saw the dawn of a new political age. And Americans were,
as Merrill Jensen has put it, "delighted and proud." [33] No

---

petitor was counteracting by every stimulant within her power every
attempt on our part to [contract?] by tribute with the Barbarian for
peace.

Great Britain had also excluded us from all commerce in our own
vessels with her colonies, and France, notwithstanding her alliance
with us during the war, had after the conclusion of the peace adopted
the same policy. She was jealous of our aggrandizement, fearful of our
principles, linked with Spain in the project of debarring us from the
navigation of the Mississippi, and settled in the determination to
shackle us.

See John Quincy Adams, *The Jubilee of the Constitution* (New York:
Samuel Colman, 1839), 74–75.

33. Jensen, *New Nation*, 85–86. For further confirmation of this view,
see Clinton Rossiter, *1787: The Grand Convention* (New York: Macmillan Co., 1966), 23, 45, 57; Echevarria, *Mirage*, 171; Max Farrand, *The
Framing of the Constitution* (New Haven and London: Yale University
Press, 1913), 1; Adrienne Koch, *Jefferson and Madison* (New York: Oxford University Press, 1964), 8–10, 21, 32; Miner, *Ratification*, 43–44; Alexander Hamilton, "Continentalist, No. IV," 1781, and "A Letter from
Phocion," 1784, in Syrett (ed.), *Papers of Hamilton*, III, 106, 492; Samuel

great democratic republic had ever before existed in the world. Theirs was to be the first. This feeling of mission, a secular version of the Puritan idea of a "City Upon a Hill," a "beacon" for the eyes of all the world to behold, was reflected in the use of words such as *Providence* and *Heaven* to describe the guiding force behind America. George Washington's *Circular To The States*, which he wrote in 1783 on retirement from command of the continental armies, is characteristic:

> The Citizens of America, placed in the most enviable condition, as the sole Lords and Proprietors of a vast Tract of Continent, comprehending all the various soils and climates of the World, and abounding with all the necessaries and conveniences of life, are . . . the Actors on a most conspicuous Theatre, which seems to be peculiarly designated by Providence for the display of human greatness and felicity. . . . Heaven has crowned all its other blessings, by giving a fairer opportunity for political happiness, than any other Nation has ever been favored with. . . . It appears to me there is an option still left to the United States of America, that it is in their choice, and depends upon their conduct, whether they will be respectable and prosperous, or contemptible and miserable as a Nation; This is the time of their political probation, this is the moment when the eyes of the whole World are turned upon them. . . . For, according to the system of Policy the States shall adopt at this moment, they will stand or fall, and by their confirmation or lapse, it is yet to be decided, whether the Revolution must ultimately be considered as a blessing or a curse; a blessing or curse, not to the present age alone, for with our fate will the destiny of unborn Millions be involved.[34]

The same buoyant sense of national pride was reflected

Adams to Richard Henry Lee, December 23, 1784, in Samuel Adams Papers, New York Public Library.
34. George Washington, "Circular to the States," June 8, 1783, in Edwin Harrison Cady (ed.), *Literature of the Early Republic* (New York: Holt, Rinehart, and Winston, 1961), 65–67.

in various actions designed to sever all remaining postwar bonds of dependence on Europe. When Harvard Medical School was founded in 1782, Dr. Benjamin Waterhouse hailed it as an important step away from reliance upon "foreign seminaries" and altogether fitting for a nation so completely independent in other ways. The founding of many other educational institutions in the immediate postwar period may also have been partially inspired by the same desire for self-reliance and excellence. Even in the realm of printing a similar spirit was afoot. Robert Aiken, the Philadelphia printer, tried to cut off the import of English Bible editions in 1782 by bringing out his own. Unfortunately, the Aiken version was so expensive and poorly printed that it put its author in the poorhouse. But more worthy of note was a special congressional resolution commending it to all good patriots. Signs of self-conscious nationalism ranged all the way from the new vogue of vulgar tobacco chewing (in preference to the typically European custom of snuff-pinching) to a tavern sign hung in crude new Terre Haute, Indiana, depicting an eagle and a lion, the former plucking out the latter's eyes.[35]

In the same vein were a vast number of literary outpourings ranging from spelling books to Fourth-of-July orations and including sermons, histories, editorials, poems, and geography texts. Some writers exuded satisfaction in anything characteristically American. Others evinced a strong belief in the improvement of man's lot that was to be the fruit of the American Revolution. David Humphreys, an aide and friend of General Washington, wrote two poems after the peace that rang with high patriotic fervor, *The Glory of*

35. Merle Curti, *The Growth of American Thought* (New York: Harper and Row, 1964), 138–40; Joseph Chamberlain Furnas, *The Americans* (New York: G. P. Putnam's Sons, 1969), 243. Professor Furnas has not precisely dated the tavern sign, but this general period is indicated.

*America* and *A Poem on the Industry of the United States of America.* In 1784, the Reverend Jedediah Morse, a Yale graduate and the "Father of American Geography," published his textbook *Geography Made Easy.* Morse believed that the natural genius of Americans had not been properly appreciated abroad due to the lack of adequate publicity. So he painted Americans and their environment in glowing color, taking time out to defend the virtues of American livestock. In 1789, he published another text, *The American Geography*, which included a laudatory history of the United States from 1607 to the adoption of the Constitution. All of his texts were staunchly American, all stressed the superiority of the United States over other countries, and all of them provided fuller accounts of his native terrain than had ever been available before.[36]

Three events of the year 1786 are noteworthy in like regard. The *Columbian Magazine* was founded in Philadelphia under the editorial leadership of Mathew Carey and Francis Hopkinson and featured an unusual amount of American fiction. The same year saw the republican poet, Philip Freneau, publish his fiercely nationalistic *Literary Importations* in which he boasted:

> Can we never be thought to have learning or grace
> Unless it be brought from that horrible place
> Where tyranny reigns with her impudent face?

And the New Haven *Gazette* featured a bitterly satirical poem known as the *Anarchiad*. Penned by such "Hartford Wits" as David Humphreys, Joel Barlow, and John Trumbull, and coming on the heels of Shays's Rebellion, it attacked, among other things, the condescending attitude of Europeans toward Americans.

36. Jensen, *New Nation*, 101–104.

Two "firsts" appeared in 1787. One was Joel Barlow's epic poem, *The Vision of Columbus*, which was expressly written to inculcate the "love of national liberty" and to show that morality, peace, and good government flow exclusively from republican principles. With its worshipful references to America's majestic mountains, broad rivers, magnificent savannahs, and alluring woodlands, it was clearly a sign of the times. It fulfilled Barlow's lifelong ambition to write an American epic and was judged to be a masterpiece by his contemporaries. The other first was the theatrical production of the first comedy ever written by a native American, *The Contrast*, by Royall Tyler. Capitalizing on popular appreciation of jingoistic themes, it contrasted the homespun dignity and practical wisdom of Americans with the effete pomposity and highflown affectation of European society. It was a great success.[37]

No discussion of the intellectual climate of the period, however, would be complete without mentioning Noah Webster, who not only epitomized the high sense of patriotic pride more than anyone else, but also connected the desire for national prestige with the need for constitutional reform. The career of this truly remarkable Connecticut-born lexicographer and philologist began with the publication in 1783 of his *Spelling Book* (*Blue-Backed Speller*) which was designed to meet American needs by standardizing American spelling and pronunciation as distinguished from prevailing British forms. It eventually sold over 600,000 copies. Webster believed that "America must be as independent in literature as she is in politics." Americans should not be forced to rely on foreigners "for books to learn the children their native language." Europe, after all, had been slipping

37. *The Father* (1789), a comedy of manners by William Dunlap (Father of the American Theater), was inspired by *The Contrast* and exploited the same sentiment of red-blooded Americanism.

into folly, corruption, and tyranny. The time was ripe for the dawning of a glorious new era. America needed a language and literature of her own. And Webster was prepared to furnish it. He was particularly contemptuous of the late British tendency to swallow final "r's" and say "secretry" for "secretary." The language, he claimed, had suffered more injurious change since the British army landed in 1768 than it had suffered in three centuries.[38] He sanctioned popular American usages such as "you was" and tried to reform spelling along simplified phonetic lines. The British form "plough" was changed to "plow." And he dropped the "u" from "honour" as "useless orthographic clutter." In fact, the Yankee schoolteacher inspired so much enthusiasm during his lecture tours of the country that plans were afoot by 1787 to radically reform the English alphabet and establish a specific letter to correspond to every distinct sound.

If Webster had been a simple scholar, his work would be germane to an essay on the role of national pride in stimulating constitutional reform. But Webster was more than this. He was, perhaps above all, an ardent nationalist. Declaring republican government to be the most perfect form ever devised, he yearned to see it strengthened through tightening the bonds of American union. He was fully aware that the fostering of a national language was a step in this direction. And he ventured beyond this into the realm of practical politics. When dissatisfaction with the Articles of Confederation was well on the rise, he published his *Sketches of American Policy* in which he argued for a stronger central government.

America is an independent empire, and ought to assume a national character. . . . Our union is so feeble, that no provi-

38. Jensen, *New Nation*, 105–107; Furnas, *Americans*, 241.

sion is made for discharging our debts. France calls for interest and that seriously. Our credit, our faith solemnly pledged, is at stake. Unless we constitute a power at the head of the state, sufficient to compel them to act in concert, I now predict not only a dissolution of our federal connection, but a rupture with our national creditors. A war in Europe may possibly suspend this event; but it must certainly take place, unless we sacrifice our jealousy to our true interest.

*Three things* demand our early and careful attention; a general diffusion of knowledge; the encouragement of industry, frugality and virtue; and a sovereign power at the head of the states. *All* are essential to our peace and prosperity; but on an energetic continental government principally depend our tranquility at home and our respectibility among foreign nations.

We ought to generalize our ideas and our measures. We ought not to consider ourselves as inhabitants of a particular state only; but as Americans.[39]

In 1789, Webster was again mixing orthography with politics. In an essay entitled "The Reforming of Spelling," he wrote:

A national language is a band of *national union*. . . . Let us then seize the present moment, and establish a *national language*, as well as a national government. Let us remember that there is a certain respect due to the opinions of other nations. As an independent people, our reputation abroad demands that in all things we should be federal; be *national*; for if we do not respect *ourselves*, we may be assured that *other nations* will not respect us. In short, let it be impressed upon the mind of every American that to neglect the means of commanding respect abroad is treason against the character and dignity of a brave independent people.[40]

39. Noah Webster, "Sketches of American Policy," 1785, in Richard Nelson Current and John Arthur Garraty, *Words That Made American History, Colonial Times to the 1870's* (Boston: Little, Brown & Co., 1962), 145–46.
40. Noah Webster, "The Reforming of Spelling," 1789, *ibid.*, 150–51.

One of the reasons men such as Noah Webster were so sensitive to the issue of national honor was that the new nation had to endure some stinging insults. The continued occupation of American frontier forts by alien troops was a serious affront. Combined with the British demand for thirteen ambassadors from the United States, it cast grave doubt upon the authority of Congress.[41]

Spanish closure of the Mississippi River touched another sensitive chord, especially since British vessels had never been stopped en route. Nor was it easy for Congress to sit idly by while Barbary corsairs terrorized American commerce in the Mediterranean and while British naval officers showed less respect for American ships than they did for those of their old enemy, France. Such incidents were invariably cited by Americans as blows to the national honor.[42]

As if events did not speak loudly enough for themselves, the United States served as a target for scathing criticism by foreign observers. According to Dr. Price, "The power

41. It is interesting in this regard that French consuls, according to the consular treaty negotiated by Franklin in 1782 (and opposed by Secretary Jay until its modification and final ratification in 1789), were supposed to present their commissions to the respective state governments.

42. New York *Packet*, January 7, 1787; *Pennsylvania Gazette*, August 30, 1786; M. Tyler to James Monroe, November 26, 1785, Philip Mazzei to James Monroe, October 5, 1785, both in James Monroe Papers, Library of Congress, Ser. 1, Vol. I; New York *Journal*, March 1, 1787; Richard Spaight to Alexander Martin, October 16, 1784, in Burnett (ed.), *Letters of Continental Congress*, VII, 601; John Adams to John Jay, May 8, 1785, in Adams (ed.), *Works of John Adams*, VIII, 243–46; Thomas Jefferson to John Adams, July 11, 1786, in *Diplomatic Correspondence, 1783–89*, I, 792. One American vessel, unfortunate enough to be driven by a gale to the shore of a British island, was confiscated and summarily sold at prize court. Another, departing from Belfast, came under fire from a British man-of-war and lost part of its rigging. When the commander of the British vessel was asked why he fired the first shot, he could give no good reason; *Pennsylvania Gazette*, October 26, 1785, June 28, July 5, 1786.

of Congress is an object of derision in Europe rather than respect.... The tumults in New England, the weakness of Congress, the difficulties and sufferings of many of the states and the knavery of Rhode Island form subjects of triumph in this country." [43]

Some of the charges were tantalizingly vague. Would the weakness of Congress not lead eventually to a reverse swing of the pendulum in the direction of dictatorship? Comte de Moustier, French minister to the United States in 1787, thought the answer was yes. Would the nation ever develop any refinement in its cultural life? Would it conform to the physiocratic dream of an agrarian society unbesmirched with sordid commercialism? There could be no reassuring answers. [44]

Outright misconceptions about America were common, ranging all the way from reports that Rhode Island was north of Massachusetts, to a listing of New Hampshire's chief exports as cocoa, cotton, and coffee (found in the French *Almanach Américain*). Many intellectuals held a persistent notion that the American climate was injurious to living organisms. The leading European authority on American questions, Corneille de Pauw, had claimed in 1768 that the climate in America, being more cold and humid than in Europe, produced animals "degenerate, small, cowardly, and a thousand times less dangerous than those of Asia and Africa." Domestic animals transported from Europe to America suffered a similar degeneration. It remained for Abbé Raynal to point out that the most important effect of the climate was on man. The proof of this was the American Indian, who had endured his environment for many centuries and was obviously the physical, moral, and

43. *Gentleman's Magazine*, LVII (July, 1787), 631.
44. Echevarria, *Mirage*, pp. xxi–xiv, 137.

intellectual inferior of his European counterpart. American Indians lacked vigor and endurance; they were "sexually frigid, perverted, unprolific, hairless, insensitive to pain, short-lived," and afflicted by a list of ills and perversions which included the eating of iguanas. Morally, they were cowardly; mentally, "they lacked intellectual ambition and curiosity and were incapable of reason." The same effects would eventually operate on European settlers; witness the fact that American colleges had not produced a single man of reputation.[45]

In such a context, one is not surprised that the most notable Americans residing abroad during these years took up their pens and collected their wits to defend the national honor. Franklin, the clever psychologist and public relations expert, knew firsthand the power of the press and went out of his way not only to publish writings of his own, but also to keep European newsmen well supplied with favorable pieces about America. Typical were his efforts to disseminate copies of the *Proceedings of the American Philosophical Society* to well-respected academicians. His good humor also served the cause well. In one instance, he found himself in the company of several other Americans, including David Humphreys, William Carmichael, and General Harmar, all of whom had been invited by the Abbé Raynal to dinner. There were about an even number of Frenchmen and Americans seated around the table. The Abbé

45. *Ibid.*, 10. See also *Pennsylvania Packet and Daily Advertiser*, December 19, 1787. De Pauw was following the general opinion of other naturalists such as Peter Kalm of Sweden and the Frenchman Georges Louis Comte de Buffon. Both Kalm, in his *Travels* (1753–1761), and Buffon, in his *Histoire Naturelle* (44 vols.; 1749–1804), had expressed the idea of degeneration. This was an age which placed great stress on the effect of climate. Montesquieu claimed that since climate affected man's character and mental capacities, the laws should be drawn to suit the climate.

began to discourse on his favorite theory of the degeneracy of life in America. Franklin, however, noticed that the Americans present happened to be conspicuously fine physical specimens, taller and much better built than their diminutive French colleagues (Abbé Raynal in particular was a shrimp!); whereupon he interjected, "M. l'Abbé, let us try this question by the fact before us. We are here one half Americans, and one half French, and it happens that the Americans have placed themselves on one side of the table, and our French friends on the other. Let both parties rise, and we will see on which side nature has degenerated." [46]

Jefferson, too, labored hard in the vineyard of public relations. He was especially disturbed by rampant reports of political chaos in America and tried to counteract them by planting articles in Etienne Luzac's pro-American *Gazette de Leyde* and other European newspapers. His exasperation in the face of consistent ignorance is clearly evident in his note to the *Journal de Paris* of August 29, 1787; "If the histories of D'Auberteuil and Longchamps and the Travels of the Abbé Robin can be published in the face of the world, and can be read and believed by those contemporary with the events these books pretend to relate, how can we expect future generations will be any better informed?" [47] He was also hard put to rebut the theory of American degeneration, so fashionable among the intelligentsia, and devoted a whole section of his *Notes on the State of Virginia* (1784) to a refutation based upon statistics and accurate descriptions of the flora and fauna of his native state. He even had his faithful correspondent, James Madison, ship him actual skeletons of creatures such as wolves to prove his points. Jefferson

46. Thomas Jefferson to Robert Walsh, December 4, 1818, in Adrienne Koch and William Peden (eds.), *The Life and Selected Writings of Thomas Jefferson* (New York: Random House, 1944), 179.
47. Quoted in Echevarria, *Mirage*, 123.

argued that American specimens were, if anything, bigger and better than those of Europe!

John Adams was no less diligent than Jefferson or Franklin. Ever poised to crush the slightest imputation against his country, he referred to French misconceptions of America as "Augean Stables." His magnum opus, *A Defense of the Constitutions of Government of the United States of America* (1787), was a three-volume reply to criticism leveled against the American frames of government and the result of long labor during his residence in London as the American minister.[48]

But despite the noble essays of such giants as Adams, most European criticism was well informed (some of it was borrowed directly from American newspapers) and therefore difficult to refute. And it was this genuine criticism which bit most sharply into the national pride, stimulating the efforts at constitutional reform. Foreigners, for example, paid great attention to the difficulty experienced by Congress in raising sufficient revenue and controlling foreign commerce. They noted with special contempt that Congress had failed to service the foreign debt.[49]

48. Franklin had published the American state constitutions while still in France in 1783. There followed a number of erudite criticisms by such notables as Marquis de Condorcet and Brissot de Warville. But Abbé Mably's critique of American political institutions, *Observations sur le gouvernement et les lois des Etats-Unis* (1784), in particular, was the spark that set Adams off. It also fired Jefferson's former neighbor, Philip Mazzei, then traveling in Europe, to write his refutation, *Recherches historiques et politiques sur les États-Unis* (1788).

49. James Madison, "Origin of the Federal Constitution," *ca.* 1833, in Hunt (ed.), *Writings of Madison*, II, 406; Richard Peters to Charles Thomson, October 20, 1783, in Burnett (ed.), *Letters of Continental Congress*, VII, 344; *State Gazette of South Carolina*, December 6, 1787; *Pennsylvania Gazette*, June 21, 1786; Report of John Jay to Congress on a Joint Letter from Adams and Jefferson, May 29, 1786, in Johnston (ed.), *Papers of John Jay*, III, 198; Elbridge Gerry to Rufus King, May 19, 1785, in King, *Rufus King*, I, 98.

How could anyone deny that these problems existed? The United States still owed French volunteer officers a large sum of back pay with interest, and Jefferson, who was acutely conscious of the national failure to pay off its debts, admitted that it would "give birth to new imputations and a relapse of credit." [50]

There could be no refutation of widespread reports that Congress was experiencing difficulty in maintaining a "working" quorum. For many weeks at a time, the lack of a nine-state majority kept Congress in a quandary and wasted valuable time. As early as 1783, Samuel Hardy, Virginia delegate to the Continental Congress and chairman of the defunct Committee of States, feared that the lack of a quorum would lessen the dignity of the federal government in the eyes of foreigners. Charles Thomson, the ever-faithful congressional secretary, had to write innumerable pleas to state governors urging them to prod their respective delegations into more responsible behavior. Yet attendance frequently dwindled to six, five, or even three states. John Hancock, elected president for one year, did not make a single personal appearance, and the problem was alarming enough to arouse considerable talk of dissolving the Confederation. Thomson expected Congress to acquire an "ill aspect in the eyes of European nations," and irascible Jacob Read, delegate from South Carolina, was perfectly outraged by the "invisible state" of the federal government, since "the eyes of Europe are upon us." [51] The Treaty of Paris lay before Congress unratified from November 26 until January 14 (1784) because the necessary nine-state delegations could not be mustered (Colonel Harmar had to serve a per-

50. Quoted in Echevarria, *Mirage*, 131.
51. Burnett, *Continental Congress*, 610–12.

sonal summons on the delegates from Connecticut and New Jersey).

As the years passed, the situation deteriorated until morale reached an all-time low following Shays's Rebellion. By this time, constitutional amendments designed to augment congressional power over finance and commerce had gone down to defeat despite overwhelming support because the Articles required the approval of every state. On only three days during the interval from November, 1786, to mid-August, 1787, were as many as ten states represented, and a working quorum was obtained on only thirty days of the congressional year. The frequent and prolonged absences of delegates were construed as signs of instability and dishonor.[52] They reflected apathy and depressed national morale more than ever. Arthur St. Clair, president of Congress, noted the scandal of the situation in a letter to the delinquent members: "What Sir must the Nations of the world think of us when they shall be informed that we have appointed an Assembly and invested it with the sole and exclusive power of peace and war, and the management of all national concerns, and during the course of almost a whole year, it has not been capable, except for a few days, for want of a sufficient number of members, to attend to these matters." [53]

52. Charles Thomson to Jacob Reed, September 27, 1784, Charles Pettit to Jeremiah Wadsworth, May 27, 1786, both in Burnett (ed.), *Letters of Continental Congress*, VII, 593; VIII, 370–71; George Washington to the president of Congress, December 14, 1784, in Fitzpatrick (ed.), *Writings of George Washington*, XXVIII, 10; Richard Henry Lee to George Washington, November 20, 1784, in Ballagh (ed.), *Letters of Lee*, II, 294.

53. Arthur St. Clair to the governors of Georgia, Maryland, Connecticut, Rhode Island, New Hampshire, and New York, August 13, 1787, in *Papers of the Continental Congress*, Microfilm Roll #24, p. 327, National Archives, Washington, D. C.

There could be no denial of the fact that the union faced ruin at the periphery as well as the center. While Congress lost itself in bickering and boredom, outlying areas were drifting dangerously away from its gravitational pull. Europeans familiar with Montesquieu's theory on the geographical limitations of popular government assumed that the United States encompassed too large an area. They doubted its survival along with such ideally small republics as Venice, Holland, and Switzerland. Among the skeptics were Frederick the Great, the Marquis de Chastellux, and Turgot, as well as the mordant Dean Josiah Tucker of Gloucester and George III. By 1786, their doubts seemed on the verge of realization. Tennessee, Kentucky, and Vermont were drawn to a foreign allegiance as were parts of Massachusetts.

The two portions of the Bay State which threatened to secede during the years 1783–1787, excluding the area affected by Shays's Rebellion, were the detached counties of York, Cumberland, and Lincoln (present-day Maine), and the important island of Nantucket. Citizens of the northern counties felt under-represented in the General Court of Massachusetts and held a convention in 1787 to consider a declaration of independence. The Nantucket community faced commercial problems which seemed insurmountable outside the folds of the British Empire. Neither movement resulted in secession; the northern counties decided to await the outcome of the Philadelphia Convention, and Nantucket decided on separation but failed to achieve it. Both, however, are significant as part of a general phenomenon affecting much of the country, and both helped to confirm European expectations of the impending downfall of the union.

The Nantucket situation is particularly interesting. Here was an island of people who made a living on large-scale whaling operations involving over three hundred vessels and five to six thousand seamen annually. Its products constituted fully half of the payment made by Massachusetts to Britain in return for manufactured goods. Before the Revolution it had enjoyed an excellent market in England for its whale oil and whale bone. After the war, however, the whalers were forced into bankruptcy by a heavy British tariff. Since they could not obtain relief from their state or from Congress, and since the island was unfit for farming, secession seemed the only recourse. The *Massachusetts Centinel* warned that the islanders were considering independence, and that this would not only deprive Massachusetts of the whale fisheries but also afford enemy warships an excellent haven just off the coast. On May 4, 1785, the island voted to become a neutral state as "the most convenient situation that the town can be placed in for the benefit of the inhabitants thereof under present circumstances." Massachusetts, of course, refused to permit the separation, but many islanders emigrated to Nova Scotia, France, and England in response to attractive settlement offers.[54] The exodus was no dire threat to the union, but in a certain sense it was as significant as the case of Tennessee or Kentucky, and for the same reason.

When American ministers were scorned for their humble deportment in the courts of Europe, the charges were again

54. Thomas Jefferson, "Observations on the Whale Fishery," November, 1788, *Diplomatic Correspondence, 1783–89*, II, 240. A fascinating and detailed account of this tightly interrelated, familial, Quaker community that had extended its prosperous whaling expeditions as far south as Cape Horn is Edouard A. Stackpole, *The Sea Hunters* (New York: J. B. Lippincott Co., 1953); quote from p. 97. See also *Gentleman's Magazine*, LVI (March, 1786), 260. A Londoner wrote his friend in Halifax, "I am very much pleased to hear that so many of the Nantucket people intend settling at Dartmouth (Nova Scotia)—what an influx of wealth and advantage they will be to you"; New York *Gazette*, July 3, 1786. The situation is well described in Stackpole, *Sea Hunters*, 1–133.

on target. Benjamin Franklin may have charmed Parisian society with his fur hat and republican simplicity, but his less experienced colleagues were at a loss when Congress could not afford to support them at the customary level of elegance.[55] Jefferson complained that Americans were "the lowest and most obscure of the whole diplomatic tribe." [56] He spent one thousand guineas in France in order to procure a proper outfit and went so heavily into debt that he despaired of ever reaching financial solvency. "I ask nothing for my time," he told Congress, "but I think my expenses should be paid in a style equal to that of those with whom I am classed." [57]

Even frugal John Adams wrote that he could not entertain as frequently or as lavishly as was required in the interest of the United States. When dining out, Adams would sit at tables set with three thousand pounds of sterling plate. Yet when he gave a formal dinner at the American embassy, his official guests dined on earthenware. He encountered icy reserve in England. His mission was not reciprocated by the Court of St. James's, and, on his arrival in London, the *Public Advertiser* stormed indignantly: "An ambassador from America! Good heavens. . . . Such a thing could never have happened in any former administration, not even that of

55. John Adams to Messrs. Willink and others, January 10, 1785, to John Jay, May 13, 1785, in Adams (ed.), *Works of John Adams*, VIII, 220, 251.
56. Thomas Jefferson to James Monroe, November 11, 1784, in Monroe Papers, Library of Congress, Ser. 1. Vol. I. Philip Mazzei, a friend of Jefferson, pointed out that during the war American ministers had made few contacts and had not been expected to establish permanent residences. Once the war ended, however, far more was expected of Americans, although their salaries remained the same. Mazzei recommended under the circumstances that Congress replace its ministers with agents of a lower rank who would not require secretaries; Philip Mazzei to James Monroe, October 5, 1785, *ibid.*
57. Thomas Jefferson to James Monroe, November 11, 1784, *ibid.*

Lord North." His wife Abigail bristled in the hostile milieu. Anxious to make a favorable impression on European society and quick to defend the social virtues of her countrywomen, she regretted the limitations of a tight budget. "Some years hence," she wrote, "it may be a pleasure to reside here in the character of American minister, but with the present salary and the present temper of the English no one need envy the embassy." [58]

Americans at home needed no embarrassing reminders from abroad of the situation as it existed. The facts were well known. Newspapers in the United States printed rumors that Adams was receiving his salary from the French ambassador. "Ought we not to blush," suggested the *Pennsylvania Gazette*, "that the ambassadors of the states are at this moment depending on foreign charity for their support. . . . If we barely should exist as a people . . . we shall necessarily receive the scorn and detestation of the world." [59]

As a result of the severe and irrefutable criticism emanating from Europe, national honor became a definite factor in the constitutional reform movement. Beginning with a congressional report in 1783 which recommended in-

58. John Adams to James Warren, August 27, 1784, in Adams (ed.), *Works of John Adams*, IX, 525; Abigail Adams to Thomas Jefferson, June 6, 1785, in Lester Jesse Cappon (ed.), *The Adams-Jefferson Letters* (2 vols.; Chapel Hill: University of North Carolina Press, 1959), I, 29; quotation from John Torrey Morse, *John Adams, Statesman* (Boston: Riverside Press, 1884), 235.

59. *Columbian Herald*, July 20 and October 2, 1786; *New Jersey Gazette*, July 24, 1786; New York *Packet*, August 24, 1786; *Pennsylvania Gazette*, June 22, 1785. Edmund Randolph warned in the Virginia ratifying convention that unless the Constitution were adopted, the American minister in London would be told, "Remember, sir, the bread you eat tomorrow depends on the bounty of the Count de Vergennes"; Jonathan Elliot (ed.), *The Debates in the Several State Conventions on the Adoption of the Federal Constitution* (5 vols., Philadelphia: J. B. Lippincott, 1861), III, 120, hereinafter cited as Elliot (ed.), *Debates in State Conventions*.

creased centralization of power in the hands of Congress "to become respectable in European eyes" and ranging through Henry Knox's advice that national honor would be a potent issue in the ratification campaign, there runs the constant theme of wounded pride and want of respect. George Washington was not the only one who resented continental arrogance. Nor was he the only one to suggest that this alone should be "sufficient to stimulate us to vest more extensive and adequate powers in the sovereign of these United States." Arguments for a constitutional convention in the spring of 1786 were peppered with allusions to world opinion. Congressmen spoke about how ludicrous the United States would appear if nothing were done to strengthen the central government. They supposed that America would become "one of the most contemptible nations on the face of the earth." Reference was made to American ambassadors who were despised as "the shadow of a shade"; it was said that the dignity of the United States was being trampled underfoot, that the flag was being insulted in enemy ports, and that there was "no body of men, vested with power to counteract such degrading measures." [60]

The movement for a 5 percent congressional impost—a driving force behind the nationalist movement from the beginning—was partially inspired and defended by the urge to appear honorable in the world's eyes. American prestige might be permanently injured if Congress were not given

60. Congressional Debate, September 26, 1783, in *Diplomatic Correspondence, 1783–89*, I, 37; Henry Knox to George Washington, December 11, 1787, in Washington Papers, Library of Congress, Ser. 4, Vol. CCXXXIX; George Washington to Governor Benjamin Harrison, January 18, 1784, in Fitzpatrick (ed.), *Writings of George Washington*, XXVII, 306; Morris, "The Confederation Period," 140–41; William Grayson to James Madison, March 22, 1786, quoted in Warren, *Making of the Constitution*, 21; *New Jersey Gazette*, May 8 and August 21, 1786; John Jay to Thomas Jefferson, July 14, 1786, quoted in Smith, *John Jay*, 106–107.

sufficient sources of revenue to "comply with engagements which the smallest nation would consider as easy to be fulfilled." This was the argument used in attempting to persuade New York to endorse a program of national taxation. And when New York finally declined to do so, dooming the impost to defeat, Washington termed it a blow to the national character.[61]

Another drive wheel in the nationalist movement—the effort to retaliate effectively against British commercial restrictions—was also grounded and defended in part on the desire for national honor. Congress first requested the power to regulate commerce in April, 1784, and it is interesting to note that the recommendation was defended on the supposition that it would prevent American trade from "being sported with." The following year, a petition signed by merchants, traders, and other inhabitants of the town of Suffolk, Virginia, recommending more power for Congress, referred to the current state of commerce as not only ruinous but also a "disgrace." Later, during the momentous sessions of the Philadelphia Convention, the New York *Journal* played engagingly on the theme of patriotism as it recounted the story of how an Englishman, when told that the United States would eventually retaliate against British restrictions, replied: "Pish! . . . what can the Americans do? They have neither government nor power. Great Britain could shut up all their ports . . . America take measures against Great Britain indeed!" [62]

61. Comte de la Luzerne to George Washington, 1787, George Washington Papers, Library of Congress, Washington, D.C., Item #102, Ser. 4, Vol. CCXXXIX; Miner, *Ratification*, 25; Alexander Hamilton, Speech before the New York Assembly, January 19, 1787, in Syrett (ed.), *Papers of Hamilton*, IV, 15; George Washington to James Duane, April 10, 1785, in Fitzpatrick (ed.), *Writings of George Washington*, XXVIII, 124.

62. Burnett (ed.), *Letters of Continental Congress*, VII, xliii; Virginia Legislative Petitions, Town of Suffolk, Nansemond County, November

It was humiliating for a nation such as the United States, with its great naval potential, to be virtually driven out of the shipping business. One nationalist writer pointed out that America enjoyed unparalleled natural advantages, including a fine coastal area and excellent rivers running into the sea, and that it had once conducted a prosperous fishing business. Was it not, he asked, all the more degrading in this case to be dependent upon foreign ships and subject to foreign influence? What good was it to have won the revolutionary war only to remain dependent upon British credit and British ships? British colonial imperialism had merely given way to a more subtle kind of imperialism.[63]

It was also humiliating for Americans to be excluded from the ports of nations whose shipping they welcomed with open arms. One editor asked: "Is it not abominable insolence in the British, after prohibiting our provisions going to their ports in our own bottoms . . . [to] imagine we can be so servile and cringing as to suffer the supplies for which they must depend on us to be carried in theirs?" Another person suggested that, in the absence of proper laws, America would have to rely on the force of "patriotism" to prevent trade with a nation (Britain) that gave daily insult. The influential Philadelphia merchant Charles Pettit agreed that "instead of supporting the respectable rank which we have assumed among nations, we have exposed our follies to their view—they treat us accordingly; they severally shut the

---

4, 1785, Virginia State Library, Richmond, Virginia; New York *Journal*, August 16, 1787. See also Bingham, *Letter from an American*, 8; James Madison to Edmund Randolph, September 13, 1783, in Hunt (ed.), *Writings of Madison*, II, 17–18; John Jay to Charles Thomson, April 7, 1784, in Johnston (ed.), *Papers of John Jay*, III, 125; New York *Packet*, May 29, 1787.

63. Tucker, *Reflections*, 8–10.

door of commercial hospitality against us, while ours being open they enter and partake with us at their pleasure." [64]

An editorial in the New York *Packet*, written while the Annapolis Report was still under consideration by Congress, was also revealing: "the little respect that is paid to the American flag and the repeated insults which subjects of the United States meet with in foreign ports, must convince the good people of this continent that it is absolutely necessary we should invest Congress with a power to regulate our commerce and to support our dignity." Preceding the editorial and lending credence to it, there appeared a petition signed by "eighteen of the most respectable sea captains from this and the neighboring states" documenting the brazen treatment which American seamen so often received while abroad. The particular case involved American crewmen in Guadeloupe who had been dragged from bed in the dead of night for reasons unknown and hustled aboard a British frigate for interrogation. Even the inveterate enemies of the British, the French, were treated with more respect than the Americans! [65]

When foreign trade restrictions could be evaded, there were still Americans who insisted on augmenting congressional power if for no other reason than to achieve self-mastery. When, for example, a French edict required American ships to obtain special passports for entrance to the French West Indies, the edict was denounced as much for its implication as for its effect. One writer asserted that congressional power would either be "enlarged or annihi-

64. *Pennsylvania Gazette*, August 3, 1785; New York *Packet*, July 21, 1785; Charles Pettit to Jeremiah Wadsworth, May 27, 1786, in Burnett (ed.), *Letters of Continental Congress*, VIII, 370.
65. New York *Packet*, January 7, 1787. The same quotation appeared in the Providence *Gazette*.

lated," for "if we must take passes before we can enter their ports to trade, I should not be surprised in the next six months to see a further edict that we should not wear our colors on the main ocean." [66]

Another argument for congressional regulation of foreign commerce was that it would increase American prestige by stimulating home industry. As long as Americans continued to buy British clothing and kept magnifying their debt to British manufacturers, they could not be truly independent. Though they had severed their political ties on the battle-field of Yorktown, economic ties continued to bind them. Congressional regulation of commerce promised to break these remaining ties by placing infant industries under the cover of a protective tariff. Groups of manufacturers in such places as Boston and Philadelphia tried to secure public protection and, when their efforts failed, joined shipping and commercial interests in support of the nationalist movement. And, as in the case of shippers and traders, they invoked the ideal of national honor. They referred to Americans as little more than "slaves to that detested nation [Britain]—that arrogant selfish people." If Congress could be vested with the requisite power, New England would excel in making such items as linen, wool, hemp, and flax. And Americans would no longer have to import hats, nails, candles, soap, and the like. A leading nationalist, Tench Coxe, speaking before the Philadelphia Association of Manufacturers in the critical year 1787, assured his audience that national regulation would rescue Americans from the "tyranny of foreign fashions." Similar language was employed by the tradesmen of Baltimore who sent a circular letter to every town in

66. *Columbian Herald*, August 28, 1786. The same quotation appeared in the *Connecticut Courant*.

Maryland, claiming that the protection of manufactures would give "true political and commercial independence." The New York Chamber of Commerce likewise asserted that Americans should look more to themselves and less to Europe, for "as in private life, so with states and kingdoms; happy and independent are they only that can help themselves." [67]

By 1787 the "City Upon a Hill" seemed in deep trouble. The beacon which was to shine before the eyes of the world was growing dim. During the previous year, the national treasury had fallen into bankruptcy after a losing battle to obtain a steady source of revenue. Its total income was less than one third of the charges for annual interest on the national debt. New York State had clamped its fatal veto on the long-brewing and popular scheme to authorize Congress to collect an import duty for a limited period of time. Indian affairs seemed ominous with unprecedented numbers of Indian raids reported from the frontier sections and the prospect of an all-out military effort by a union of tribal confederations ever more likely. This was also a time when threats of secession and plans for a dissolution of the union came closest to realization. Congress could hardly operate. It was without funds and without sufficient attendance. Even the movement to transfer power over foreign commerce from the states to the central government was foundering. And never had congressional impotence been as graphically revealed as during Shays's Rebellion in the fall of 1786. Young John Marshall of Virginia viewed the disturbances in Massachusetts as casting a shadow over "the bright pros-

67. Tench Coxe, *An Address to an Assembly of the Friends of Manufactures* (Philadelphia: Aitken and Son, 1787), 25; *New Jersey Gazette*, September 18, 1786; Boston *Gazette*, October 31, 1785, January 9, 1786.

pect which the revolution in America and the establishment of our free governments had opened to the votaries of liberty throughout the globe." [68]

Events were reaching a climax. The champions of the national reputation could not have been more disturbed. Far more was at stake than the fate of a single nation. The future of all mankind had reached a crossroads. The normally lighthearted and brilliant sophisticate, Gouverneur Morris, became utterly serious during the Constitutional Convention when he indicated that "the whole human race" stood to be vitally affected. Testy Elbridge Gerry of Massachusetts agreed. Certainly if they failed at Philadelphia they would disappoint "not only America but the whole world." And the scholarly Madison assessed the role of the delegates as one which would "decide forever the fate of republican government." [69]

68. All of the above quotations are from Roger Hamilton Brown, *The Republic in Peril: 1812* (New York: Columbia University Press, 1964), 5–6. For other evidence of the effect of Shays's Rebellion and the excessive issuance of paper money on the national pride, see George Washington to Henry Lee, October 31, 1786, to James Madison, November 5, 1786, to Thomas Johnson, November 12, 1786, and to Henry Knox, December 26, 1786, all in Fitzpatrick (ed.), *Writings of George Washington*, XXIX, 33–35, 50–52, 60–61, 121–25; Tench Coxe, *An Enquiry into the Principles on Which a Commercial System for the United States Should Be Founded* (Philadelphia: Robert Aitken, 1787), 51.

69. Madison's opening speeches in the Virginia ratifying convention were entirely concerned with the exigencies of national security and national honor. See also Madison's contribution to *The Federalist*, No. 37; Nicholas Gilman to Joseph Gilman, September 18, 1787, New Hampshire Miscellaneous Correspondence MSS, Library of Congress, Vol. I; Robert R. Livingston, Speech before the New York State Society of the Cincinnati, July 4, 1787, quoted in Dangerfield, *Livingston*, 211; Hanson, "Remarks," and James Iredell, "Answers to Mr. Mason's Objections to the New Constitution," in P. L. Ford (ed.), *Pamphlets on the Constitution*, 244, 250–51, 369–70; Lynn Montross, *Reluctant Rebels—The Story of the Continental Congress, 1774–1789* (New York: Harper, 1950), 415; Oliver Ellsworth, "The Letters of a Landholder," and Hugh Williamson, "Remarks on the New Plan of Government," in P. L. Ford (ed.), *Essays on the Constitution*, 142, 402–403; *State Gazette of South Carolina*, November

Opinions such as these were expressed too often and by too many individuals of undoubted sincerity to be dismissed as mere rhetoric. They reflected a genuine concern and deserve greater emphasis than they have received in past efforts to explain the scrapping of the Articles of Confederation. The national pride was remarkably sensitive. It had been wounded. And its pain called forth great remedial efforts.

26, 1787; New York *Packet*, September 28, 1786; *Pennsylvania Packet*, October 9 and December 19, 1787.

# IV

# The Culmination:
# Philadelphia, 1787

No sooner had the Constitutional Convention begun than the delegates were asked to consider America's position in a hostile world. Governor Randolph of Virginia opened his keynote address with a warning that the Confederation was vulnerable to foreign attack. First on his list of problems under the Articles was that of national security. Congress could not punish a state for acting against a foreign power in violation of a treaty or the Law of Nations. It might therefore be involved in needless wars, and without sufficient money or manpower. "Are we not," queried Randolph, "on the eve of war which is only prevented by the hopes from this convention?" [1] Soon after Randolph's thrust, the young Charles Pinckney (not to be confused with an older cousin of the same name who was also a delegate) presented a set of resolutions aimed at the defense of the states "against all designs and leagues that may be injurious to their interests and against all foes and attacks offered to or made upon . . . any of them." Hamilton excoriated the Confederation for deficiency in "all matters in which foreigners are concerned."

1. Farrand (ed.), *Records of Federal Convention*, I, 24–26.

He criticized the Articles for giving Congress the "power of treaty" without the "power of execution," the responsibility for the common defense without the power to raise troops or money, and the "power to contract debts without the power to pay." Wars, he pointed out, were always imminent and had been waged over such trifling issues as the duchess of Marlborough's glove. As a confederation, the United States would always live in fear of foreign influence, conquest, and dismemberment; witness the case of Poland. What was needed in the federal government was not only a strong soul but "strong organs by which that soul is to operate." [2]

There was overwhelming consensus on the need for increased national power in four areas: taxation, military establishment, regulation of foreign commerce, and treaty enforcement. Some would differ on the question of how these powers should be exercised and where they should be lodged, but on the question of transferring power in the area of foreign relations from the state to the federal level there was virtual unanimity.

The most basic and dangerous of the new powers was that of taxation. Whereas the Confederation congress had depended entirely on the largesse of state legislatures, the new government would draw revenue directly from individuals. From this flowed the power to maintain an army and navy of indeterminate size which would in turn help to break the Indian power, drive the British out of the northern posts, force open the mouth of the Mississippi, and subdue the Barbary pirates. Captive sailors could be ransomed, and the foreign debt paid. All of these benefits had to be weighed, of course, against the possibility of centralized

2. *Ibid.*, I, 304, 308, 473–74; III, 604–605.

tyranny, but there was little doubt that the need justified the risk.[3]

Next in importance was the power to maintain a military establishment. Under the Articles, Congress had been obliged to requisition the states for all troops except in time of war. Under the new system, Congress would not only have the money but also the authority to raise troops directly, to nationalize the militia of the various states, and to maintain a navy. There was opposition, naturally, to so liberal a dispensation of the power of the sword. The New Jersey Plan included grants to the national government in all major areas except this one. Elbridge Gerry would have preferred that the power be exercised only in time of war, to which the nationalists replied that preparations for war are normally made in peacetime. He would also have felt more comfortable if the convention had placed an absolute limit on the size of a standing army—three thousand, for example. But his proposal was unanimously rejected. Some wanted to limit defense appropriations to one year, but this was voted down on the assumption that in practice congressmen could be counted upon to act prudently and it would be awkward to require an annual appropriation from a biennial legislature.[4]

What is remarkable is that there were so few voices to match Gerry's. The fear of standing armies had taken root in America long before the Revolution and was a hallowed part of the British tradition, dating back to the days of the Stuarts and beyond. The best explanation seems to be that the delegates perceived a sufficient threat to the national security to justify the risk of tyranny. The anxiety generated by Shays's Rebellion may have been a consideration in the

3. Prior to 1787, nine of the states had maintained their own navies.
4. Farrand (ed.), *Records of Federal Convention*, II, 329–30, 509.

minds of some, although not for Gerry. The revolt exposed the impotence of Congress and showed the need for strong executive power—points pressed home in the convention by Randolph, Pinckney, and Hamilton. While Knox had been unable to put troops in the field, Governor Bowdoin, operating under a new Massachusetts constitution, had exercised his extensive prerogative and crushed the rebels during a legislative adjournment. The lesson was clear: there was need for a strong national executive, and such an office would prove effective. A civil officer, in this case Bowdoin, had wielded war powers without falling prey to a military take-over.[5]

Perhaps as important as raising and supporting federal troops was the power to command state militia. In a sense, this would determine whether the country was to be a mere league or a powerful national unit. Control over militia was an absolute necessity for federal law enforcement. Interestingly, the power to call up the militia met little resistance. But some welcomed it as a substitute for dependence on the army and wanted to describe the militia as a precaution "against the danger of standing armies in time of peace." The most they could obtain, however, was an authorization for the states to staff and train their own forces. The militia was left at the disposal of the central government and did not preclude a standing army.[6]

5. Not surprisingly, when George Mason, Luther Martin, and Gerry himself turned their backs on the Constitution, they listed standing armies as a principal grievance. Antifederalists attacked the army clause almost to a man; Bernard Donahoe and Marshall Smelser, "The Congressional Power to Raise Armies: The Constitutional and Ratifying Conventions, 1787–1788," *Review of Politics,* XXXIII (April, 1971), 202–204; Harry M. Ward, *The Department of War, 1781–1795* (Pittsburgh: Pittsburgh University Press, 1962), 81.

6. Arthur Taylor Prescott (comp.), *Drafting the Federal Constitution* (Baton Rouge: Louisiana State University Press, 1941), 525. See also *ibid.,* 517–25; Ward, *Department of War,* 96.

The third reform in the area of foreign relations was the long-awaited provision for federal regulation of commerce. Of the three changes thus far discussed, this was the most radical and far-reaching in that it necessitated other reforms in the basic design of government. The Annapolis Report of 1786 maintained that "the power of regulating trade is of such comprehensive extent, and will enter so far into the general system of the federal government, that to give it efficacy and to obviate questions and doubts concerning its precise nature and limits, may require a correspondent adjustment of other parts of the federal system." And this belief seems to have been widely held. As mentioned earlier, Rufus King could not envision the commerce power without a federal judiciary, and Madison felt that it would have to include interstate as well as foreign commerce. Whatever the implications, this concept was used to defend the Constitution against some of its more conservative critics during the ratification debates, and it must have been a major factor in promoting the Virginia Plan over the New Jersey Plan.[7]

Few delegates doubted the need for broad federal power in this area although some desired strict limitations. Southerners, contrary to opinion, were positively eager to retaliate against foreign trade restrictions. Maryland and Virginia had been the first to enact discriminatory duties against British ships and goods. Even Georgia engaged in retaliation of this kind. The Virginians, Randolph, Madison, and Monroe, were unreserved in support of federal regulation. Madison had written to Jefferson in March, 1786, "Most of our political evils may be traced to our commercial ones," and the Annapolis Report had won unanimous endorsement by the

7. Prescott, *Drafting the Federal Constitution*, 6; Randolph, "Letter," in P. L. Ford (ed.), *Pamphlets on the Constitution*, 267; Sherman, "A Citizen," in P. L. Ford (ed.), *Essays on the Constitution*, 238.

Virginia House of Delegates. There was a feeling, which Washington shared, that the South could break a northern monopoly of the carrying trade by building its own ships. Georgia was in the process of developing a shipping business and would soon ship more than one third of its exports in local bottoms. In South Carolina, locally owned ships carried about a fourth of the rice and indigo exports. Virginia merchants were building their own export fleet to carry tobacco.[8]

At the same time, the South feared export taxes because of its unique dependence on the overseas sale of tobacco, rice, and indigo. It seemed likely that the North would favor such a tax in order to bludgeon Britain into opening her West Indies. Southerners also anticipated a northern attempt to bar the import of slaves, and they were far from unanimous in their belief that they could avert a northern monopoly of the carrying trade. To protect themselves, they demanded a prohibition against taxes on all exports and the importation of slaves as well as against the passage of navigation acts with less than a two-thirds majority.[9]

Delegates from the northern and middle states felt that export taxes and navigation acts would be indispensable for promoting commerce with all foreign countries and especially Britain. They argued that by forcing London to open its sugar islands to American ships, both North and South would benefit. The South should be prepared to make certain concessions to the North in return for the military protection afforded by Yankee ships and soldiers. Federal con-

8. Jensen, *New Nation*, 401; James Madison to George Washington, November 8, 1786, in Hunt (ed.), *Writings of Madison*, II, 283; George Washington to James McHenry, August 22, 1785, in Fitzpatrick (ed.), *Writings of George Washington*, XXVIII, 229; McDonald, *We The People*, 131–32, 213, 382.

9. Nettels, *Emergence of National Economy*, 103.

trol of exports would prevent the states with good harbors from exploiting more isolated areas such as Connecticut and New Jersey; but most important, it would strengthen the president's hand in negotiating "favorable treaties of commerce." The threat of a tax on lumber, flour, or livestock, Gouverneur Morris suggested, would be a powerful inducement for Britain to open her Caribbean ports.[10]

When the Committee of Detail made its report on August 6, the northern delegates were outraged.[11] The committee had ruled out exports taxes and required a two-thirds majority for navigation acts. To add insult to injury, it had recommended that no obstacles be placed in the path of the importation of slaves. Men such as Rufus King and Gouverneur Morris, feeling they had been more than liberal in agreeing to the representation of slaves in Congress, now reverted to the issue of slavery in order to extract commercial concessions. Morris attacked slavery as a "nefarious institution" which was "the curse of heaven on the states where it prevailed." Was it not inconsistent for the South to ask the North for protection while allowing slaves to jeopardize its security? Was the first object of the national government not "defense against foreign aggression?" And did the South also wish to deny its brethren their natural advantages in the realm of commerce?

A week later, there was prolonged debate on the question of export taxes with both sides evenly matched. The topic was again raised on August 21 in connection with the slave trade and navigation acts, and the erratic Luther Martin of Maryland gave three reasons for blocking the slave

10. Farrand (ed.), *Records of Federal Convention*, II, 306–307, 360–62.
11. On July 24, 1787, the convention appointed John Rutledge, Edmund Randolph, Nathaniel Gorham, Oliver Ellsworth, and James Wilson a Committee of Detail to shape a constitution from the resolutions thus far agreed upon.

trade: without federal limitation, the trade would continue to grow as a result of the representation of slaves in Congress; slaves would weaken the defense of the area which the North would be bound to protect; and chattel traffic was inconsistent with the character of the American people. This was too much for John Rutledge of South Carolina. "Religion and humanity," he exclaimed, "have nothing to do with this question. Interest alone is the governing principle with nations. The true question at present is whether the southern states shall or shall not be parties to the Union." George Mason of Virginia then reminded Rutledge of the "pernicious effect" of slavery on the manners of the owner class: "Every master of slaves is born a petty tyrant." He recalled the history of slave insurrections in Greece and Sicily and insisted that it was absolutely essential for the general government to halt the increase of slavery. Had Cromwell not ordered his lieutenants to spark a servile insurrection in Virginia should his subjects prove defiant? These were strong words, coming from the distinguished framer of the Virginia Bill of Rights—too strong to go unchallenged. The two Pinckneys of South Carolina rushed into the fray claiming that if slavery was wrong, it was practiced by all the world, modern as well as ancient. In every age, half of mankind had lived in fetters. Besides, the Deep South could not do without slaves even if it so desired. John Dickinson of Delaware rejoined that although England and France permitted slavery, slaves were excluded from both of their kingdoms. As for Greece and Rome, they had been made to suffer by the evil of their ways.

A familiar suggestion finally brought the discussion to a close—one that had averted disaster on many an occasion since May 25: namely, that the question be referred to committee. Gouverneur Morris, the leading talker of the convention, now rose to suggest that the question of export taxes, the slave trade, and navigation acts be ironed out in a bundle by the same committee so as to "form a bargain among the northern and southern states." His motion passed, and the entire question was referred to a committee of eleven. Two days later, on August 24, a plan was reported which mollified the North in two ways. First, it allowed Congress to pass navigation acts by majority rather than two-thirds vote. Second, it allowed for congressional control of the slave trade beginning in 1800 (extended in debate to 1808). Only the prohibition against export taxes remained. The die had at last been cast. Morris' bargain had been struck. And the second great compromise of the convention became a *fait accompli*.

There was one last moment of suspense when young Pinckney burst out unexpectedly against the principle of majority rule for navigation acts. But he was obviously out of tune with the rest of his colleagues who were firmly resigned to the committee compromise. The older Pinckney reiterated the idea of southern reliance upon the military power of the North and suggested that a grateful South would surely want its northern brethren to reap their share of the general prosperity. He admitted coming to Philadelphia with prejudice against "the strong eastern states," but he had to admit that their people were "as liberal and candid as any men whatever." One by one, various voices chimed in to overwhelm the dissident member and move on with the proceedings. Gouverneur Morris was sure that navigation acts would increase American shipping to such a degree that southern produce would travel more cheaply than ever. Unless American bottoms and seamen found employment, there would be little chance of having the kind of a navy which would be needed to shield the southern coast. The cerebral Madison, taking his time as usual, opined that congressional regulation of commerce would benefit southern as well as northern shipping. Rutledge reminded the delegates of the need to secure "the great object" of the West India trade for which navigation acts would be vital. Nathaniel Gorham of Massachusetts remembered that the main purpose of the convention was to centralize control over commerce. He was not about to accept another defeat after conceding the principle of free exports. And so it went, with the tide running in one direction and protests by Randolph and Mason buried in short order.[12]

The last of the critical powers for the conduct of foreign relations, treaty enforcement, was in part a product of the other three. There had to be a means of guaranteeing that United States treaties would be honored by states and individuals. Congressional files contained legal complaints from every nation to which the country was bound by treaty. The most familiar case concerned prewar debts still owed to British merchants, but there were many other broken pledges including ones with France, Holland, Sweden, and the Indians, as well as a general usurpation of congressional prerogative by the states. One of the critical but less well-known instances occurred in 1783 when the states allowed a premature resumption of trade with Britain before Congress had officially indicated that the war was over. The result was disastrous for diplomatic efforts under way at the time to convince the British to make commercial concessions. It was Madison who, more than anyone else, was responsible for driving these points home to the delegates. He

12. Adrienne Koch (ed.), *Notes of Debates in the Federal Convention of 1787 Reported by James Madison* (Columbus: Ohio University Press, 1966), 409–12, 502–507, 547–51; Prescott, *Drafting the Federal Constitution*, 503–508; Rossiter, *Grand Convention*, 215–18; Farrand (ed.), *Records of Federal Convention*, II, 374, 449–53

attacked the New Jersey Plan for its failure to ensure the enforcement of treaties and the Law of Nations. The Virginia Plan, for which he was fighting, provided not only for regulation of foreign commerce but also for a military establishment and a congressional veto over state laws. The veto scheme was defeated on July 17, but the machinery for treaty enforcement was bolstered by two legal safeguards: treaties were ranked with the highest law of the land, and the Supreme Court was vested with original jurisdiction in all cases involving foreign nations.[13]

It is hard to say which of the four powers was most vital since each was dependent upon the other. The entire structure rested upon its fiscal base, and without the military establishment there would be little leverage for commercial bargaining, treaty enforcement, or revenue. In the absence of commercial success, revenue would dry up, and the navy would suffer from want of a merchant marine nursery. Treaty enforcement was a prerequisite for maintaining peace and fostering trade. All were vital.

At the same time, there was one consideration which entirely transcended the question of national versus state power: namely, the proper role for the executive branch. Under the Articles, Congress had acted as its own executive, with Jay in the role of glorified clerk. The New Yorker had complained about how often Congress failed to function for lack of a quorum. Even with a quorum, Congress could not agree on a course of action. Much of the business had been conducted by committees suffering from frequent membership changes and overlapping jurisdiction. The multiplicity of these groups encouraged obstruction, and committee members often disagreed so bitterly that, in order to represent diverse points of view, they attached several agents to

13. Farrand (ed.), *Records of Federal Convention*, I, 164, 316; II, 28.

a legation when a single individual would have been more than adequate. Large policy questions took a back seat to the trivia of patronage and economy.[14]

Another problem with the old system had been the ephemeral nature of Congress itself. Delegates had been constantly on the move in the early years, shifting their headquarters from Philadelphia to Princeton, to Annapolis, and to Trenton before settling in New York (where Jay rented two rooms in Fraunce's Tavern). When in session, the peripatetics were plagued with absenteeism. When they were out of session, which was over half the year, there was no agency to conduct foreign relations since Jay lacked substantial executive power. Jefferson suggested a permanent committee of the states to act as a carry-over when Congress was not meeting, and his suggestion was followed. But the committee was so restricted that it was practically useless. It could neither send nor replace envoys or even reply to foreign correspondence. In reality, it was nothing but a watchdog.

To make matters worse, there had been constant friction between internationalists and isolationists. The former included such men as Madison, Hamilton, and Livingston who wanted a sizable foreign service with ministers at five or six of the principal maritime courts. Among the latter were Benjamin Rush, Elbridge Gerry, Charles Dana, Arthur Lee, Stephen Higginson, Samuel Osgood, David Howell, and James Monroe, all of whom hoped to practice strict economy by reducing the foreign service to a skeleton. John Francis Mercer of Virginia, Daniel Carroll of Maryland,

14. These problems have been explored in a doctoral dissertation by George Clayton Wood, *Congressional Control of Foreign Relations During the American Revolution, 1774–1789* (Allentown, Pa.: H. R. Haas and Co., 1919). They are also mentioned in Gilbert, *To the Farewell Address*, 79–81.

and Hugh Williamson of North Carolina headed a powerful movement to eliminate ministers entirely and conduct
all foreign business at home (even Jefferson envied the se-
clusion of China). Most of the isolationists feared the influence of monarchy and resented the power which France
had exerted over American councils during the Revolution.
They remembered how Congress had been reduced to near
servility by the wiles of La Luzerne, and they were now
determined to have independence in fact as well as in name.

In the years 1783 to 1789 it was the isolationists who
held sway. The number of ministers dwindled to two in
1784. Salaries sagged from $11,111 to $9,000, and ministerial tenure was cut to three years. When Adams left the
Hague in 1785 to go on to London, his post remained va-
cant because no one would serve for $4,500. The work of
negotiating commercial treaties with a list of twenty-two
nations was entrusted to a temporary commission of three:
Adams, Franklin, and Jefferson. Congress waited six precious months to decide on the members and then failed to
send them their commissions along with their instructions.
The result was predictable. Even the giants of American
diplomacy could not stretch themselves thin enough to per-
form a task of this magnitude. Only two nations out of
twenty-two signed agreements, and of these, one (Prussia)
had been in the process of negotiation prior to the appoint-
ment of the commission. There were, of course, reasons
more basic than the shortage of personnel to explain Europe's diplomatic reserve; but the foreign service was not
the asset it might have been.[15]

In view of these shortcomings and Secretary Jay's insis-

15. Very helpful along these lines is Howard J. Phillips, "*The United
States Diplomatic Establishment in the Critical Period, 1783–1789*" (Ph.D.
dissertation, Notre Dame, 1968), especially pp. 55, 84, 91, 106–107, 122–
23, 353, 356.

tence on the need for a strong executive, one might have expected some concern on the part of the Constitutional Convention. Instead, however, the delegates assumed that diplomatic negotiations *per se* would be rare, that foreign relations would be commercial in nature, and that treaties would be few. Thus, while the New Jersey and Virginia Plans provided for an executive branch, there was little indication prior to September that the president would emerge as more than a diplomatic figurehead. Hamilton had spoken on June 18 in favor of an executive with a dominant role in foreign relations. But this proposal was ignored along with the rest of his speech, and the New Yorker does not seem to have pushed his point. The report of the Committee of Detail on August 6 vested the Senate rather than the executive with the power to negotiate treaties and appoint ambassadors.[16] On August 15, Mason and Mercer warned of senatorial power and presented a case for including the House of Representatives in the ratification process. A week later, two other large-state men, Gouverneur Morris and James Wilson of Pennsylvania, declared their support for a House role, explaining that treaties should be rare and formed only under the most favorable conditions. They should not, therefore, be formed easily. "The more difficulty in making treaties, the more value will be set on them."

16. This was one of the reasons for extending the Senate term to six years. Only a longer term would allow the necessary amount of stability and expertise. Wilson argued that the Senate must "be made respectable in the eyes of foreign nations." Why, he asked, had Congress not obtained a commercial treaty with Great Britain? Was it not partly, perhaps, because of a lack of confidence in the stability of Congress? He insisted that the long term, combined with the principle of partial change in membership every two years, would ensure the continuity, stability, and dignity necessary for the proper conduct of foreign affairs. The fundamental reason for the long term was, of course, the idea that the Senate should act as a conservative check on the House. See Farrand (ed.), *Records of Federal Convention,* I, 421–26, 433.

The learned Dr. Johnson of Connecticut was not convinced, however. There seemed to him something of "a solecism in saying that the acts of a minister with plenipotentiary powers of one body should depend for ratification on another body." In the end, Johnson's view prevailed and Morris' motion to include the House in treaty ratification was voted down decisively, eight to one.

Madison then spoke briefly about making the president "an agent in treaties" since the Senate represented the states alone," and with Morris' support he succeeded in having the whole treaty clause recommitted.

It is important to note that the Committee of Detail had not yet reported to the convention on diplomatic powers. Nor did it ever do so. On August 31, it was replaced by a new Committee on Remaining Business, composed of one member from each state, and on September 4 this new committee reported a much enhanced presidential role—one which bore a striking resemblance to Hamilton's plan. "The President, by and with the advice and consent of the Senate" was to "have power to make treaties; and he shall nominate and by and with the advice and consent of the Senate shall appoint ambassadors . . . ." [17] Three days then elapsed, and when the subject came up for discussion, the convention was grinding into its last week under great pressure for adjournment. There was a brief return to the question of a House role. Wilson, who had not given up on his original motion, now argued that the advantages of excluding the House of Representatives from the treaty process would be

17. It may be significant that both Madison and Morris, who had taken the lead in urging that the president be "an agent in treaties," were appointed to represent their states on this new committee. Other members were Rufus King (a friend of Hamilton and Jay), Williamson and Carroll (friends of Madison), Gilman, Sherman, Brearly, Dickinson, Butler, and Baldwin. None of these had served on the Committee of Detail.

outweighed by the danger of forcing an unpopular decision. Arch-Yankee Roger Sherman from the small state of
Connecticut disagreed with Wilson and led the opposition
which again squelched the idea of a House role by a vote
of ten to one. The question was dead. Wilson then objected
to the Senate's role in appointing ambassadors because it
would undermine executive responsibility. Again, he found
few to agree with him, and his objection was overridden.[18]

The next question arose with regard to treaty approval:
what kind of a Senate majority should be required? Wilson
and King argued for a simple majority. They were not in
favor of allowing the few to control the many. Delegates
from the South, on the other hand, spoke up for a two-
thirds rule. The Jay-Gardoqui talks had convinced them
that the federal government would sacrifice vital navigation
rights on the Mississippi if the subject were left to the disposal of a simple majority. In addition, Congress had alien-
ated many frontiersmen in the Southwest by its Indian policy. The Treaty of Hopewell had been repugnant to land
speculators, and New Englanders harbored similar fears
concerning their fishery rights off Newfoundland. There
were those, too, who were isolationist enough in their outlook to want to discourage treaties in any form. Madison
offered a compromise which would keep the two-thirds rule
but exempt peace treaties from executive approval. Butler
of South Carolina seconded the idea as a necessary safeguard against presidential ambition. Had the delegates not
heard of the recent perfidy of the Dutch Stadtholder or

18. Farrand (ed.), *Records of Federal Convention*, I, 292; II, 394, 538–
39; Koch (ed.), *Notes*, 460–61, 520–21, 575, 597–98. The constitution which
Edmund Randolph drafted for his Committee of Detail vested diplomatic
powers in the legislature as a whole until Randolph revised it to favor
the Senate. Two of Wilson's copies placed these powers in the Senate
from the beginning.

the artful tricks of the duke of Marlborough in prolonging a war which he was conducting? Gerry countered with the remark that peace treaties were not as innocuous as they might sound. They could easily become the instrument for bartering away minority interests (i.e. the fisheries or western access to the Gulf of Mexico). Gerry's view prevailed. Madison offered a second compromise which would exempt peace treaties from the two-thirds rule, but this too was voted down after initial acceptance. One last effort to reduce executive power by allowing the Senate to *make* as well as *approve* treaties was handily defeated. Thus there were no modifications of the structure established in committee. The question of diplomatic powers was promptly turned over to the Committee on Style, and the key member of this committee, Gouverneur Morris, decided to list all diplomatic clauses under the heading of executive powers. Morris, of course, was an ardent nationalist and firm believer in elite leadership.[19]

Towering above the responsibility for making treaties and appointing ambassadors was the executive war power. This ultimately included the command of the armed forces and the emergency war power. Most delegates agreed on the need to make good use of executive speed, secrecy, and efficiency, and there was no opposition to the Commander-in-Chief clause. But the Committee of Detail, in its report of August 4, lodged the power to "make" war in the legislature. Young Pinckney took exception to this clause as soon as it

19. Hugh Williamson to James Madison, June 2, 1788, in Farrand (ed.), *Records of Federal Convention*, III, 306; Whitaker, *Spanish-American Frontier*, 124–26; R. Earl McLendon, "Origins of the Two-Thirds Rule in Senate Action Upon Treaties," *American Historical Review*, XXXVI (1931), 772; Farrand (ed.), *Records of Federal Convention*, II, 540–41, 549; Dexter Perkins, *The American Approach to Foreign Policy* (New York: Atheneum, 1968), 191–92; Koch (ed.), *Notes of Debates*, 599–604; Phillips, *Diplomatic Establishment*, 301, 361–62.

came up for discussion on August 17. He felt that the House would not be capable of acting rapidly enough and that the Senate alone should receive the power. Butler thought the Senate as objectionable as the House and suggested the executive as the proper agency. Madison and Gerry then moved to substitute the word "declare" for "make," leaving the president "the power to repel sudden attacks." Sherman was concerned that Madison's motion might allow the president to start a war, and he didn't want the legislative power narrowed so much. But Madison and Gerry won by a vote of seven to two. Thus, there would be nothing to prevent the president from deploying troops in the critical period between the outbreak of hostilities and a formal declaration of war.[20]

In summary, the more nationalist-minded delegates succeeded in building up executive prerogative to a remarkable degree. One may wonder what might have transpired if such isolationists as Osgood, Higginson, and Monroe had been present. Things might also have been different had it not been for the awesome figure of George Washington presiding over the convention from beginning to end. It was obvious that Washington would be the nation's first choice for president and that he would have as many terms as he desired. His popularity and good sense must have presented a constant challenge to the opponents of executive power. But the nationalists also knew how to engage in debate; they were adept at infiltrating key committees, and they could count on the failures of the Confederation to plead their case. British precedent was on their side, too, although they

20. Farrand (ed.), *Records of Federal Conventon*, II, 318–19; Koch (ed.), *Notes of Debates*, 475–76. The principle of executive control in this area was a part of Pinckney's plan (Farrand [ed.], *Records of Federal Convention*, III, 598, 599, 606, 607) and encountered little opposition in the Convention.

rarely referred to it. When all was said and done, there was a minimum of floor debate on the diplomatic powers, and the momentous shift from Senate to president occurred at the very end of the session when tempers were short and patience wearing thin. Perhaps young Pinckney was correct when he reminisced in 1818:

> The great diplomatic power given to the President was never intended to have been given to him while the Convention continued in that patient and coolly deliberate situation in which they had been for nearly the whole of the preceding . . . months of their session, nor was it until within the last week or ten days that almost the whole of the executive department was altered. I can assure you as a fact that for more than four months . . . the power of exclusively making treaties, appointing public ministers and judges of the Supreme Court was given to the Senate after numerous debates.[21]

Even the idea of a group similar to the British Privy Council which would act as a check upon arbitrary presidential power was brushed aside with little discussion. On August 18, Oliver Ellsworth of Connecticut noted that the president had not yet been given a council. He envisioned an advisory group consisting of the president of the Senate, the chief justice, and the ministers of foreign and domestic affairs, war, finance, and the merchant marine. Young Pinckney and Gouverneur Morris proposed a council of similar composition but without the president of the Senate. The executive would be free to consult or not to consult as he pleased, and he might call for a written opinion from one or more of the members. In addition, there would be a secretary to serve both the council and the president (a secretary of state). The plan was referred to the Committee of Detail which recommended a slightly enlarged version. This,

21. Phillips, *Diplomatic Establishment*, 321–22, 325.

in turn, went back to committee where it was discarded on the apparent assumption that the president would inevitably dominate his council and thereby acquire even greater power. The idea was not yet dead, however, for on September 7 Colonel Mason warned his colleagues that to reject an executive council was to embark on an experiment which even "the most despotic governments" had not dared to try—even the Grand Signor himself had "his Divan." Mason's ideal council would be more powerful than anything yet proposed and would consist of six members, two from each section of the country (south, north, and middle area), with a rotation and term similar to that of the Senate. The key stipulation was that it would be appointed by the legislature or the Senate. Franklin found himself in agreement with Mason because he did not think the delegates were sufficiently aware of the danger to be apprehended from appointments made by an individual. "Experience shewed that caprice, the intrigues of favorites and mistresses, etc. were . . . the means most prevalent in monarchies." Among the instances of abuse, he mentioned the many bad colonial governors appointed by Great Britain. Surely a council would not only be "a check on a bad President but a relief to a good one." Wilson, Dickenson, and Madison concurred. But King attacked the scheme as costly and tending to lend additional influence to an already powerful central government. When the discussion came to an end, Mason's motion was voted down, eight to three.[22] The final Constitution therefore provided only for executive departments. It enabled the president to require the opinion of "the principal officer in each of the executive departments," leaving the

22. Farrand (ed.), *Records of Federal Convention*, II, 329, 342–43, 539; Koch (ed.), *Notes of Debates*, 481, 487–88, 509–10, 600–601.

actual designation of departments to the first legislature.[23]

The last decision to reflect the impact of external affairs was the question of how to secure the nation against foreign subversion. As mentioned above, there was strong apprehension that the nation would be defenseless against the kind of influence which France had insinuated into American councils during the war. Secretary Jay, who was especially sensitive to the problem, suggested to Washington during the convention that it might be "wise and reasonable to provide a strong check to the admission of foreigners into the administration of our national government," and he specifically advised that the president be required to be a natural born citizen.[24] Not everyone, of course, favored restrictive measures. Some of the delegates were themselves foreigners, and others pointed to the outstanding record of aliens who had fought in the Revolution. Nevertheless, the final draft included a number of requirements, in addition to the obvious one of a president who was either native-born or a citizen at the time of the adoption of the Constitution, which reflected majority opinion.

One clause was lifted verbatim from the old constitution: that no official "shall, without the consent of the Congress, accept of any present, emolument, office or title, of

23. Article II, Section II. An act was promptly passed in the first session of Congress officially establishing a Department of Foreign Affairs; Bemis, "John Jay," 275. The only question which arose after ratification was whether or not there should be a separate department for home affairs. Since it seemed at the time that there would not be sufficient work to justify such an addition, foreign affairs and home affairs were combined under one department, the Department of State. Home affairs consisted of such matters as communications between the executive and the states, keeping the great seal, and affixing it to all commissions of officers appointed by the president; *ibid.*; Gaillard Hunt, *The Department of State of the United States, Its History and Functions* (New Haven: Yale University Press, 1914), 69–70, 73.

24. John Jay to George Washington, July 25, 1787, in Johnston (ed.), *Papers of John Jay*, III, 250.

any kind whatever, from any king, prince, or foreign state." Young Pinckney stressed the need to protect American envoys from foreign influence. Edmund Randolph, in later testimony before the Virginia ratifying convention, alluded to a snuff box with a portrait of Louis XVI which had been given to Franklin during his term as minister to France and asserted that the provision was designed "to exclude corruption and foreign influence." And a Federalist pamphleteer assured his readers that "the influence which foreign powers may attempt to exercise in our affairs was foreseen, and a wholesome provision has been made against it; for no person holding an office under the United States is permitted to enjoy any foreign honors, powers, or emoluments." [25]

The terms of citizenship required of representatives and senators were predicated on the assumption that the longer an immigrant remained in America, the more detached from his native country he would become. A senator, because of his special role in foreign affairs, should be particularly free from alien influence, and the Committee of Detail suggested a citizenship requirement for senators of four years. Gouverneur Morris, however, claimed that if it took seven years to learn to be a shoemaker, "fourteen at least are necessary to learn the trade of American legislator" and "eradicate the affections of education and native attachments." He would be the last to discourage immigration, but he would not be "polite at the expense of prudence." He believed in hospitality, but should there not be limits? Certain Indian tribes had reportedly gone so far as to offer their wives and daughters to strangers! Was this a proper example for the United States? "Admit a Frenchman into your Senate and he will study to increase the commerce of France: an Englishman,

25. The Constitution, Article I, Section IX; Farrand (ed.), *Records of Federal Convention*, II, 389; III, 327; Coxe, *A Brief Examination*, 150.

he will feel an equal bias in favor of that of England." Pierce Butler of South Carolina, who was himself foreign-born, agreed with Morris that immigrants brought with them "not only attachments to other countries but also foreign ideas of government." He mentioned the severity of British law in this regard. In opposition to the policy of exclusion stood Mason, Madison, and Ellsworth who stressed that such a rule would discourage immigration. Franklin and Randolph took a middle position, suggesting nine years as a suitable period, and this proved to be the acceptable ground of agreement.[26]

There was also a citizenship requirement for members of the House, based on similar principles. The Committee of Detail had proposed a period of three years, but Mason argued successfully for seven, assuring his colleagues that he harbored no prejudice toward immigrants, but that he did not wish to see foreigners and adventurers making laws. His motion was approved by every state except Connecticut. Some delegates felt that even seven years was too brief a period. Gerry wanted eligibility restricted to natives. "Foreign powers," he warned, "will intermeddle in our affairs, and spare no expense to influence them. Persons having foreign attachments will be sent among us and insinuated into councils. . . . Everyone knows the vast sums laid out in Europe for secret services." There were other opinions as well. Hugh Williamson of North Carolina suggested nine years instead of seven; Hamilton was in favor of letting the state legislatures decide; and Madison opposed any restrictions whatever. Wilson also took a liberal position, unwilling to violate pledges which had already been made to prospective immigrants. He read a clause in the Pennsylvania constitution which promised immigrants the rights of citizenship

26. Farrand (ed.), *Records of Federal Convention*, II, 235–36, 238–39, 243.

after only two years' residence. Mason countered with a warning that immigrants would bring especially strong pressure to bear upon commercial legislation. If, for example, "persons among us attached to Great Britain should work themselves into our councils, a turn might be given to our affairs and particularly to our commercial regulations which might have pernicious consequences. The great houses of British merchants would spare no pains to insinuate the instruments of their views into the government." Mason held his ground to the end, and the seven year plan received unanimous approval.[27]

The debates over citizenship and titles were not the only ones which reflected a fear of foreign subversion. On a number of other occasions spokesmen for diverse causes voiced a similar apprehension. Gouverneur Morris raised the question in connection with the presidency, arguing successfully for an impeachment provision and citing the familiar case of Charles II who had accepted bribes from Louis XIV. Wilson tried to defend the Virginia Plan for a congressional veto over state laws on the basis that some states might be "used by foreign powers as engines against the whole." Men such as Gerry, King, and Morris even invoked the fear of subversion in an unsuccessful effort to restrict western representation in Congress. They claimed that the western states, soon to be admitted to the union, would be under the influence of hordes of recent immigrants loyal to their native country. Should such states be allowed to overshadow the seaboard states in congressional power? In another instance, Hamilton and Madison helped to discredit the New Jersey Plan (which retained the concept of confederation by sovereign states) by warning that foreign nations would be quick to exploit the least sign of dissension within the union. One state would be played off against another, as was the case

27. *Ibid.*, II, 178, 216, 268, 271–72.

with the Amphictionic Council, Charlemagne's empire, and the Swiss cantons, all of which had fallen prey to external forces due to internal discord.[28]

Having considered the relationship between foreign affairs and the Philadelphia Convention in terms of specific provisions written into the new Constitution, there is one final observation to be made. Throughout all the deliberations there was the expectation that each provision, and especially the Constitution *in toto*, would be a great tonic for the national spirit. This idea was mentioned several times in debate and was universally assumed. By placing the country on a footing of strength and reliability, the new government would acquire prestige in the eyes of the world. There would be no more demand for thirteen ambassadors to represent the states individually. There would be no more foreign charges of chaos and impotence. The federal government would at last exercise unquestioned authority in the area of taxation, military operations, commerce, and treaties. John Adams, on his return from England in the spring of 1788, reported that the Constitution was "spoken of by the English minister as an admirable form of government . . . which if adopted will place the American character in a new point of view highly deserving respect." And Gouverneur Morris wrote proudly that America would soon be "as much respected abroad as she has for some time past been disregarded." [29]

It only remained for the friends of the Constitution to secure its adoption.

28. *Ibid.*, I, 172, 285, 319; II, 3, 68–69.
29. Henry Knox to George Washington, May 25, 1788, in Washington Papers, Library of Congress, Ser. 4, Vol. CCXL; Gouverneur Morris to a gentleman in France, 1787, in Mrs. Anne Cary (Morris) Maudslay (ed.), *The Diary and Letters of Gouverneur Morris* (2 vols.; New York: Charles Scribner's Sons, 1888), I, 18.

# V

# The
# Final Test

*If we are to be one nation in any respect, it clearly ought to be in respect to other nations.*[1]

What transpired in Philadelphia during the hot summer of 1787 has been called a "miracle"—a miracle of statesmanship, of scholarly application, of political expertise.[2] Just as miraculous, however, was the skill with which the proponents of constitutional reform presented their case to the public. It has been suggested that they worked so quickly that the opposition never had time to organize, that they were favored by the newspapers, that they benefited from the superior prestige of their leaders, and that perhaps they succeeded through sheer good fortune. All of this may be true. But in light of the difficulties which lay before them, they campaigned in a very winning manner. They had to sell the country a completely new frame of government. Moreover, many whose approval they sought tended to be

1. James Madison, quoted in Rossiter (ed.), *Federalist Papers*, No. 42, p. 264.
2. Bowen, *Miracle at Philadelphia.*

167

unfamiliar with continental problems and therefore unappreciative of the remedies offered. The average man would tend to resist the onrushing forces of change. He would be sensitive to any threat, however remote, to his newly won freedom. In particular he would be strongly biased against any plan which reminded him of the British imperial system, characterized by a strong central government with power to tax and maintain standing armies. Finally, state and local leaders were not anxious to see continental power augmented at their own expense.

Throughout the ratification campaign Antifederalists criticized the Constitution mainly for concentrating too much power in the hands of the central government without sufficient checks and balances. State governments, they argued, would lose power. The country would fall into the hands of a privileged few. The rich would oppress the poor. One geographical section would victimize another. The Constitution would degenerate into a bill of tyranny. Arguments such as these stressed the cultural, economic, and political diversity of the country and were divisive in nature. As such they were well suited to the obstructionist cause.[3]

Federalists, on the other hand, were obliged to emphasize unity and a harmony of interests. The question can therefore be put: how did they conduct their side of the great debate? How did they approach the issues, and where did they concentrate their attention? Which arguments did they fasten upon as having the greatest common appeal for

3. A classic example of this was the testimony of Amos Singletary in the Massachusetts ratifying convention; Elliot (ed.), *Debates in State Conventions*, II, 101–102, 147. For a good discussion of Antifederalist fears, see Cecilia M. Kenyon, "Men of Little Faith: The Anti-Federalists on the Nature of Representative Government," *William and Mary Quarterly*, XII, Ser. 3 (January, 1955), 3–42; see also Main, *Antifederalists*, Chaps. 6, 7.

such a variety of people as lived from Maine to Georgia, and from the tidewater regions of Virginia to the Mississippi Valley? Did they shift their line of argument from location to location, or did they rely on certain stock themes regardless of the neighborhood?

The key to consensus lay in several issues related to foreign affairs. In state ratifying conventions and in pieces of propaganda, Federalists stressed the weak condition of American defense. The Constitution, with its provisions for a standing army and navy, would reduce the likelihood of invasion and increase America's ability to triumph in the event of war. It would also bring relief from commercial distress by allowing Congress to retaliate against British trade restrictions. Moreover, it promised to bolster national pride and enable the United States to take a dignified place among the countries of the world. These were the winning issues.

*The Federalist*, a series of eighty-five articles which appeared in New York newspapers between October 27, 1787, and August, 1788, is a good illustration of the way in which the Constitution was presented to the people.[4] Out of the

4. *The Federalist* not only appeared in the most widely circulated newspapers but was a chief source of reference in the Virginia and New York ratifying conventions and was more widely read than any other tract of the controversy; Rossiter (ed.), *Federalist Papers*, viii, xi; Monaghan, *John Jay*, 291. *The Federalist's* influence is also reflected in such letters as Richard Stuart to James Madison, April 5, 1788, in James Madison Papers, Library of Congress, Ser. 1, Vol. VIII. Apparently, the series of articles was widely circulated in individual correspondence among Federalists. Washington forwarded available issues of *The Federalist* to Richmond for publication, and the secretary of Congress, Charles Thomson, sent a copy of it to James McHenry who exerted great influence on behalf of the Constitution throughout the Maryland ratifying convention; George Washington to James Madison, December 7, 1787, in Fitzpatrick (ed.), *Writings of George Washington*, XXIX, 331; Charles Thomson to James McHenry, April 19, 1788, in Burnett (ed.), *Letters of Continental Congress*, VIII, 721–22.

first thirty-six articles, twenty-five concerned national insecurity. These twenty-five anticipated all the major arguments used during the campaign. The subject of military weakness was discussed in numbers 3, 4, 14, 23–32, 34, and 36; the possibility of a dissolution of the union and foreign intervention in numbers 5–8 and 18–20; commercial distress and the need for congressional power to retaliate against foreign trade restrictions in numbers 11, 12, 22, and 23; national honor in number 15; and treaty enforcement in number 22. Nearly every argument sprang from the concept of a foreign threat. Characteristic was a statement by Madison in which he denied the Antifederalist claim that republican government could not be extended to the outlying areas of a country as large as the United States. Border communities, he pointed out, would be the first to benefit from a closer union because they would receive increased military support. He deplored the lack of protection for settlers on the frontier and condemned continued British occupation of the frontier posts, attributing these ills to two basic conditions: the want of an adequate army and the depressed state of the treasury.[5] His reply to Antifederalist critics who feared that too strong a central government might undermine states' rights was clever. He pointed out that since the national government was intended primarily for the purpose of defense, its operations would be "most extensive and important in times of war and danger; those of the state government in times of peace and security." Therefore, if the Antifederalists proved correct in their prediction that war would not occur, the state governments would continue to hold sway. Indeed, the more power given to the national government to cope with a potential state of war, the less likely

5. Rossiter (ed.), *Federalist Papers*, No. 14, p. 103.

would be a state of war in which such power would be exercised.[6]

Hamilton, as well as Madison, made much of the theme of national insecurity. He justified direct and unlimited taxation on the basis that it was a wartime necessity for obtaining foreign credit and a steady revenue. In summing up his argument for such taxation he affirmed that the government should not be disarmed "of a single weapon which in any possible contingency might be usefully employed for the general defense and security." In the same vein he asked, "Is public credit an indispensable resource in time of public danger?" America had very little. "Is respectability in the eyes of foreign powers a safeguard against foreign encroachments? . . . Our Ambassadors abroad are the mere pageants of mimic sovereignty." [7]

The remainder of *The Federalist* was far more concerned with procedural clauses in the Constitution than with the underlying reasons for constitutional reform. Yet even here the subject of foreign relations was frequently injected.[8] Madison, in defending the long House and Senate terms against those who desired a higher rate of turnover in public office, pointed out the problems of a high rate of change in government personnel:

> It forfeits the respect and confidence of other nations, and all the advantages connected with national character. An individual who is observed to be inconstant to his plans, or perhaps to carry on his affairs without any plan at all, is marked at once by all prudent people as a speedy victim to his own unsteadiness and folly. . . . One nation is to another what one individual is to another. . . . But the best instruction on this subject is unhappily conveyed to America by the example of

6. *Ibid.*, No. 45, p. 293.
7. *Ibid.*, No. 15, p. 107; No. 36, p. 223.
8. *Ibid.*, Nos. 42, 53, 62–64, 75.

her own situation. She finds that she is held in no respect by her friends; that she is the derision of her enemies; and that she is a prey to every nation which has an interest in speculating on her fluctuating councils and embarrassed affairs.[9]

He added further that, without a select and stable government, "the national councils will not possess that sensibility to the opinion of the world which is perhaps not less necessary in order to merit than it is to obtain its respect and confidence." John Jay referred especially to senators when he remarked that their diplomatic duties would demand that they take the time to acquire "exact information . . . to become perfectly acquainted with our national concerns, and to form and introduce a system for the management of them." [10]

This point received additional clarification later in the New York ratifying convention where Robert R. Livingston explained that the office of senator "requires a comprehensive knowledge of foreign politics and an extensive acquaintance with characters whom, in this capacity they have to negotiate with, together with such an intimate conception of our best interests relative to foreign powers, as can only be derived from much experience in this business." [11]

The House term was also defended in a context of foreign relations. Federalists maintained that congressmen as well as senators would need a knowledge of foreign affairs because the regulation of commerce would entail an understanding of treaties between the United States and foreign countries and a knowledge of the trade regulations of other nations. Since such knowledge was not available on the state

9. *Ibid.*, No. 62, pp. 380–81.
10. *Ibid.*, No. 63, p. 382; No. 64, p. 392.
11. Alexander Hamilton supported Livingston on this issue, and James Iredell said the same thing in the North Carolina convention; Elliot (ed.), *Debates in State Conventions*, II, 291, 302, 306; IV, 41.

level, the newly elected congressman should be allowed sufficient time in office to acquire it.[12]

But any discussion of *The Federalist* in the context of foreign affairs would be incomplete without mentioning John Jay, who, as secretary for foreign affairs, was at the time the best known of its three authors. Jay had taken an important part in the peace negotiations, and now at the age of forty-two his prestige was said to exceed the combined fame of his younger colleagues, Madison and Hamilton.[13] Because of illness, he contributed only five articles to *The Federalist*. Yet, after an introductory article by Hamilton, it was he who actually launched the series, and it was his articles which set the tone for the rest of the series by emphasizing the foreign threat.[14]

In addition to his contribution to *The Federalist*, Jay published *An Address to the People of New York on the Subject of the Constitution* which appeared in April, 1788. It was an extremely popular and influential tract which

12. Rossiter (ed.), *Federalist Papers*, No. 53, p. 334. This argument came up again in the Massachusetts convention when Cabot of Beverley argued that the House would have to be specially qualified in its spending capacity to decide on the advisability of raising funds to support a war or implement a treaty; Elliot (ed.), *Debates in State Conventions*, II, 25; and John Dickinson wrote that the two houses of Congress would be "not only legislative but also diplomatic bodies," requiring a "competent knowledge of foreign affairs relative to the states"; John Dickinson, "The Letters of Fabius on the Federal Constitution," No. 2, in P. L. Ford (ed.), *Pamphlets on the Constitution*, 170.

13. Madison was thirty-six, Hamilton thirty. Indicative of Jay's great popularity was the fact that out of a total of 2,836 votes cast in New York City for delegates to the state ratifying convention, he received 2,735 while Governor Clinton polled only 134; John Jay, *Second Letter on Dawson's Introduction to "The Federalist"* (New York: American News Co., 1864), 26; Monaghan, *John Jay*, 294. Jay assumed a prominent role at the state convention, being chosen by the Federalists to move the adoption of the Constitution and to draft New York's circular letter to the other states; Jay, *Second Letter*, 48.

14. Rossiter (ed.), *Federalist Papers*, Nos. 2–5 and 64.

characteristically placed heavy emphasis on foreign affairs.[15] Congress could declare war, exclaimed Jay, but could not raise men or money to wage it. It could make peace but could not enforce it. It could make commercial treaties but could not execute them. Consequently:

> Almost every national object of every kind is at this day un-provided for; and other nations taking the advantage of its imbecility, are daily multiplying commercial restraints upon us. Our fur trade is gone to Canada and British garrisons keep the keys of it. Our shipyards have almost ceased to disturb the repose of the neighborhood by the noise of the axe and hammer; and while foreign flags fly triumphantly above our highest houses, the American stars seldom do more than shed a few feeble rays about the humble masts of river sloops and coasting schooners. The greater part of our hardy seamen are plowing the ocean in foreign pay; and not a few of our in-genious shipwrights are now building vessels on alien shores. Although our increasing agriculture and industry extend and multiply our productions, yet they constantly diminish in value; and although we permit all nations to fill our country with their merchandise, yet their best markets are shut against us. Is there an English, or a French, or a Spanish island or port in the West Indies, to which an American vessel can carry a cargo of flour for sale? Not one. The Algerines ex-clude us from the Mediterranean, and adjacent countries, and we are neither able to purchase, nor to command the free use of those seas.[16]

15. Monaghan, *John Jay*, 292. Washington recommended it for its "good sense, for able observations, temper and moderation." According to S. B. Webb, the pamphlet "had a most astonishing influence in con-verting antifederalism to a knowledge and belief that the new constitu-tion was their only political salvation." And Noah Webster felt that it contained "a brief recapitulation of the most striking arguments in favor of adopting the proposed Federal Constitution"; quoted in P. L. Ford (ed.), *Pamphlets on the Constitution*, 67. E. W. Spaulding agreed that the *Address* was one of the most influential of all Federalist works; Ernest Wilder Spaulding, *New York in the Critical Period, 1783–1789* (New York: Columbia University Press, 1932), 8.

16. Jay, "Address," in P. L. Ford (ed.), *Pamphlets on the Constitution*, 73.

The convention which met to resolve these problems, continued Jay, drafted a plan which was the best possible under the circumstances. He emphasized the threat of a dissolution of the union and warned of the danger of foreign influence in any future convention. Should a future convention fail to agree on a plan—and the likelihood of this would increase as time passed and factions grew stronger—"then every state would be a little nation, jealous of its neighbors, and anxious to strengthen itself by foreign alliances against its former friends." New York State would be threatened by Connecticut and New Jersey, her great harbor imperiled, and the people of Long Island exposed.[17]

While Madison, Hamilton, and Jay were making their case for ratification in New York, other writers were presenting arguments in a similar vein elsewhere. Noah Webster's *Examination into the Leading Principles of the Federal Constitution* was not so much a defense of the Constitution as a rebuttal of specific criticisms. Nevertheless, mention was made of the foreign debt problem and the danger of foreign invasion. Likewise, Alexander Hanson's *Remarks on the Proposed Plan of a Federal Government*, though mostly a defense of specific constitutional clauses, touched on the issue of war and national honor. In Pennsylvania, Tench Coxe applauded the new Constitution on the basis of its safeguards against subversion and external attack. And John Dickinson's *Letters of Fabius on the Federal Constitution*, although mostly philosophical in tone, ended with a consideration of foreign hostility.[18]

From the South, also, came familiar arguments. Edmund

17. *Ibid.*, 81–84.
18. Noah Webster, "An Examination into the Leading Principles of the Federal Constitution"; "Remarks"; Tench Coxe, "An Examination of the Constitution for the United States of America"; Dickinson, "Fabius," Nos. 5 and 9, *ibid.*, 29–61, 133–50, 188, 192–93, 215, 244–51.

Randolph's *Letter on the Federal Convention* concentrated almost entirely on the advantages of the new Constitution in the area of foreign relations. Randolph argued that war would be inevitable under the Articles and the United States would just as inevitably suffer defeat through incompetence. James Iredell, in answer to George Mason's objections, published a pamphlet on national honor and the threat of European and Indian attack. And David Ramsay, in his *Address to the Freemen of South Carolina on the Federal Constitution*, concerned himself mostly with the issue of defense against foreign aggression.[19]

Of the various issues related to foreign affairs, one in particular served the Federalists well, namely the military weakness and insecurity of the Confederation government. Perhaps a letter from Henry Knox to George Washington came as close as anything to being an indication of party strategy: "As a war between France and England seems inevitable and a general war in Europe probable, the result may be highly beneficial to this country.... The war will impress on the fears of the people of the United States the necessity of a general government to defend them against the insults and invasions of the Europeans.... This subject being forcibly impressed on the public mind will have its full effect unless we are devoted to destruction." [20] Knox not only expressed the prevalent feeling of insecurity, he

19. Randolph, "Letter"; Iredell, "Observations"; Ramsay, "Address," *ibid.*, 262–70, 365–70, 373–80. The heavy emphasis which the Federalists placed on the issues of national security, national honor, and foreign commerce is illustrated also in Oliver Ellsworth, "Letters"; Williamson, "Remarks"; and Charles Pinckney, "Letter of a Steady and Open Republican," in P. L. Ford (ed.), *Essays on the Constitution*.

20. Henry Knox to George Washington, December 11, 1787, in Washington Papers, Library of Congress, Ser. 4, Vol. CCXXXIX.

also suggested that this feeling might be used as a means of winning support for the Constitution.[21]

Federalists followed Knox's suggestion closely. Typical of their stress on the likelihood of war was the following:

> Wars have been, and, we must suppose, will continue to be frequent. A war has generally happened among the European nations as often as once in twelve or fifteen years, for a century past; and for more than one third of this period, the English, French and Spaniards have been in a state of war. The territories of two of these nations border upon our country. England is at heart inimical to us; Spain is jealous.... It would be no strange thing if within ten years the injustice of England or Spain should force us into a war; it would be strange if it should not within fifteen or twenty years.[22]

Many theories were advanced to explain how the next war would come. The foreign debt was considered by some as a likely source of conflict unless Congress could be assured of a steady source of revenue under the new Constitution. Foreign creditors would not be patient indefinitely while America continued to renege on its fiscal responsibilities. Sooner or later they would seek revenge by attacking American commerce. British presence in the frontier posts was also cited as a powder keg to watch.[23]

Pelatiah Webster warned that the United States would become embroiled abroad unless some federal authority was

21. This would seem especially plausible in light of Forrest McDonald's observation that Federalists drew much of their support from the ranks of soldiers and officers who had fought in the Revolution; Forrest McDonald, "The Anti-Federalists, 1788–1789," *Wisconsin Magazine of History*, XLVI (Spring, 1963), 207–209.

22. New York *Journal*, March 29, 1787.

23. Jay, "Address," in P. L. Ford (ed.), *Pamphlets on the Constitution*, 83; James Bowdoin in Massachusetts, in Elliot (ed.), *Debates in State Conventions*, II, 82; Alexander Hamilton, "Speech before the New York Assembly," March 28, 1787, in Syrett (ed.), *Papers of Hamilton*, IV, 134–35.

established "to punish any individual or state, who shall violate our treaties with foreign nations, insult their dignity or abuse their citizens, and compel due reparation in all such cases." This was a common theme. William Davie echoed it in the North Carolina convention, recounting how a thief who had stolen a Dutch vessel took refuge in Rhode Island and how that state, by refusing to hand the thief over to Dutch authorities, "might have involved the whole Union in a war." Hugh Williamson cited, as another example, the case of a state which refused to allow foreign creditors to collect debts guaranteed to them by a national treaty. But the great champion of this point of view was Edmund Randolph who insistently urged the need for some agency which would prevent war by enforcing the Law of Nations upon recalcitrant states. In a letter to the Virginia House of Delegates, he wrote:

> If we examine the Constitution and laws of the several states, it is immediately discovered that the law of nations is unprovided with sanctions in many cases which deeply affect public dignity and public justice. The letter, however, of the Confederation does not permit Congress to remedy these defects. . . . Is it not a political phenomenon that the head of the Confederacy should be doomed to be plunged into war from its wretched impotency to check offenses against this law; and sentenced to witness in unavailing anguish the infraction of their engagements to foreign sovereigns?[24]

Once Federalists could demonstrate the likelihood of war,

24. Pelatiah Webster, "The Weakness of Brutus Exposed, or Some Remarks in Vindication of the Constitution Proposed by the Late Federal Convention against the Objections and Gloomy Fears of the Writer Humbly Offered to the Public," November 4, 1787, in P. L. Ford (ed.), *Pamphlets on the Constitution*, 121; Elliot (ed.), *Debates in State Conventions*, IV, 19; Williamson, "Remarks," in P. L. Ford (ed.), *Essays on the Constitution*, 400; Randolph, "Letter," in P. L. Ford (ed.), *Pamphlets on the Constitution*, 262–63.

the next step was to show that the Confederation government would be unable to cope with it. James Madison took as his major theme in the Virginia ratifying convention the inadequacy of the Confederation during the late war, its oppression of the people in some instances, the disillusionment of Washington as commanding general, and his postwar recommendations for a stronger central government. Madison argued that the state militias were no substitute for a federal army, for "without uniformity of discipline . . . the country might be overrun and conquered by foreign armies." Under the old requisition system one section of the country, feeling less threatened than another, might be unwilling to pay its share of the cost of defense. There would be the problem of partial payments, the problem of discipline, and the problem of federal finance should the usual state revenue from import duties dry up during hostilities.[25] Edmund Randolph warned that militias would be poorly trained and not as zealous as they had been in 1776. Their use on the front would cause a dangerous decline in agricultural production. He also attacked the requisition system: "After a war shall be inevitable, the requisitions of Congress for quotas of men or money will again prove unproductive and fallacious." Recalling revolutionary days, he could not forget how the army, on a sudden challenge, marched into war "on the mere recommendation of Congress"; but he wondered if, in the future, the same enthusiasm would prevail. And if not, "where shall we find protection?" Requisitions would be balked, and any attempt of Congress to coerce a particular state might induce that state to seek foreign support. Thus, radical new powers must be entrusted to the

25. Elliot (ed.), *Debates in State Conventions,* III, 90–95, 133, 248–49, 253. Similar remarks were made by John Marshall, Edmund Randolph, and Francis Corbin; *ibid.,* III, 109, 115, 227–29.

national government and the Confederation must be altered "in its very essence." [26]

When Antifederalists insisted that it would be time enough to organize a defense when war broke out, the reply was that a standing army would be necessary to strike an immediate blow against the enemy. In a sneak attack, the enemy would allow no time for response. "Half a dozen regiments from Canada or New Spain, might lay whole provinces under contribution while we were disputing who has power to pay and raise an army." As one newspaper put it: "In case of a war with any formidable power, how will an army be raised and equipped? . . . While the states are disputing whether they shall grant the federal requisitions or not any enemy may penetrate into the heart of the country, and cut off some members of the Union." [27] When a suggestion was made to continue the old requisition system and resort to direct federal taxation only if the former should fail, it was shown that this system would inevitably put the central government in conflict with one or more of the states which refused to comply with congressional requisitions. Friction, in turn, would create an opening for foreign intervention and aggrandizement. Was America to wait until she was attacked? She was "circumscribed with enemies from Maine to Georgia." In an emergency, it would take precious time to obtain a representation of the required number of states in Congress, then to go through the process of pleading with the various state legislatures. A stitch in time would save nine. The very power to lay direct taxes would itself act as a deterrent to invasion.[28]

26. Randolph, "Letter," in P. L. Ford (ed.), *Pamphlets on the Constitution*, 263–67.

27. Ellsworth, "Letters," No. 5, in P. L. Ford (ed.), *Essays on the Constitution*, 157; *State Gazette of South Carolina*, January 3, 1788.

28. Randolph in Virginia, T. Sedgwick, Christopher Gore, and E. Pierce in Massachusetts, in Elliot (ed.), *Debates in State Conventions*, II, 61, 66–67, 76; III, 116–18.

Certain states, naturally, were more impressed with the military benefits of the Constitution than others. The southern states in particular evidenced a strong feeling of insecurity. They were faced with the prospect of full-scale Indian hostilities, and the experience of being conquered and occupied by British armies was still fresh in their memories. Georgia was actually fighting large numbers of Indians during the ratification campaign, and there can be no doubt that her rapid and enthusiastic endorsement of the Constitution resulted in part from her embattled condition. Nor can it be doubted that the Georgia struggle influenced South Carolina's decision only a few months later. South Carolinians deemed themselves sufficiently threatened to authorize their own General Andrew Pickens to raise a volunteer company for the defense of Georgia.[29] On May 5, 1788, just before South Carolina voted to accept the Constitution, a Charleston newspaper asked its readers: "How long can we be free from Indian cruelties and depredations sometime since begun in Georgia?"[30]

The excellent use of the security issue in South Carolina is illustrated by the following appeal by the noted historian and politician, David Ramsay:

> Our local weakness particularly proves it to be for the advantage of South Carolina to strengthen the federal government; for we are inadequate to secure ourselves from more powerful neighbors.... The Congress are authorized to provide and maintain a navy—our coast in its whole extent needs the protection thereof.... If this state is to be invaded by a maritime force, to whom can we apply for immediate aid?

29. *Gazette of the State of Georgia*, October 11, 1787.

30. *State Gazette of South Carolina*, May 5, 1788. Marvin Zahniser has written that "South Carolina's exposed position during the Revolutionary War had shown that the state could be effectively defended only in concert with the other states, and Pinckney knew this better than most"; Marvin Zahniser, *Charles Cotesworth Pinckney* (Chapel Hill: University of North Carolina Press, 1967), 86–87.

To Virginia and North Carolina? Before they can march by land to our assistance, the country may be overrun. The Eastern states, abounding in men and ships, can sooner relieve us than our next door neighbors.[31]

Considering what might happen if the national debt were not paid off, he warned that the United States owed several million dollars to France, Spain, and Holland. If the foreign debt were not paid, who would lose? The southern states. Southern exports, because they were the most valuable, would be the first to be captured in a war, and raids would be made on their defenseless coasts.

Charles Cotesworth Pinckney pleaded with the delegates to the South Carolina ratifying convention to allow northern merchants a virtual monopoly of southern commerce under the new Constitution in order to be assured of their naval support in case of attack. Hoping to soften the attitude of his fellow planters toward the New England manufacturing and commercial classes, he pointed out that because of the late war and present state of commerce, "they have lost everything but their country and freedom. It is notorious that some ports to the eastward which used to fit out one hundred and fifty sail of vessels do now fit out thirty; that their trade of shipbuilding which used to be very considerable is now annihilated; that their fisheries are trifling, and their mariners in want of bread. Surely . . . we should let them in some measure, partake of our prosperity." [32] Pinckney was trying to do two things. By describing the depressed state of the northern economy, he wished to per-

31. Ramsay, "Address," in P. L. Ford (ed.), *Pamphlets on the Constitution*, 373–77.
32. Elliot (ed.), *Debates in State Conventions*, IV, 284–85. Charles Pinckney, not to be confused with his distant cousin, Charles Cotesworth Pinckney, argued the same way in the South Carolina convention (although he had spoken differently in Philadelphia); *ibid.*, IV, 331. See also Farrand (ed.), *Records of Federal Convention*, II, 449.

suade his state to endorse the principle of congressional regulation of commerce even though southerners feared this might lead to a northern monopoly of the southern carrying trade. But more important, he was reminding his audience that northern distress was partly because of the fact that the North had come to the aid of the South during the war and that such assistance might well be needed in the future.

In both North Carolina and Virginia, Federalists echoed Pinckney in maintaining that a most important consideration was national defense. James Iredell pressed the need for a strong standing army and warned that "to refuse this power would be to invite insults and attacks from other nations. . . . The British government is not friendly to us. They dread the rising glory of America." He even suggested that the British government had "formed a scheme to attack New York next April with ten thousand men." [33] Edmund Randolph based his remarks on Virginia's openness to foreign attack. The Tidewater State, with its many navigable rivers emptying into Chesapeake Bay, was plainly vulnerable to naval attack. And "let us look at the land. . . . Cast your eyes to the western country that is inhabited by cruel savages who may be incited by the gold of foreign enemies." Nor did he forget to warn of the danger of a slave uprising in the hour of greatest peril.[34]

In contrast to southerners, the people of New England felt more secure and had less to fear from a war. The Yankee farmers remembered that although several of their

33. Iredell in North Carolina, in Elliot (ed.), *Debates in State Conventions*, IV, 96. William Davie also concentrated heavily on the weakness of his state in case of attack; *ibid.*, IV, 17–19.
34. Randolph in Virginia, *ibid.*, III, 72–73. For similar remarks by Randolph, Madison, Corbin, and Marshall, see *ibid.*, III, 76, 90–91, 95, 109, 112, 115–18, 226–27, 229, 248–49.

coastal towns had been shelled and burned during the war, yeoman armies had faced up to the British redcoats with marked success. The troops of George III which had fled from Boston on St. Patrick's Day, 1776, had never returned to fight again on New England soil. Subsequently, the greatest victory of the war prior to Yorktown had been won in the North at Saratoga.

But the fact that New England was relatively strong and fearless did not deter the Federalists from making use of the security issue. They called attention to the fact that New Hampshire, like Georgia, lay adjacent to enemy territory. One pamphleteer warned the citizens of the White Mountain State: "Trust not to any complaisance of those British provinces on your northern borders, or those artful men who govern them, who were selected on purpose to beguile your politics, and divide and weaken the union. When the hour for permanent connection . . . is past, the teeth of the lion will again be made bare, and you must be either devoured, or become its jackal to hunt for prey in the other states." A few regiments of Canadian troops could march through New Hampshire and put down all resistance along the way. Troops from other states would have to come to the rescue. But if New Hampshire refused to ratify, such out-of-state aid might be withheld.[35] Even though Massachusetts was the strongest of any state militarily, Fisher Ames still argued along familiar lines in the state convention: "What security has this single state against foreign enemies? Could we defend the mast country which the Britons so much desire?" Judge Francis Dana was certain that Nova Scotia and New Brunswick were full of Tories and refugees standing "ready to attack and devour these states, one by one." And the Honorable William Phillips of Boston pro-

35. Ellsworth, "Letters," No. 10, in Ford (ed.), *Essays*, 190–91.

claimed, "We are verging towards destruction. . . . Let us take the means to prevent war by granting to Congress the power of raising an army. If a declaration of War is made against this country . . . before Congress could collect the means to withstand this enemy, they would penetrate into the bowels of our country." [36]

In the Connecticut convention, national defense was cited as the most compelling reason for ratification. Oliver Ellsworth, referring to the geographical encirclement of America by foreign nations, compared it to a similar ring of hostile powers which once encompassed the Hebrew people, the infant Roman state, and the English. All these peoples, he noted, were conquered by inferior forces because of their lack of unity. He then appealed to Yankee thrift by reminding the delegates that the larger the nation, the less the cost of defense per person. England's burden of taxes, for example, was only about one half that of a smaller nation such as the Netherlands. [37]

New York Federalists could capitalize on past history. The Empire State had been a principal theater of war and of Indian raids during the Revolution, and its chief city had endured a seven-year occupation by British troops. It was the one area that Washington had tried at all costs, but failed, to hold. Robert R. Livingston gave a detailed analysis of New York's exposure to attack in the state convention. He pointed out that Long Island and Staten Island were indefensible. New York would be threatened on the west by hostile Indians, on the east by a potentially hostile Vermont, and it would be laid open to sudden attack from the British-held posts, five of which were within the state's borders.

36. Elliot (ed.), *Debates in State Conventions*, II, 43, 158. Similar remarks came from Sedgwick, Gore, and Pierce; see note 28 above.

37. Ellsworth in Connecticut, *ibid.*, II, 185–86.

The Hudson River would be an irresistible avenue of attack which would make New York the probable "theater of operations" in wartime. James Duane strongly resented the British troops which remained on New York soil and considered this "the highest insult to our sovereignty." He saw the British presence as creating an immediate need for military power and eventually a large army and navy. In any case, he hoped to see the United States strong enough in his lifetime to redress any injuries.[38]

Yet after all was said that could be said by Federalists on the lack of preparation for another war, there were still those who remained unconvinced either because they did not believe another war very likely, or because they believed the existing system of defense adequate for an emergency. For these persons the Federalists modified their line of argument. They reasoned that the likelihood of war was directly related to the nation's defense posture. Weakness would invite attack.[39] Madison told the delegates to the Virginia ratifying convention that "the best way to avoid danger is to be in a capacity to withstand it." What, he asked prophetically, would be the position of the United States as a neutral carrier, believing in the principle of freedom of the seas, if war broke out, as was most likely, between France and England? "A neutral nation ought to be respectable or else it will be insulted and attacked." [40] Benjamin Rush of

38. *Ibid.*, II, 212, 232, 379. The vulnerability of New York and Long Island was also stressed in *The Federalist*, Nos. 25 and 41.

39. Hanson, "Remarks," in P. L. Ford (ed.), *Pamphlets on the Constitution*, 244–45.

40. Hunt (ed.), *Writings of Madison*, V, 150–51, 169. In *The Federalist*, No. 41, Madison had also stressed the idea that Virginia and Maryland could easily be attacked from the sea. For the same theme see the *New York Journal*, March 29, 1787; Pelatiah Webster, "Remarks on the Address of Sixteen Members of the Assembly of Pennsylvania, to Their Constituents, Dated September 29, 1787, with Some Strictures on Their Objects to the Constitution Recommended by the Late Federal Convention,

Philadelphia had the Quakers of his city in mind when he assured them that the new government would mean, among other things, "the prevention of war." [41] James Wilson, a neighbor of Rush in Philadelphia, also seemed to be making a special appeal to the peace-lovers of the area when he quoted the celebrated French statesman, Jacques Necker, to the effect that America was young, pure, and felicitous and should remain so by shunning involvement in European conflicts. "An efficient government," said Wilson, "will not hurry us into war; it is calculated to guard against it." [42]

For those hardy New Englanders who had no fear of war and felt no need for additional military backing, the Federalists had another argument. Yankee soldiers who had fought to liberate their southern brethren during the Revolution and had borne a disproportionate burden of the war's cost would feel obligated in their own interest to do the same thing again in any future invasion of the South. Therefore, even if they themselves were not in need of military assistance, would it not pay them to support a national army which would tap each state for a proportionate number of troops? Had not Massachusetts and New Hampshire furnished half of the Continental army for the first two or three years of the war? Had not the Bay State, in particular, borne "an unequal burden" and "never been fairly compensated?" [43]

Frequently, Federalists ignored the condition of national

Humbly Offered to the Public. By a Citizen of Philadelphia," in McMaster and Stone (eds.), *Pennsylvania and the Federal Constitution*, 101; *Virginia Independent Chronicle*, June 13, 1787.

41. *State Gazette of South Carolina*, December 24, 1787.

42. Wilson in Pennsylvania, in Elliot (ed.), *Debates in State Conventions*, II, 528.

43. James Varnum and Reverend Mr. Thatcher in Massachusetts, *ibid.*, II, 78, 142. Oliver Ellsworth also pointed this out in the Connecticut convention; *ibid.*, II, 188.

defense altogether and urged a closer union on the assumption that the nation was threatened with dissolution by outside forces. The residents of New Hampshire were warned that their "British neighbors . . . will not fail by their emissaries to seminate such jealousies as favor their own designs." Charles Pinckney asserted that George III had spies in every state and was hoping to separate the southern states from the Confederacy and see them eventually revert to his control.[44] Britain was accused of dumping cheap copper coins on America to debase her currency.[45] And one newspaper editor queried: "What American can without horror, indignation and grief reflect that a fatal disunion may basely throw under foreign domination, the plains of Saratoga, Yorktown, or the Cowpens?"[46] John Jay made use of this argument, it appeared in pamphlets by Alexander Hanson and Edmund Randolph, and Madison made extensive use of it in the Virginia ratifying convention.[47] The Reverend Mr. Thatcher concerned himself in the Massachusetts convention with the possible secession of the counties of Maine and Plymouth. How could the Confederacy protect the states from foreign powers, he asked, when the states themselves were in danger of breaking up: "Conceive the number of states increased, their boundaries lessened, their interests clashing; how easy a prey to foreign power! How liable to war among themselves!"[48]

44. Ellsworth, "Letters," No. 10 and Charles Pinckney, "Letter," in P. L. Ford (ed.), *Essays on the Constitution*, 191, 411–12. This charge also appeared in the *State Gazette of South Carolina*, May 5, 1788.

45. *Gazette of the State of Georgia*, August 16, 1787.

46. *Trenton* (N.J.) *Mercury and Weekly Advertiser*, September 25, 1787.

47. Jay, "Address," in P. L. Ford (ed.), *Pamphlets on the Constitution*, 82; Hanson, "Remarks," *ibid.*, 248; Randolph, "Letter," *ibid.*, 268–70; Elliot (ed.), *Debates in State Conventions*, III, 79, 90–91, 129–30.

48. *Ibid.*, II, 144, 146. The same theme was used in the New York convention; *ibid.*, II, 219.

Federalists purported to know of various foreign plots which would succeed if the Constitution were not adopted. In one instance they warned that Britain and Morocco had agreed to partition America and appoint such Tories and ex-patriots as Silas Deane, Joseph Galloway, and Benedict Arnold to the office of state governor.[49]

The Antifederalists were furious at such tactics and tried to counteract them by printing Federalist-style propaganda so exaggerated as to be ludicrous. One pamphlet of this type described an Algerian spy who was prepared to offer his country's support to both the Shaysites and Rhode Island if a dissolution of the union could be obtained. He would provide Rhode Island with a large sum of money accompanied by "one hundred thousand saphis and janizaries." And "in return for protection, Rhode Island would be permitted to pay their tribute to the Sultan in a certain number of virgins."[50] An article which appeared in the *Independent Gazetteer* of October 15, 1787, accused the Federalists of deceiving the people into believing that opposition to the Constitution arose chiefly "from foreigners and foreign agents," of filling the papers "with ludicrous pieces under the signatures of 'Britons,' 'Gauls,' 'Spaniards,' and even 'Turks' "; whereas, in reality, foreign agents were all in favor of the Constitution and "bellowing forth its praises."[51]

Both Federalist and Antifederalist claims in this case were exaggerated. Foreign agents were not uniformly in favor of the Constitution. Neither did they engage in the type of

49. *Independent Gazetteer*, September 20, 1787, quoted in McMaster and Stone (eds.), *Pennsylvania and the Federal Constitution*, 122.

50. Peter Markoe, *The Algerine Spy in Pennsylvania: or Letters Written by a Native of Algiers on the Affairs of the United States in America, from the Close of the Year 1783 to the Meeting of the Convention* (Prichard and Hall, 1787), 105, 114–15.

51. *Independent Gazetteer*, October 15, 1787, quoted in McMaster and Stone (eds.), *Pennsylvania and the Federal Constitution*, 163–64.

plots suggested by Federalist writers. But friends of the Constitution and enemies alike tried to exploit the popular fear of subversion by identifying their adversaries with foreign influence. Antifederalists were said to be anxious for a return to prewar conditions. They were called "the secret abettors of the interests of Great Britain." Twenty irreconcilables in the Massachusetts ratifying convention were labeled British sympathizers because they had fought under Daniel Shays.[52] In Connecticut, where patriotic sentiment was still burning strongly, Oliver Ellsworth asserted, "The first to oppose a federal government will be the old friends of Great Britain who in their hearts cursed the prosperity of your arms and have ever since delighted in the perplexity of your councils. Many of these men are still with us and for several years their hopes of a reunion with Britain have been high." [53] Conversely, Federalists were said to be rich and high-living, haughty and aristocratic in manner. They were contemptuous of the common man and conspiring with George III to destroy American liberty.[54]

52. *State Gazette of South Carolina*, March 31, 1788; *Independent Gazetteer*, September 20, 1787, quoted in McMaster and Stone (eds.), *Pennsylvania and the Federal Constitution*, 121. It is interesting in this connection that many individuals, including George Washington and James Madison, regarded Shays's Rebellion as the work of British spies and sympathizers; see *Massachusetts Centinel*, April 2, May 21, 1785 (for background); *New Jersey Gazette*, October 9, 1786; New York *Journal*, September 28, 1786; *Pennsylvania Gazette*, September 27, December 20, 1786; George Washington to David Humphreys, December 26, 1786, in Fitzpatrick (ed.), *Writings of George Washington*, XXIX, 126; James Madison to Edmund Pendleton, January 9, 1787, in Hunt (ed.), *Writings of Madison*, II, 307.

53. Ellsworth, "Letters," No. 2, in P. L. Ford (ed.), *Essays on the Constitution*, 143; Isaac Lee to William Lee, July 18, 1785, in Perkins Papers, Clements Library.

54. James Winthrop, "The Letters of Agrippa," No. 11, in P. L. Ford (ed.), *Essays on the Constitution*, 89; *Independent Gazetteer*, October 15, 1787, quoted in McMaster and Stone (eds.), *Pennsylvania and the Federal Constitution*, 164.

A second major issue which Federalists stressed in the ratification campaign was that of commercial distress. Next to national insecurity, the Federalists could find no topic which appealed to more people in more places than the need to retaliate against foreign trade restrictions, particularly the British Orders in Council.

In heavily commercial centers such as Boston, New York (the entire Hudson Valley), and Philadelphia there was no doubt about the benefits of congressional regulation. These people were directly affected by the decline in American commerce and shipbuilding. Native fishermen, shipowners, shipbuilders, carpenters, and the many craftsmen adversely affected by the British Orders could easily be won over on the commercial issue. Federalists naturally promised a great revival in shipbuilding if the Constitution were adopted. The most outstanding issue in the Massachusetts convention, for example, was that of American shipping. One delegate pointed out indignantly that British bottoms were carrying three quarters of all Delaware's imports and exports. Surely the Bay State, with its tradition of maritime industry, should have a share of this traffic. Ship carpenters were assured that they would not have to look for work in England. And manufacturers were reminded that they would benefit by the passage of federal tariff legislation.[55]

55. J. Choate, Thomas Russell, Thomas Dawes, James Bowdoin in Massachusetts, and William Davie in North Carolina, in Elliot (ed.), *Debates in State Conventions*, II, 58–59, 79, 129–30, 139; IV, 20; Jay, "Address," in P. L. Ford (ed.), *Pamphlets on the Constitution*, 73; *Virginia Independent Chronicle*, June 13, August 1, December 5, 1787, June 2, 1788. Alfred F. Young has found, in a study of New York state politics, that the prospect for commercial gain was the most important issue in assuring Federalist control of New York where "middling" mechanics and farmers joined wealthy merchants in a strong desire for renewed access to the British West Indies. He also concludes that the entire Hudson Valley was engaged in commercial agriculture; Young, *Democratic Republicans*, 79, 91, 100, 102.

In less commercial areas a healthy foreign trade might not be as vital as in major ports such as Boston and Philadelphia. But Federalists went to great lengths to demonstrate that everyone had reason for concern in one way or another. William Davie reminded the farmers and wealthy planters of North Carolina that commerce was "the nurse" of agriculture, and Madison told his fellow Virginians that the two occupations were interdependent.[56] Alexander Hamilton appealed to every kind of group in *The Federalist* Number 12, including the "assiduous merchant," the "laborious husbandman, the active mechanic, and the industrious manufacturer." But he was especially intent upon having the ear of farmers when he argued that revenue obtained from duties on commercial imports would render all taxes on land unnecessary. Land values would increase. Agricultural produce would have a "free vent," and the supply of circulating specie would be more plentiful. Wheat farmers would be able to ship their surplus produce to the British West Indies. Cheese and barley exports would increase. And farmers in general would escape from too heavy a tax burden since most revenue would come from import duties rather than land taxes.[57]

In the South, where people were somewhat less interested personally in commerce and feared a northern monopoly of the carrying trade, Federalists appealed to the popular ha-

56. Elliot (ed.), *Debates in State Conventions*, III, 345; IV, 20. Recent interpretations of the period have pointed out that farmers as a group were by no means uninterested in the potential commercial benefits of the Constitution. A surprisingly large number produced some kind of surplus for export; Nettels, *Emergence of National Economy*, 93; Young, *Democratic Republicans*, 69, 91.

57. *Independent Gazetteer*, September 20, 1787, quoted in McMaster and Stone (eds.), *Pennsylvania and the Federal Constitution* 121–23; *Pennsylvania Gazette*, November 14, 1787; Bowdoin in Massachusetts, in Elliot (ed.), *Debates in State Conventions*, II, 130; Rossiter (ed.), *Federalist Papers*, No. 12, p. 92.

tred of Great Britain and the strong sense of national honor. St. George Tucker pointed out the folly of depending on the merchants, ships, and manufactures of "our enemy," the British. Other spokesmen for the Constitution insisted that exclusion must be met by exclusion. Foreign discrimination must be counteracted by appropriate retaliatory legislation in Congress. What had been the answer of the Court of St. James's to Mr. Adams' plea for mutuality in commercial relations? Such as would insult the pride of any man of feeling and independence! In South Carolina, Charles Pinckney and other Federalists led off the state convention with a discussion of commercial distress and the humiliating position of American foreign ministers. David Ramsay insisted, "We certainly ought to have a navigation act, and we assuredly ought to give a preference though not a monopoly to our own shipping." Similarly, Henry Lee and Edmund Randolph maintained in the Virginia convention that all evils could be traced to the stagnation of American foreign commerce and that national measures should aim to bring about a policy of reciprocity on the part of Great Britain.[58]

Such arguments were unanswerable because no one would deny that the commerce clause in the Constitution could be used to apply pressure on Great Britain. Even Patrick Henry, who minimized nearly every other Federalist argument, tacitly admitted that the new government could be a boon to commerce. James Monroe, who opposed the Constitution in Virginia because of the grant to Congress of direct taxing power, felt that the power to regulate com-

58. Tucker, *Reflections*, 4–6; Edmund Randolph's Letter to the Speaker of the Virginia House of Delegates, and William Davie in North Carolina, in Elliot (ed.), *Debates in State Conventions*, I, 484; IV, 18; *ibid.*, IV, 253–84, 321; Ramsay, "Address," in P. L. Ford (ed.), *Pamphlets on the Constitution*, 376–77; Elliot (ed.), *Debates in State Conventions*, I, 484; III, 43, 78.

merce would be a prerequisite for any "proper federal government." George Bryan, Antifederalist of Pennsylvania, did not try to deny the commercial advantages of the Constitution. Nor did Samuel Adams have any reservations on this issue, although his support for the new government was doubtful at first. He recalled the chagrin and failure of Cousin John's mission in London.[59]

The issues of commercial distress and national insecurity were alike in many ways. Both depended in some measure upon granting Congress the power to fulfill its treaty commitments. Britain could not be deprived of its excuse for occupying the posts unless Congress could enable British merchants to collect the prewar debts owed to them by Americans.[60] Nor could the Court of St. James's be expected to negotiate a commercial treaty until Congress acquired the power to speak authoritatively for all the states.[61] Both issues appealed to a wide cross section of economic and geographic groups, depending on the method of presentation. Finally, both appealed to the prevalent spirit of anglophobia. Britain must be compelled to drop its discrimination against American ships, and British troops must evacuate American soil.

Closely allied to the use which Federalists made of the

59. For evidence of Antifederalist recognition of Federalist arguments with regard to foreign commerce, see Elliot (ed.), *Debates in State Conventions*, II, 123–24; III, 137–76, 214.

60. For this argument, see Oliver Ellsworth in Connecticut, Robert R. Livingston in New York, James Wilson in Pennsylvania, Frances Corbin and George Nicholas in Virginia, in Elliot (ed.), *Debates in State Conventions*, II, 189, 213, 489–90; III, 104–105, 238–39; also the *Pennsylvania Packet* which assured its readers on November 23, 1787, that "in all probability the first good consequence arising from a firm and respectable government will be the relinquishment of the western posts."

61. For examples of this argument, see James Madison in Virginia, in Elliot (ed.), *Debates in State Conventions*, III, 135–36; Williamson, "Remarks," in P. L. Ford (ed.), *Essays on the Constitution*, 402.

spirit of anglophobia was their appeal to the country's sense of patriotic pride.[62] In the various ratifying conventions they insisted that America would be great if the Constitution were adopted, despised if rejected. They warned of the inevitable dissolution of the Confederation under the Articles and pointed out how contemptible the states would become as independent entities. Humiliation would be unavoidable without an invigorated union. They ran through the whole catalog of insults borne by the United States since 1783.[63] They referred to American ambassadors as ciphers, and to Americans, generally, as "slaves to Europe." [64] Sometimes the image of America as a slave among nations was implied rather than stated directly, as was the case in the Massachusetts ratifying convention when Captain Snow testified that in the course of his extensive travels, he had

62. Madison's opening speeches in the Virginia ratifying convention were entirely concerned with the exigencies of national security and national honor. See also Madison's *The Federalist*, No. 37; Nicholas Gilman to Honorable Joseph Gilman, September 18, 1787, in New Hampshire Miscellaneous Papers MSS, Library of Congress, Vol. I; Robert R. Livingston, Speech before the New York Society of the Cincinnati, July 4, 1787, quoted in Dangerfield, *Livingston*, 211; Hanson, "Remarks," and James Iredell, "Observations," in P. L. Ford (ed.), *Pamphlets on the Constitution*, 244, 250–51, 369–70; Lynn Montross, *Reluctant Rebels*, 415; Ellsworth, "Letters," and Williamson, "Remarks," in P. L. Ford (ed.), *Essays on the Constitution*, 142, 402–403; *State Gazette of South Carolina*, November 26, 1787; New York *Packet*, September 28, 1786; *Pennsylvania Packet*, October 9 and December 19, 1787.

63. Remarks by Reverend Thatcher in Massachusetts, Thomas McKean and Charles Wilson in Pennsylvania, James Iredell in North Carolina, C. C. Pinckney in South Carolina, and Edmund Randolph in Virginia, in Elliot (ed.), *Debates in State Conventions*, II, 43, 142–48, 379, 526, 542; III, 81; IV, 99, 282; James Iredell, "To the People of the State of North Carolina," and "To the People of the District of Edenton," in Hugh Talmage Lefler (ed.), *A Plea for Federal Union, North Carolina, 1788* (Charlottesville: University of Virginia Press, 1947), 35, 49–50; *Virginia Independent Chronicle*, December 5, 1787.

64. Remarks of Samuel Adams and William Dawes in the Massachusetts ratifying convention, in Elliot (ed.), *Debates in State Conventions*, II, 58–59, 123–24.

found his country "held in the same light by foreign nations as a well-behaved Negro in a gentleman's family." [65]

Proponents of the Constitution spoke in Old Testament language and likened the proposed new form of government to "an ark for the preservation of the remains of the justice and liberties of the world." Heaven was preparing the infant America for greatness and preserving it miraculously in times of crisis, first during the Revolution, and again in 1787. "The goodness of our God was truly apparent," proclaimed the *Pennsylvania Gazette* in the aftermath of the Philadelphia Convention. Such language echoed the traditional concept of America as "a city upon a hill" and was used by Dr. Benjamin Rush who gave as his main reason for supporting the Constitution the influence which the example of a good government might have upon the nations of Europe.[66]

In comparing Federalist with Antifederalist literature, it is interesting to note the fundamental difference in emphasis. Antifederalists rarely discussed foreign affairs. Richard Henry Lee's celebrated *Letters of a Federal Farmer* mentioned it only once to assert that there was "no danger of invasions." [67] George Mason, in his *Objections*, said not a word on the subject. Patrick Henry, in the Virginia convention, carefully separated domestic concerns from foreign pressures and addressed himself to the former. And Elbridge Gerry, in his *Observations on the New Constitution*, flatly denied the danger of foreign conquest while focusing nine tenths of his attention on the danger of aristocratic tyranny.

Most of the time, when Antifederalists turned to the sub-

65. *Ibid.*, II, 34.
66. *State Gazette of South Carolina*, December 6, 1787; *Pennsylvania Gazette*, November 14, 1787; *Pennsylvania Packet*, December 19, 1787.
67. Lee, "Letters," No. 1, in P. L. Ford (ed.), *Pamphlets on the Constitution*, 281.

ject of foreign affairs, they accepted Federalist arguments but doubted whether the good which would result from a stronger position in foreign affairs would outweigh the risks of central power. They questioned whether they should "swallow a large bone for the sake of a little meat." The one issue related to foreign affairs which Antifederalists did stress heavily, particularly in the South, was that of the federal treaty-making power. They argued that the two-thirds rule for Senate approval of treaties would not protect those who had an interest in the navigation of the Mississippi River. The North would gain the ascendancy over the South and would naturally favor its own commercial interests. Rather than aiding in the development of western lands, northerners would consider it a threat to their already scarce labor supply. They would try instead to halt the flow of westward migration and keep the West dependent upon the East. They might also use their political power to conclude prejudicial treaties with the Indians. In the Virginia convention, Henry, Grayson, and others laid great emphasis on these issues in an effort to woo the delegates from Kentucky. Throughout the first half of the convention, they repeatedly returned to "their favorite business" which, according to one delegate, was the "scuffle for Kentucky votes." [68] Yet their case was not, perhaps, as compelling as it might have been since many southern leaders such as Richard Henry Lee and George Washington had sided with John Jay in his negotiations with Gardoqui.[69] Moreover,

---

68. George Nicholas in Virginia and General Thompson in Massachusetts, in Elliot (ed.), *Debates in State Conventions*, II, 80–81; III, 502.

69. George Washington to Richard Henry Lee, July 26, 1786, in Fitzpatrick (ed.), *Writings of George Washington*, XXVIII, 484–85; Richard Henry Lee to George Washington, July 15, 1787, in Ballagh (ed.), *Letters of Lee*, II, 426. They doubted that the United States could defend its right of navigation in view of Spain's superior military power. They also recognized the large economic benefit to be derived from increased

it was argued that only a stronger federal government could vindicate American rights. Frontiersmen and investors in western lands could expect military assistance from the new government in keeping the Mississippi River open to American commerce (although this hope tended to be offset by the fear that navigation rights might be yielded by treaty), in clearing the West of hostile Indians, and in forcing the British to vacate their strongholds on American soil.[70]

On rare but memorable occasions, the friends and enemies of the Constitution did come to grips. Melancton Smith attempted to refute every one of Jay's arguments point by point. He denied the benefit of commercial treaties with foreign nations and maintained strongly that no foreign nation threatened the United States. But one of the cleverest and most remarkable of all Antifederalist writers was James Winthrop, a librarian at Harvard College and a descendent of the first John Winthrop. He is one of the few Antifederalists who tried to turn the subject of foreign relations to his own advantage.

Wherever possible, Winthrop would associate Federalists with foreigners. He mischievously suggested that topics relating to foreign affairs had provided Federalists with "some of the plausible reasons . . . in favor of their plan, as derived from the sentiments of foreigners." He accused Federalists of being soft on monarchy and affirmed that "some of their

---

trade with Spain. Finally, they hoped to keep the West dependent upon the East and to strengthen the bonds of union by extending river navigation inland and by building roads to link both sections of the country together.

70. John Marshall in Virginia, in Elliot (ed.), *Debates in State Conventions*, III, 223, 231; James Madison to George Nicholas, April 8, 1788, in Madison Papers, Library of Congress, Ser. 1, Vol. IX. Professor Nettels makes this point very clearly; Nettels, *Emergence of National Economy*, 93.

leaders . . . have formed pretty strong attachments to foreign nations, whether those attachments arose from their being educated under a royal government, from a former unfortunate mistake in politics, or from the agencies for foreigners." To cement the association further, he pointed out that, in the case of Federalists as well as monarchists, "power and high life are their idols." [71]

Winthrop also exploited the issue of subversion, a favorite of Federalists, by indicating that foreign influence would insinuate itself all the more as a result of the "multiplication of officers" under the Constitution as well as the long terms proposed for representatives and senators. The outcome, as he saw it, could only be that "we must be involved in all the quarrels of European powers." And with pen dipped in irony he added, "This is the only sense in which the Philadelphia system will render us more respectable in the eyes of foreigners." [72]

Where Federalists made political capital out of the issue of national honor, Winthrop tried to turn the tables by remarking, "Once surrender the rights of internal legislation and taxation, and instead of being respected abroad, foreigners will laugh at us, and posterity will lament our folly." [73]

In disarming fashion, he accepted the Federalist argument that foreign commerce must be centrally regulated but claimed that a simple amendment to the Articles would suffice without swallowing the bone. He wanted, in addition, a guarantee that Congress "shall not by treaty or other-

71. "Agrippa," No. 11, in P. L. Ford (ed.), *Essays on the Constitution,* 89. Federalist leaders did, in fact, tend to be relatively well-to-do, and, as is indicated later in this essay, a disproportionate number were indeed educated "under a royal government."

72. "Agrippa," No. 11, *ibid.,* 88; No. 14, *ibid.,* 104; No. 11, *ibid.,* 88–89.

73. "Agrippa," No. 9, *ibid.,* 81. Here, as well as elsewhere, Winthrop was proven wrong by subsequent events.

wise give a preference to the ports of one state over those of another." [74]

Finally, he made light of the problem of treaty enforcement. The Dutch Confederacy never had any problems in this regard even though it had to consult all the states. Moreover, the Federalists were mistaken in believing that British reluctance to sign a commercial treaty was owing to distrust. Rather, their reluctance was caused by resentment. The British would bend the knee and place self-interest before pride once they recognized the desperate situation of Nova Scotia and their West Indian possessions. [75]

Winthrop alone among leading Antifederalists met his antagonists squarely on their own ground, exploiting their favorite issues and stabbing at their arguments on national security. Significantly, he avoided the military question. But in a statement of fourteen reservations to the Philadelphia plan and in his advocacy of a simple amendment to the Articles, he set forth a concrete and constructive plan of his own.

One reason there were so few Winthrops among Antifederalists and so many Jays among Federalists was that the discussion of foreign affairs put the Constitution in the best light for the most people. Few persons anywhere in

74. "Agrippa," No. 10, *ibid*, 84. This was his strongest argument, although it could be argued that Congress had tried and failed to obtain such an amendment under the articles. Federalists also argued that the commerce power was so radical in itself that it would necessitate many other innovations such as a national judiciary and some means of coercion, i.e. taxation and army.

75. "Agrippa," No. 11, *ibid.*, 89–90. In fact, what the Federalists claimed was that congressional inability to regulate trade provided Britain with an *excuse* for withholding trade concessions, but that her real motive was twofold: to strengthen her own merchant marine and naval power while injuring that of the United States. Hence, congressional power, while eliminating possible distrust, was primarily intended to *force* British concessions by threat of retaliatory trade restrictions.

the country would deny that external forces threatened the Confederacy. Few would disapprove of a stronger national defense. There could be no mistake about the challenges facing American commerce or the need to strengthen the diplomatic bargaining power of Congress. No one, moreover, would deny that national insecurity resulted partially from constitutional weakness. Thus Federalists could achieve more of a consensus on the question of ends than they could on the question of means.

Another reason for the emphasis on foreign affairs can be found in the makeup of the Federalists themselves. For a number of reasons Federalists were apt to have a deeper interest and a broader knowledge in the area of foreign affairs than their opponents. Many were shipowners engaged in transatlantic trade, merchants anxious to penetrate European markets, or farmers who desired greater access to the British West Indies. As such, they could well appreciate the advantages of a strong bargaining position in foreign affairs not only for themselves, but also for the nation as a whole. In other words, while the mercantile class which supported the Constitution did so out of immediate self-interest, they also did so because their business dealings with foreign countries impressed upon them in concrete terms the universal need for benefits such as those offered by the Constitution.[76]

It is a striking fact that the men who were officially concerned with foreign affairs in this period supported the Constitution without exception. Robert R. Livingston, who served as secretary for foreign affairs from August 10, 1781, to December 2, 1782, was a leading Federalist, as was his successor, Elias Boudinot. James McClurg, whom Madison

---

76. Jackson Turner Main has found the mercantile class to be the most outstanding and significant of all groups in support of the Constitution; Main, *Antifederalists*, 271.

nominated for secretary for foreign affairs, was another chief exponent, as was Gouverneur Morris, who was heavily involved in diplomatic matters and who later became American minister to France.[77] John Jay, who was recognized as a leading advocate for constitutional reform on both the state and national level, served throughout the years 1785–1789 as secretary for foreign affairs.[78] William Samuel Johnson, who led the Federalist forces in Connecticut, had once defended his state's right to western lands as a colonial agent before the British House of Commons. Stephen Higginson, who mobilized support for the Constitution in Massachusetts, had testified before a parliamentary committee on the subject of New England commerce and resources.[79] Such men were in no sense unaware of the exigencies of foreign relations. Other friends of the Constitution with outstanding records in the diplomatic arena included John Adams, Benjamin Franklin, and Thomas Jefferson.

In addition to official diplomatic experience, education abroad was also apt to impress a person with the importance of foreign affairs. Training at a foreign university helped to foster an awareness of America's unique position in the world and of the power of foreign countries to influence

77. Morris drafted the *Report on Lord North's Conciliation Offer* (1778), a public paper on the significance of the Franco-American Alliance (1778), the instructions for Benjamin Franklin's mission to Paris, and the instructions for obtaining a treaty of peace and commerce with Great Britain (1779); *Dictionary of American Biography, s.v.* "Morris, Gouverneur."

78. Jay's influence is reflected in the following: Louis Guillaume Otto to Comte de Vergennes, January 10, 1786, in Bancroft, *Formation of the Constitution,* I, 479; Jensen, *New Nation,* 366; Monaghan, *John Jay,* Chap. 13; Bemis, "John Jay," *American Secretaries,* I, 202.

79. Higginson played no major role in the ratification controversy, but he did recommend to General Knox a plan for the adoption of the Constitution; *Dictionary of American Biography, s.v.* "Higginson, Samuel."

American development. The Federalists who studied or worked in Europe greatly outnumbered their counterparts among Antifederalists. They included Thomas Mifflin, Jared Ingersoll, Charles Pinckney, Charles Cotesworth Pinckney, Thomas Pinckney, John Rutledge, Arthur Lee, Joseph Jones, Hugh Williamson, Richard Dobbs Spaight, William Houston, Daniel Carroll, Charles Carroll of Carrollton, John Dickinson, John Blair, James McClurg, and Benjamin Rush. John Hancock received a year of training in London in the business of transatlantic shipping. The only prominent Antifederalists educated abroad were Theodorick Bland, William Grayson, Willie Jones, and Richard Henry Lee. And of these, Grayson opposed the Constitution in part because it was not strong enough in the area of foreign affairs, and Lee advocated a national government which would extend "exclusively to all foreign concerns." [80]

Foreign birth and upbringing was another element likely to foster a cosmopolitan outlook. To be born and raised abroad was to be more aware of the existence of a world beyond state and national boundaries. Federalist leaders born outside America included Alexander Hamilton, James Wilson, Robert Morris, Thomas Fitzsimmons, Pierce Butler, William Patterson, William Davie, James McHenry (all of whom were framers), not to mention George Read, James Iredell, and St. George Tucker. In contrast, almost all Antifederalist notables were native-born.[81]

Still another factor contributing to the Federalist mentality was that of national political experience. Many of the leading Federalists had served in the revolutionary war

80. William Grayson to William Short, November 10, 1787, in Burnett (ed.), *Letters of Continental Congress*, VIII, 678; Lee, "Letters," No. 1, in P. L. Ford (ed.), *Pamphlets on the Constitution*, 287.
81. Exceptions to the rule were George Bryan, Adeanus Burke, and Rawlins Lowndes.

either as soldiers on the continental line or as delegates to Congress.[82] Such experience tended to stimulate a "continental approach to things," especially with respect to foreign affairs, which impinged upon congressmen far more than it did upon state or local leaders.[83] Jefferson remarked to Madison that a term in Congress had an enlightening influence upon local politicians: "They see the affairs of the Confederacy from a high ground; they learn the importance of the union, and befriend federal measures when they return. Those who never come here [to Congress] see our affairs insulated." [84]

Yet, if the concepts of foreign background and national experience are useful in explaining why Federalists dealt effectively with topics related to foreign affairs and perhaps why specific individuals became Federalists, they do not

82. In 1955, Cecilia Kenyon designated the Antifederalist philosophy as one of localism as opposed to nationalism; Kenyon, "Men of Little Faith." The theory was then expounded in subsequent articles including Elkins and McKitrick, "The Founding Fathers: Young Men of the Revolution"; John P. Roche, "The Founding Fathers: A Reform Caucus in Action"; and McDonald, "Anti-Federalists," 207–209.

83. Roche, "Founding Fathers," 801. According to Roche, "Congressmen were constantly forced to take the broad view of American prestige, were compelled to listen to frustrated envoys in Britain, France, and Spain. From considerations such as these, a 'continental' ideology developed which seems to have demanded a revision of our domestic institutions primarily on the ground that only by invigorating our general government could we assume our rightful place in the international arena."

84. Thomas Jefferson to James Madison, February 20, 1784, in Bancroft, *Formation of the Constitution*, I, 345. Congressional experience in itself was, of course, not enough to assure unreserved support for the nationalist movement. Monroe encountered substantial congressional opposition in 1785 when he sponsored his amendment for congressional regulation of foreign commerce. Madison remarked at the time that even in Congress there were minds unaccustomed to think nationally, let alone globally, and that these would be least sympathetic to the Monroe plan; James Madison to James Monroe, August 7, 1785, in Hunt (ed.), *Writings of Madison*, II, 157. Nor did all congressmen support the Constitution. Exceptions were Richard Henry Lee, John Francis Mercer, Timothy Bloodworth, and William Grayson.

necessarily explain why these same individuals chose a particular method of appealing to the general public. Federalists might have given more emphasis to the domestic anxiety manifested by Shays's Rebellion. They might have spoken at length about the importance of law and order and the sanctity of private property. Issues such as paper money and stay laws had great attraction for many; likewise the idea of retiring the national debt. These issues, however, were divisive in that they tended to set poor against rich, debtors against creditors, West against East. For this reason, Federalists strove wisely to minimize them. They sought, rather, to stress the ways in which the Constitution would benefit all the people, concentrating on two or three basic issues such as national insecurity and commercial distress. Regardless of what economic or geographic group they addressed, these issues could be used with appropriate modifications to forge a national consensus.

To say that foreign affairs was a powerful weapon in the hands of the Federalists is not, of course, to deny the importance of other issues of a domestic nature. One must assume that considerations of internal order and protection of property were strong motives in the constitutional movement from the beginning. However, because nearly everyone wanted the government strengthened in the area of foreign affairs, this issue provided Federalists with a basis for national consensus and the primary theme of their campaign rhetoric.

Many Americans did not believe that the federal government should play a strong role on the domestic scene. The idea of central government reaching down to regulate life at the local level was repugnant to a major segment of the population. This had been evident even before the Revolution. Had Britain been content to regulate American commerce in the interest of imperial trade there would have been few objections. But when the Court of St. James's interposed troops and taxes at the local level, disaffection spread rapidly. Many objections to the Constitution arose from a similar fear that federal power would usurp the authority of local government. A standing army had to be defended, therefore, as a precaution against foreign invasion. Direct taxation could only be defended as a response to national insecurity and humiliation.[85] On the exigencies of foreign affairs there was little disagreement. Thomas Jefferson wrote that the purpose of the central power should be "to make us one nation as to foreign concerns, and keep us distinct in domestic ones." [86] The principal task for Federalists, therefore, was to demonstrate that the exigencies of foreign affairs were sufficient to justify the significant increase in national power represented by the Constitution. And in this they succeeded.

85. Main has written that this was the most divisive issue of the period; *Antifederalists*, 72.

86. Thomas Jefferson to James Madison, December 16, 1786, in Julian Parks Boyd (ed.), *Papers of Thomas Jefferson* (17 vols.; Princeton: Princeton University Press, 1950–), X, 603.

# Epilogue

Final adoption of the Constitution was the signal for a great effusion of patriotic pride. "Tis done!" exulted Dr. Rush. "We have become a nation. America has ceased to be the only power in the world that has derived no benefit from her declaration of independence. . . . We are no longer the scoff of our enemies." By all indications, it looked as if Europe would be favorably impressed. Leaders such as Henry Knox and George Washington foresaw a future without insult, and the country was soon in the grip of a rising spirit of nationalism which was described in 1791 by Sir John Temple, the British consul in Boston, as "a vast alteration in the minds and sentiments of the people in general." [1]

But one question remains. If the Constitution was largely intended to strengthen the national position in foreign re-

1. Benjamin Rush, "Observations on the Federal Procession in Philadelphia," July 9, 1788, in Butterfield (ed.), *Letters of Benjamin Rush*, I, 475; Henry Knox to George Washington, May 25, 1788, in Washington Papers, Library of Congress, Ser. 4, Vol. CCXL; George Washington to Sir Edward Newenham, August 29, 1788, in Fitzpatrick (ed.), *Writings of George Washington*, XXX, 71–72; Ritcheson, *Aftermath of Revolution*, 107.

lations, did it accomplish its objective? Did it actually make the country more secure? Did it, in fact, bolster our commercial position?

From a military standpoint, the answer is clear. Federal income and expenditures increased rapidly and were greater for the year 1792 than they had been for the five-year period, 1784 —1789. In spite of continued provocation from Europe and initial reverses along the frontier, the government dealt more effectively with its enemies.

In the case of the Barbary pirates, President Washington was authorized on May 8, 1792, to spend forty thousand dollars for the ransom of thirteen American captives in Algiers. The Senate even suggested that a similar sum be used as an initial down payment for the purchase of peace, and it voted fifty thousand dollars to support an immediate mission to Algiers.[2] When news arrived in 1793 that eleven American ships had fallen prey to the Algerines, Congress was in a position to order the construction of six warships. Finally, when the Dey agreed to make peace and release the prisoners for the sum of $642,000 plus a guaranteed annual tribute of $21,000, Washington could and did accept these terms, exorbitant as they were.[3] The following year, eighty-two seamen, the sole survivors of the epidemics, hard labor, and drunken brawls of the Algerine captivity, were released. The Algerines, of course, were soon again on the

2. Irwin, *Diplomatic Relations*, 55–56.

3. Congress may have made a mistake by accepting these terms at their face value and halting the construction of three out of six of its newly planned frigates. Instead of purchasing an expensive agreement it might have been wiser to go ahead with the shipbuilding program while insisting on more reasonable terms of settlement. The price of a seventy-four-gun ship stood at about a third of a million dollars. But the United States paid thirty times this sum in ransom and tribute over a twelve-year period; Marshall Smelser, *The Democratic Republic, 1801–1815* (New York: Harper and Row, 1968), 58, 61. On the other hand, Great Britain continued to pay tribute despite its overwhelming naval power.

rampage. By 1815, they had incarcerated 450 Americans and were only halted when a battle-hardened squadron of ten ships led by Commodore Stephen Decatur subdued a defiant Dey under the mouth of the cannon. The case of the other North African states was similar. The ruler of Tripoli and the Bey of Tunis signed peace treaties in 1796 and 1797 respectively; but they became dissatisfied when they discovered what a high price the Algerines had exacted. Since the United States would not alter the amount of its payments, the corsairs were again unleashed, not to be recalled until met by superior force.[4] Yet, despite the time and expense involved in eliminating Barbary blackmail, the government was able to act with some degree of effectiveness as a result of its new revenue power.

Another illustration of the potency of the federal government was its record during two years of undeclared war with France. Many observers, including James Madison, had predicted that a European war was about to break, and, once it did, a weak United States would be obliged to watch helplessly while the warring powers made sport of its commerce. When prophecy became fact and the decision was made to challenge France to a contest on the high seas, the administration was able not only to add ten thousand troops to the regular army and establish a provisional army of fifteen thousand, but also to supply fourteen frigates to a navy which had consisted of only a few revenue cutters. The fourteen men-of-war then proved their mettle by sinking eighty-five enemy craft with only one serious loss of their own. The result was the Franco-American Convention of 1800 which brought the fighting to a close, absolved the country from its embarrassing military alliance of 1778, salvaged its honor, and opened the path for Jefferson's even-

4. Barnby, *Prisoners of Algiers*, 215–16, 303.

tual purchase of Lousiana. None of this might ever have been possible without a revenue system capable of support-ing a massive military buildup on short notice.[5]

A more vigorous central administration was also able to nip western secessionist movements in the bud. The mere prospect of a stronger government in July, 1788, was enough to prevent a Kentucky convention from taking the advice of separatist leaders such as James Wilkinson, Harry Innes, and Benjamin Sebastian. Once in office, the Wash-ington administration moved quickly to satisfy the hopes and needs of frontiersmen. Hamilton's unequivocal affirma-tion of American rights on the Mississippi and the appoint-ment of Jefferson rather than Jay as secretary of state were reassuring to those with fresh memories of the abortive Jay-Gardoqui talks. The army was given additional forces and funds for an immediate campaign against the Miami and Wabash Indians with a twofold purpose: to relieve the Ken-tucky settlements from external pressure and provide a local market for their surplus farm produce (a large army would have to be fed). At the same time, the government endeared itself to westerners, whose loyalty to Congress had once been doubtful, by putting them on the federal payroll. By March of 1792, James Wilkinson, John Sevier, and James Robertson had all become brigadier generals in the United States army. Benjamin Sebastian had been named attorney general in his district, Harry Innes became a federal judge for the district of Kentucky, and William Blount was ap-pointed governor of the Southwest Territory. Even Alex-ander McGillivray was "bought off" with the honorary title of brigadier general and an annual pension of eighteen thou-

5. By December 19, 1801, the regular army consisted of 3,794 men and 248 officers. It might also be noted that the fourteen frigates included three which had been ordered in 1794 to counter the Barbary threat but had never been completed; Weigley, *History of U.S. Army*, 104.

sand dollars.[6] One marvels at what can be accomplished by the prudent application of money!

Southerners were pleased when Secretary of State Jefferson scrapped the Cherokee Treaty of Hopewell (1785) and negotiated a new one at Holston on July 2, 1791, extending the national boundary one hundred additional miles down the Tennessee River. They were also gratified to hear that the Creeks had been persuaded to cede a large area to white settlement (although not as much as Georgia wanted).[7] The people of Franklin and Cumberland were heartened by a grant of territorial status and the prospect of statehood in the near future. And Washington was able to thwart the secessionist schemes of the Yazoo Land Company promoters by obtaining the cooperation of the Choctaws, Chickasaws, and Creeks in the Treaty of New York.[8]

In the battle for men's loyalties, much depended upon federal military initiative in the Northwest. A major offensive against Brant's Indian confederation had been impossible during the Confederation period. But Congress was now

6. When the Spaniards heard of the American offer to McGillivray, they more than matched it by raising his salary as Indian agent from six hundred to thirty-five hundred dollars per year. To encourage the emigration of American pioneers, they were offering land grants, commercial opportunities, and (most unusual) religious toleration. Jefferson laughingly compared this to settling the Goths at the gates of Rome. He hoped a hundred thousand Americans would take advantage of Madrid's hospitality. Little did he know what the effect of such a policy would be in West Florida and Texas; Whitaker, *Spanish-American Frontier*, 103.

7. This was arranged by the Treaty of New York in 1790. It should be noted that the Washington administration took steps to enforce white as well as red obedience to treaties and boundary lines. Congress made provision in 1794 for additional frontier garrisons. There were also efforts to open a regular trade and to introduce civilization among the Indians through agriculture, spinning, and weaving. In 1796, Congress initiated a federal factory system which included federal trading posts on the frontier to relieve the Indian from his reliance on dishonest private merchants.

8. All of the above information comes from Whitaker, *Spanish-American Frontier*, 119–39.

free to act. On April 30, 1790, it voted to increase the number of enlisted men from 672 to 1,216. General Harmar was authorized to lead three hundred regular troops and twelve hundred militia from Fort Washington (Cincinnati) north to the Maumee River for an attack on the Miami and Wabash villages. Although Harmar burned several settlements in the course of his expedition, he allowed his forces to be fatally divided and had to retreat. The following year, Congress voted another increase in the size of the army, this time to three thousand men, and the troops swung into action under General Arthur St. Clair. Again they were thrown back with heavy losses, but Congress refused to be discouraged. In 1792 it voted a third time to augment the size of the regular army, heeding General Knox's request for five thousand men. The new army, the Legion of the United States, was to consist of four sublegions of 1,280 men each, headed by a brigadier general, and unlike its predecessors it did not depend upon militia or short-term volunteers. The new commander, "Mad Anthony" Wayne, took plenty of time to drill his men; he forced them to dig earthworks until their hands were raw; and on August 20, 1794, in the decisive Battle of Fallen Timbers, his patience was rewarded.

Meanwhile, the people of Kentucky had entered the union, and Congress had voted to erect additional forts and arsenals. It had also authorized the construction of six frigates, ostensibly to deal with the Barbary pirates, but obviously mindful of Great Britain.

The British could not overlook the evidence of America's growing power. For ten years they had been under pressure to yield the frontier posts. Now they were at war with France. Federal courts were in the process of compelling Americans to pay their prewar debts so as to lessen the cause for complaint about American violation of the treaty.

Congress was flexing its military muscle. It is not surprising, therefore, that the Court of St. James's agreed to withdraw its garrisons from American soil under the terms of Jay's Treaty. And it is perhaps symbolic that the treaty was signed soon after the definitive reports of Wayne's victory reached London.[9] Jay's Treaty brought peace to the Northwest. It helped persuade the Indians to sign the Treaty of Greenville in 1795 whereby they gave up most of present-day Ohio. Federal lands in the area could be offered for sale, and the army could look to the southwest.

Madrid kept a keen eye on these developments and acted accordingly. Federal treaties of 1790 and 1791 with the Creeks and Cherokees, Kentucky's entry into the union on June 1, 1792, the imminent entry of Tennessee, and the Battle of Fallen Timbers gave the impression that the United States was master of its house. In 1795, Spain yielded free navigation of the Mississippi, the right of deposit at New Orleans, and all land claims above the 31st parallel (including forts at Natchez and Walnut Hills).

Admittedly, the motivation behind British and Spanish concessions was complex. Britain's hope that America would not side with France during the war and her desire to make it easier for Washington to enforce his Proclamation of Neutrality weighed heavily in the diplomatic scales. Spain's fear of an Anglo-American alliance stemming from the Jay mission to London in 1794 and her own withdrawal from the First Coalition must also be taken into account.[10] How-

---

9. Ritcheson, *Aftermath of Revolution*, 147–48, 261–62, 319, 321. Wayne's dispatches were published in London on November 12 following rumors of his victory, and Jay signed the treaty on November 19, *ibid.*, 321; Bemis, *Jay's Treaty*, 345. The First Coalition against revolutionary France was breaking up and the Irish were threatening a full-scale rebellion as well.

10. Bemis, *Pinckney's Treaty*, 313–14; Whitaker, *Spanish-American Frontier*, 218, 221. It should also be noted that Spain devised an escape

ever, the military power commanded by Washington and supported by the new revenue system was as large a factor as any.

In assessing the impact of the Constitution on the American economy, there is a problem. On the one hand, all branches of industry and commerce were booming by 1797; the balance of trade had shifted favorably; there was a striking increase in the size of the native-built merchant marine (from 202,000 tons in 1789 to 1,425,000 in 1810); and a golden age of American shipping spanned the years 1793–1807.[11] On the other hand, these developments flowed from several causes rather than one. Poor harvests in Europe and the outbreak of war in 1793 stimulated a greater European demand for American food, raw materials, and transportation services. It also forced the combatants to suspend or relax their restrictions on American access to the West Indies. In addition, the trade with China and the East Indies had begun to increase at a rapid tempo by 1789, resuscitating the American shipbuilding industry. One might still argue, however, that the new Constitution served the economy well.

Two acts, passed in July of 1789, defined the economic policy of the new government. The Tariff Act laid a minimum tax of 5 percent on all imports and as much as 50 percent on such items as tobacco, indigo, and ships. Originally

---

valve in 1790 by opening the Mississippi to American shipping at a duty rate of 15 percent, reducible to 6 percent at the discretion of Governor Miró. Eighteen American vessels passed New Orleans in 1790 as compared to none the previous year. But for most farmers, the duty was prohibitively high.

11. In the years 1785 to 1791, imports had been two or three times greater than exports, constituting an unfavorable balance of $52,372,875, whereas, from 1795 to 1801, exports exceeded imports by $89,374,315; Thompson, *History*, 84–85. See also Nettels, *Emergence of National Economy*, 233; Clark, *History of Manufactures*, I, 237–38.

designed only for revenue, it conceded a great deal to the protectionists in its final form by taxing imports such as carriages, gunpowder, paints, and glass. It aided farmers by taxing imported beer, ale, cider, cheese, malt, and leather goods. It also encouraged maritime interests by allowing a 10 percent discount on all goods imported in native ships and imposing a high tax on oriental products imported by foreign vessels. President Washington, who complained that his countrymen were still "subject to British prejudices," signed the Tariff Act on July 4 to highlight its meaning as a second declaration of independence.[12] A second piece of legislation, the Tonnage Act, encouraged American shippers and shipbuilders by laying a duty of fifty cents per ton on vessels built and owned abroad, thirty cents on vessels owned abroad but built in America, and six cents on vessels both built and owned by natives. Moreover, in the case of the six-cent duty, shipmasters were only required to pay the tax once a year. Americans were thus given a virtual monopoly of the fishing and coasting trade.[13]

The new tariff policy held two special advantages. One was its nationwide scope. Actual rates were not as high as they had been in some of the states of the Confederation.[14] But they stood to be more effective because they were uniform. Long before 1789, northern industries had been capable of producing enough merchandise to supply out-of-state markets. However, because out-of-state tariff rates were too low to shield them from British competition, they

12. Thompson, *History,* 52, 61–62. On December 5, 1791, Hamilton issued his *Report on Manufactures* which confirmed the protective policy, provided a strong rational foundation for it, and helped to ensure its acceptance by the Adams and Jefferson administrations. See also Nettels, *Emergence of National Economy,* 109.
13. Nettels, *Emergence of National Economy,* 111.
14. Jensen, *New Nation,* 300; Setser, *Commercial Reciprocity,* 65.

could not realize their potential. Now, American goods and ships were guaranteed uniform protection in all states of the union. There would be less likelihood of last-minute rate changes, and one would only need to be familiar with one schedule instead of thirteen or more.[15]

The second advantage of the new laws was the fact that Congress could adjust them at any time to favor one trading partner over another. The desire to retaliate against foreign trade restrictions had been an important factor in the movement for constitutional reform down to 1787, and Madison's followers never lost their enthusiasm for a program of discrimination against British commerce. They tried to write a provision into the Tonnage Act of 1789 which would have subjected British vessels to a tax of sixty cents per ton, as compared to only thirty cents for French shipping. And such a bill passed the House. But it could not get through the Senate without being shorn of its discriminatory clauses.[16] Similar attempts in subsequent years on the part of the Jeffersonians also failed despite Madison's insistence that discrimination was an object "for which the government was in great degree instituted." Summoning Clio to his side at one point, the Virginia scholar recalled that "as early as the year succeeding the peace, the effect of the foreign policy [of Britain] which began to be felt in our trade and navigation excited universal attention and inquietude." He then went on to relate how Congress had failed to obtain the power to regulate foreign trade as a result of a "radical vice" in the political system, how state efforts had proved equally fruitless, and how this experience had produced measures which culminated in the establishment

15. Nettels, *Emergence of National Economy*, 70–71.
16. Certain schedules amounted to *de facto* discrimination. Rum, for example, which was apt to be British, was taxed more heavily than brandy (apt to be French); Setser, *Commercial Reciprocity*, 107.

of a government competent to regulate commerce and vindicate commercial rights. He continued, "As these were the first objects of the people in the steps taken for establishing the present government, they were universally expected to be among the first fruits of its operation. In this expectation the public were disappointed. An attempt was made in different forms and received the repeated sanction of this branch of the Legislature, but they expired in the Senate." [17]

Madison's argument failed for a variety of reasons. Many farmers, shipowners, and shipbuilders had lost interest in a trade war with Great Britain due to the more prosperous conditions which had developed since 1786 when the constitutional reform movement was at its apex. By 1789, a steadily growing trade with the East Indies, the Orient, and food-starved Europe had taken the edge off the desire to challenge Britain on her navigation laws. Second, the postwar expectation of a large increase in the Franco-American trade had proven unrealistic. Americans continued to prefer British goods over French, and they remained as dependent as ever upon traditional sources of credit in Glasgow and Liverpool. Nor did the French Revolution alter the picture. On the contrary, French duties on American fish, whale oil, and salted provisions rose to new heights by 1791, and French restrictions made it nearly impossible to ship tobacco to France aboard American ships. By 1794, many Americans had begun to regard Britain as a bulwark against the increasingly radical trend of French politics. Third, the whole financial program and credit structure of the new government depended heavily on the Anglo-American trade, as

17. *Debates and Proceedings in the Congress of the United States* (42 vols.; Washington, D. C.: U.S. Government Printing Office, 1934–62), 3rd Congress, First Sess., 155, 210. For all of Madison's argument, see *ibid.*, 155–225.

Hamilton pointed out so emphatically. Finally, it was argued that a trade war might lead to full-fledged hostilities which the new nation could ill afford. Domestic manufacturing could not yet supply the country should imports fall off. Nor was the American merchant fleet large enough to fill all of the country's transportation needs.[18]

Events themselves played into the hands of the Hamiltonians who argued that diplomatic channels should be explored before resorting to force. Whenever Madison stood on the verge of pushing his program to victory, his opponents were able to cite a good reason for delay. First there was the mission of Gouverneur Morris to London in 1790. When Morris failed to make headway, the Federalists counseled forbearance on the theory that the British had just decided to send the United States a minister plenipotentiary; this was a sign of good will which should be tested. When the minister revealed that he had come without power to negotiate, the Jeffersonians again pressed for discriminatory measures. But this time Hamilton was saved by the indiscretions of Citizen Genêt. Meanwhile, the outbreak of war on the Continent and Washington's Proclamation of Neutrality meant that the nation could no longer engage in commercial discrimination without being drawn into the fighting. Finally, when Britain added injury to insult by seizing American ships in the Caribbean under secret Orders in Council, Madison was thwarted by the decision to send John Jay to London. The Republicans, hoping to pass a nonintercourse bill, were now forced to settle for an un-

18. For a clear statement of the Hamiltonian position in the House of Representatives, see the remarks by William Smith of South Carolina, given on January 3, 1794, *ibid.*, 174–209. For the change which took place in Hamilton's thought since his publication of *The Federalist*, No. 11, see Setser, *Commercial Reciprocity*, 101–103; Combs, *Jay Treaty*, 39–40, 62.

popular embargo which was allowed to expire after two months.

What is significant, though, is that the mere threat of commercial retaliation helped to bring results. Combined with war on the Continent, it inspired enough fear in the king's ministers to cause them to violate an age-old tradition and open their West Indian colonies to American ships of limited tonnage. Without the threat of action made possible by the new Constitution, it is unlikely that Jay would ever have secured the concessions that he did, inadequate as they may have seemed at the time.[19]

Thus, while the impact of the Constitution on foreign relations in the years immediately after 1789 cannot be assessed with absolute precision, there is little doubt that the new government served the purpose for which it was intended, in commerce as well as defense. There were no instant miracles. The British did not abandon the frontier in 1790; the pirates did not sink into perpetual obscurity; the United States continued to endure insult from abroad; it remained relatively weak. For the first time, however, Americans were flexing a powerful set of muscles. And, in this sense, the hope of Philadelphia had become a reality.

19. Setser, *Commercial Reciprocity*, 130; Ritcheson, *Aftermath of Revolution*, 319. After 1815, it became quite evident that the British would trim their sails to avoid commercial retaliation by Congress. When Congress did move in this direction, Britain opened her West Indies. Jackson was president at the time, and it was one of the highlights of his record in foreign relations.

# Bibliography

PRIMARY SOURCES

*Official Records*

Carter, Clarence Edwin, ed. *Territorial Papers of the United States.* 26 vols. Washington, D.C.: U.S. Government Printing Office, 1934–1962.

*Debates and Proceedings in the Congress of the United States.* 42 vols. Washington, D.C.: Gales and Seaton, 1834–1856.

*Diplomatic Correspondence of the United States of America, from the Signing of the Definitive Treaty of Peace, September 10, 1783, to the Adoption of the Constitution, March 4, 1789.* 3 vols. Washington, D.C.: Blair and Ives, 1837.

*Documentary History of the Constitution of the United States of America, 1786–1870.* 5 vols. Washington, D.C.: Department of State, 1894–1905.

Elliot, Jonathan, ed. *The Debates in the Several State Conventions on the Adoption of the Federal Constitution.* 5 vols. Philadelphia: J. B. Lippincott and Co., 1861.

Farrand, Max, ed. *The Records of the Federal Convention of 1787.* 4 vols. New Haven: Yale University Press, 1911.

Ford, Worthington Chauncey, *et al.*, eds. *Journals of the Continental Congress, 1774–1789.* 34 vols. Washington, D.C.: U.S. Government Printing Office, 1904–1937.

Grant, W. L., James Munro, and A. W. Fitzroy, eds. *Acts of the Privy Council of England, Colonial Series.* 6 vols. Hereford and London, 1908–1912.

Lowrie, Walter, and Matthew St. Clair Clarke, eds. *American State Papers: Documents, Legislative and Executive, of the Congress of the United States, From the First to the Third Session of the Thirteenth Congress, Inclusive: Commencing March 3, 1789, and Ending March 3, 1815.* 38 vols. Washington, D.C.: Gales and Seaton, 1832–1861.

*Papers of the Continental Congress,* Microfilm. National Archives.

*Secret Journals of the Acts and Proceedings of Congress.* 4 vols. Boston: Thomas B. Wait, 1821.

Wharton, Francis, ed. *The Revolutionary Diplomatic Correspondence of the United States.* 6 vols. Washington, D.C.: U.S. Government Printing Office, 1889.

### Manuscript Collections

American Philosophical Society, Philadelphia
    Benjamin Franklin Papers
William L. Clements Library, Ann Arbor, Michigan
    Josiah Harmar Papers
    Perkins Papers
Columbia University, New York
    John Jay Papers
    Gouverneur Morris Papers
Connecticut Historical Society, Hartford
    Jeremiah Wadsworth Papers
Historical Society of Pennsylvania, Philadelphia
    George Bryan Papers
    Pierce Butler Papers
    Benjamin Franklin Papers
    John Langdon Papers
    James Wilson Papers
Library of Congress, Washington, D.C.
    John Adams Papers
    Samuel, John, and William Augustus Atlee Papers
    Charles Carroll of Carrollton Papers
    Connecticut Miscellaneous Papers

Nathan Dane Papers
Benjamin Franklin Papers
Alexander Hamilton Papers
Harry Innes Papers
Thomas Jefferson Papers
William Samuel Johnson Papers
Rufus King Papers
John Lamb Papers
Henry and John Laurens Papers
Lee Family Papers
James Madison Papers
Massachusetts Miscellaneous Papers, Force Transcripts
James Monroe Papers
Robert Morris Papers
New Hampshire Miscellaneous Papers
Pinckney Family Papers
Edmund Randolph Papers
Joseph Reed Papers
Shippen Family Papers
Charles Thomson Papers
Nicholas Van Dyke Papers
Jeremiah Wadsworth Papers
George Washington Papers
Massachusetts Historical Society Collections, Boston
    Belknap Papers
    Henry Knox Papers
    Pickering Papers
    Warren-Adams Letters
New-York Historical Society, New York
    King Papers
    John Lamb Papers
    Robert R. Livingston Papers
    Philip Schuyler Papers
New York Public Library, New York
    Samuel Adams Papers
    Emmet Collection
Pennsylvania State Archives, Harrisburg
    Records of the Pennsylvania Assembly
Philadelphia Free Library, Philadelphia
    Benjamin Rush Papers

Virginia State Library, Richmond
Virginia Legislative Petition Collection

*Collected Works*

Adams, Charles Francis, ed. *The Works of John Adams, Second President of the United States; with a Life of the Author, Notes and Illustrations*. 10 vols. Boston: Little, Brown & Co., 1850–1856.

Ballagh, James Curtis, ed. *The Letters of Richard Henry Lee*. 2 vols. New York: Macmillan Co., 1911–1914.

Bigelow, John, ed. and comp. *The Works of Benjamin Franklin, Including the Private as Well as the Official and Scientific Correspondence Together With the Unmutilated and Correct Version of the Autobiography*. 12 vols. New York: G. P. Putnam's Sons, The Knickerbocker Press, 1904.

Borden, Morton, ed. *The Antifederalist Papers*. East Lansing: Michigan State University Press, 1965.

Boyd, Julian Parks, ed. *Papers of Thomas Jefferson*. 17 vols. Princeton: Princeton University Press, 1950–.

Burnett, Edmund Cody, ed. *Letters of Members of the Continental Congress*. 8 vols. Washington, D.C.: Carnegie Institution, 1921–1936.

Butterfield, Lyman Henry, ed. *Letters of Benjamin Rush*. 2 vols. Princeton: Princeton University Press, 1951.

Cappon, Lester Jesse, ed. *The Adams-Jefferson Letters*. 2 vols. Chapel Hill: University of North Carolina Press, 1959.

Cushing, Harry Alonzo, ed. *The Writings of Samuel Adams*. 4 vols. New York: G. P. Putnam's Sons, 1904–1908.

Dewitt, John H., ed. "Journal of Governor John Sevier," *Tennessee Historical Magazine*, V (October, 1919), 156–94; V (January, 1920), 232–64; VI (April, 1920), 18–68.

Fitzpatrick, John Clement, ed. *The Writings of George Washington from the Original Manuscript Sources, 1745–1799*. 39 vols. Washington, D.C.: U.S. Government Printing Office, 1931–1944.

Ford, Paul Leicester, ed. *Essays on the Constitution of the United States, Published During Its Discussion by the People, 1787–1788*. Brooklyn: n.p., 1892.

_____, ed. *Pamphlets on the Constitution of the United States, Published During Its Discussion by the People, 1787–1788.* Brooklyn: n.p., 1888.

_____, ed. *The Works of Thomas Jefferson.* 12 vols. New York and London: G. P. Putnam's Sons, 1904–1905.

Ford, Worthington Chauncey, ed. *Letters of Joseph Jones of Virginia.* Washington, D.C.: Department of State, 1889.

Hamilton, Stanislaus Murray, ed. *The Writings of James Monroe Including a Collection of His Public and Private Papers and Correspondence Now for The First Time Printed.* 7 vols. New York and London: G. P. Putnam's Sons, 1898–1903.

Hammond, Otis Grant, ed. *Letters and Papers of Major-General John Sullivan, Continental Army.* 3 vols. Concord: New Hampshire Historical Society, 1930–1939.

Hart, Albert Bushnell, ed. *American History Told by Contemporaries.* 5 vols. New York: Macmillan Co., 1897–1929.

Hunt, Gaillard, ed. *The Writings of James Madison.* 9 vols. New York: G. P. Putnam's Sons, 1900–1910.

Jameson, John Franklin, ed. "Letters of Stephen Higginson, 1783–1804," *Annual Report of the American Historical Association for the Year 1896.* 2 vols. Washington, D.C.: U.S. Government Printing Office, 1897; I, 704–841.

Johnston, Henry Phelps, ed. *The Correspondence and Public Papers of John Jay.* 4 vols. New York: G. P. Putnam's Sons, 1890–1893.

Kenyon, Cecilia M., ed. *The Antifederalists.* Indianapolis: Bobbs-Merrill Co., 1966.

Koch, Adrienne, ed. *Notes of Debates in the Federal Convention of 1787 Reported by James Madison.* Columbus: University of Ohio Press, 1966.

Lefler, Hugh Talmage, ed. *A Plea for Federal Union, North Carolina, 1788.* Charlottesville: University of Virginia Press, 1947.

Lipscomb, Andrew Adgate, ed. *The Writings of Thomas Jefferson.* 20 vols. Washington, D.C.: Thomas Jefferson Memorial Association of the United States, 1903–1904.

Lodge, Henry Cabot, ed. *The Works of Alexander Hamilton.* 12 vols. New York and London: G. P. Putnam's Sons, 1903.

McMaster, John Bach and Frederick Dawson Stone, eds. *Penn-*

*sylvania and the Federal Constitution.* Lancaster, Pa.: Inquirer Printing and Publishing Co., Printers, 1888.

Rossiter, Clinton, ed. *The Federalist Papers.* New York: New American Library, 1961.

Smyth, Albert Henry, ed. *The Writings of Benjamin Franklin.* 10 vols. New York and London: Macmillan Co., 1905–1907.

Syrett, Harold Coffin, ed. *Papers of Alexander Hamilton.* 13 vols. New York: Columbia University Press, 1961–.

Thornborough, Gayle, ed. *Outpost on the Wabash, 1787–91: Letters of Brigadier General Josiah Harmar and Major John Francis Hamtramck.* Indianapolis: Indiana Historical Society, 1957.

### Memoirs and Journals

Butterfield, Lyman Henry, ed. *Diary and Autobiography of John Adams.* 4 vols. New York: Atheneum, 1961.

Lee, Richard Henry. *Memoir of the Life of Richard Henry Lee, and His Correspondence with the Most Distinguished Men in America and Europe, Illustrative of Their Characters, and of the Events of the American Revolution.* 2 vols. Philadelphia: H. C. Carey and I. Lea, 1825.

Maudslay, Mrs. Anne Cary Morris, ed. *The Diary and Letters of Gouverneur Morris.* 2 vols. New York: Charles Scribner's Sons, 1888.

Wilkinson, James. *Memoirs of My Own Times.* 3 vols. Philadelphia: Abraham Small, 1816.

### Travelers' Accounts

Brissot de Warville, Jacques Pierre. *New Travels in the United States of America: Including the Commerce of America with Europe: Particularly with France and Great Britain.* 2 vols. London: J. S. Jordan, 1794.

Chastellux, Marquis de. *Travels in North America in the Years 1780, 1781, and 1782.* 2 vols. London: n.p., 1787.

Schoepf, Johann David. *Travels in the Confederation (1783–1784) from the German of Johann David Schoepf.* Translated and edited by Alfred J. Morrison. 2 vols. Philadelphia: W. J. Campbell, 1911.

Smyth, John Ferdinand Dalziel. *The United States of America:*

*A Tour in the United States of America Containing An Account of the Present Situation of That Country: The Population, Agriculture, Commerce, Customs, and Manners of the Inhabitants.* 2 vols. London: n.p., 1784.

*Newspapers and Magazines (1785–1788)*

Boston *Gazette*
Charleston (S.C.) *City Gazette or Daily Advertiser*
Charleston (S.C.) *Evening Gazette or Daily Advertiser*
Charleston (S.C.) *Morning Post*
*Columbian Herald* (Charleston, S.C.)
*Connecticut Courant* (Hartford)
*Gazette of the State of Georgia* (Savannah)
*Gentleman's Magazine* (London)
*Georgia State Gazette* (Augusta)
*Maryland Gazette* (Annapolis)
*Maryland Journal* (Annapolis)
*Massachusetts Centinel* (Boston)
*New Jersey Gazette* (Trenton)
New York *Daily Advertiser*
New York *Journal*
New York *Packet*
*North Carolina Gazette* (New Bern)
*Pennsylvania Gazette* (Philadelphia)
*Pennsylvania Herald* (Philadelphia)
*Pennsylvania Packet and Daily Advertiser* (Philadelphia)
*South Carolina Gazette and General Advertiser* (Charleston)
*State Gazette of South Carolina* (Charleston)
Trenton (N.J.) *Mercury and Weekly Advertiser*
*Virginia Gazette* (Richmond)
*Virginia Independent Chronicle* (Richmond)

*Pamphlets and Political Tracts*

Adams, John. *A Defence of the Constitutions of Government of the United States of America.* 2 vols. Boston: E. Freeman, 1788.
Adams, John Quincy. *The Jubilee of the Constitution.* New York: Samuel Colman, 1839.
Barton, Thomas. *The Conduct of the Paxton Men, Impartially*

*Represented with Some Remarks on the Narrative.* Philadelphia: Andrew Stuart, 1764.

Barton, William. *The True Interest of the United States, and Particularly of Pennsylvania, Considered; With Respect to the Advantages Resulting from a State Paper-Money, with Some Observations on the Subject of a Bank and On Agriculture, Manufactures and Commerce.* Philadelphia: Charles Cist, 1786.

Bingham, William. *Letter from An American Now Resident in London to a Member of Parliament on the Subject of the Restraining Proclamation and Containing Strictures on Lord Sheffield's Pamphlet on the Commerce of the American States.* Philadelphia: Robert Bell, 1784.

Bryan, Samuel. *To the People of Pennsylvania.* Philadelphia: n.p., 1787.

Burke, Aedanus. *Considerations on the Society or Order of the Cincinnati.* Philadelphia: Robert Bell, 1783.

Chalmers, George. *Opinions on Interesting Subjects of Public Law and Commercial Policy: Arising from American Independence.* London: J. Debrett, 1784.

Champion, Richard. *Considerations on the Present Situation of Great Britain and the United States of North America With a View to Their Future Commercial Connections.* London: J. Stockdale, 1784.

*The Commercial Conduct of the United States Considered by a Citizen of New York.* New York: S. and J. Loudon, 1786.

Coxe, Tench. *An Address to an Assembly of the Friends of Manufactures.* Philadelphia: Aitken and Son, 1787.

———. *A Brief Examination of Lord Sheffield's Observations on the Commerce of the United States.* Philadelphia: M. Carey, 1791.

———. *An Enquiry into the Principles on Which a Commercial System for the United States Should Be Founded.* Philadelphia: Robert Aitken, 1787.

Edwards, Brian. *Thoughts on the Late Proceedings of Government Respecting the Trade of the West India Islands with the United States of North America.* London: T. Cadell, 1784.

*A Few Salutary Hints, Pointing Out the Policy and Conse-*

quences of *Admitting British Subjects to Engross Our Trade and Become Our Citizens.* New York: S. Kollock, 1786.

*Fragments on the Confederation of the American States.* Philadelphia: Thomas Dobson, 1787.

*A Free and Candid Review of a Tract Entitled "Observations on the Commerce of the United States."* London: n.p., 1784.

Gibbes, Sir Philip, bart. *Reflections on the Proclamation of the Second of July 1783, Relative to the Trade Between the United States of America and the West-India Islands; Addressed to the Right Honourable William Pitt, First Lord of the Treasury and Chancellor of the Exchequer.* London: n.p., 1783.

Hanson, Alexander Contee. *Remarks on the Proposed Plan of a Federal Government.* Annapolis, Md.: Frederick Green, 1788.

Holroyd, John Baker, first earl of Sheffield. *Observations on the Commerce of the American States with Europe and the West Indies.* London: J. Debrett, 1783.

Jackson, Jonathan. *Thoughts Upon the Political Situation of the United States of America in Which That of Massachusetts is More Particularly Considered.* Worcester, Mass.: n.p., 1788.

Langdon, Samuel. *The Republic of the Israelites: An Example to the American States.* Exeter, N.H.: Lamson and Ranlet, 1788.

Markoe, Peter. *The Algerine Spy in Pennsylvania: or Letters Written by a Native of Algiers on the Affairs of the United States in America, from the Close of the Year 1783 to the Meeting of the Convention.* Philadelphia: Pritchard and Hall, 1787.

Pinckney, Charles. *Observations on the Plan of Government Submitted to the Federal Convention.* New York: Francis Childs, 1787.

*The Political Establishments of the United States of America in a Candid Review of Their Deficiencies, Together With a Proposal of Reformation, Humbly Addressed to the Citizens of America, By a Fellow Citizen.* Philadelphia: Robert Bell, 1784.

Tucker, St. George. *Reflections on the Policy and Necessity of*

*Encouraging the Commerce of the Citizens of the United States of America and of Granting Them Exclusive Privileges of Trade.* Richmond and New York: Sam and John Loudon, 1786.

Webster, Noah. *An Examination into the Leading Principles of the Federal Constitution.* Philadelphia: Pritchard and Hall, 1787.

Webster, Pelatiah. *A Dissertation on the Political Union and Constitution of the Thirteen United States of North America: Which is Necessary to Their Preservation and Happiness, Humbly Offered to the Public by a Citizen of Philadelphia.* Philadelphia: T. Bradford, 1783.

————. *An Essay on Credit in Which the Doctrine of Banks is Considered and Some Remarks are Made on the Present State of the Bank of North America.* Philadelphia: E. Oswald, 1786.

————. *Remarks on the Address of Sixteen Members of the Assembly of Pennsylvania, to Their Constituents, Dated September 29, 1787, with Some Strictures on Their Objections to the Constitution Recommended by the Late Federal Convention, Humbly Offered to the Public. By a Citizen of Philadelphia.* Philadelphia: Eleazer Oswald at the coffeehouse, 1787.

### Collections of Documents

Morison, Samuel Eliot, ed. *Sources and Documents Illustrating the American Revolution 1764–1788 and the Formation of the Federal Constitution.* Oxford: The Clarendon Press, 1962.

Tansill, Charles Callan. *Documents Illustrative of the Formation of the Union of the American States.* Washington, D.C.: U.S. Government Printing Office, 1927.

### SECONDARY SOURCES

Abernethy, Thomas Perkins. *The South in the New Nation, 1789–1819.* Baton Rouge: Louisiana State University Press, 1961.

Alden, John Richard. *The South in the Revolution, 1763–1789.* Vol. III of *A History of the South.* Edited by Wendell Stephenson. Baton Rouge: Louisiana State University Press, 1957.

Amory, Thomas Coffin. *Life of James Sullivan: With Selections from His Writings.* 2 vols. Boston: Phillips, Sampson, & Co., 1859.

Austin, James Trecothick. *The Life of Elbridge Gerry.* 2 vols. Boston: Wills and Lilly, 1828–1829.

Bancroft, George. *History of the Formation of the Constitution of the United States of America.* 2 vols. New York: D. Appleton & Co., 1882.

Banks, Ronald F. *Maine Becomes A State: The Movement to Separate Maine from Massachusetts, 1785–1820.* Middletown, Conn.: Wesleyan University Press, 1970.

Barnby, Henry G. *The Prisoners of Algiers: An Account of the Forgotten American-Algerian War, 1785–1797.* New York: Oxford University Press, 1966.

Barry, Richard Hayes. *Mr. Rutledge of South Carolina.* New York: Dull, Sloan & Pearce, 1942.

Batchellor, Albert Stillman. *A Brief View of the Influences that Moved in the Adoption of the Federal Constitution by the State of New Hampshire.* Concord, N.H.: Rumford Press, 1900.

Bates, Frank Greene. *Rhode Island and the Formation of the Union.* New York: Macmillan Co., 1898.

Beard, Charles Austin. *An Economic Interpretation of the Constitution of the United States.* New York: Macmillan Co., 1913.

————. *The Enduring Federalist.* New York: Frederick Ungar Publishing Co., 1959.

Beatty, Hubert Irving. "Why Form a More Perfect Union? A Study of the Origins of the Constitutional Convention of 1787." Ph.D. dissertation, Stanford University, 1962.

Bell, Herbert C. "British Commercial Policy in the West Indies, 1783–1793." *Economic History Review,* XXXI (1916), 440–41.

Bemis, Samuel Flagg. *Jay's Treaty: A Study in Commerce and Diplomacy.* New York: Macmillan Co., 1923.

————. *John Jay, Secretary for Foreign Affairs for the Continental Congress, September 21, 1784, to September 15,*

*1789.* Vol. I of *The American Secretaries of State and Their Diplomacy, 1776–1925.* Edited by Samuel Flagg Bemis. 10 vols. New York: Alfred A. Knopf, 1927–1929.

————. *Pinckney's Treaty, America's Advantage from Europe's Distresses, 1783–1800.* Rev. ed. New Haven: Yale University Press, 1960.

————. "Relations Between the Vermont Separatists and Great Britain, 1789–1791." *American Historical Review,* XXI (April, 1916), 547–60.

Berry, Jane M. "The Indian Policy of Spain in the Southwest, 1783–1795." *Mississippi Valley Historical Review,* III (March, 1917), 462–77.

Beveridge, Albert Jeremiah. *The Life of John Marshall.* 4 vols. in 2. New York: Houghton Mifflin Co., 1929.

Bishop, Hillman Metcalf. "Why Rhode Island Opposed the Federal Constitution." *Rhode Island History,* VIII (January, 1949), 1–10; VIII (April, 1949), 33–44; VIII (July, 1949), 85–95; VIII (October, 1949), 115–26.

Bixler, Raymond. *The Open Door on the Old Barbary Coast.* New York: Pageant Press, 1959.

Boehm, D. and E. Schwartz. "Jefferson and the Theory of Degeneracy." *American Quarterly,* IX (Winter, 1957), 448–53.

Bolkhovitinov, Nikolai Nikolaevich. *Stanovlenie Russko-Amerikanshkikh otnoshenii, 1775–1815.* Moscow: Izdatel'stvo "Nauka," 1966.

Boorstin, Daniel Joseph. *The Lost World of Thomas Jefferson.* Boston: Beacon Press, 1960.

Bowen, Catherine Drinker. *Miracle at Philadelphia.* Boston: Little, Brown and Co., 1966.

Brant, Irving. *James Madison.* 6 vols. Indianapolis: Bobbs-Merrill Co., 1941–1961.

Brigham, Clarence Saunders. *History and Bibliography of American Newspapers, 1690–1820.* 2 vols. Worcester, Mass.: American Antiquarian Society, 1947.

Brown, Alan S. "The Role of the Army in Western Settlement: Josiah Harmar's Command, 1785–1790." *Pennsylvania Magazine of History and Biography,* XVIII (April, 1969), 161–78.

Brown, Robert Eldon. *Charles Beard and the Constitution: A Critical Analysis of "An Economic Interpretation of the*

*Constitution.*" Princeton: Princeton University Press, 1956.

————. *Reinterpretation of the Formation of the American Constitution.* Boston: Boston University Press, 1963.

Brown, Roger Hamilton. *The Republic in Peril: 1812.* New York: Columbia University Press, 1964.

Brunhouse, Robert Levere. *The Counter Revolution in Pennsylvania, 1776–1790.* New York: Octagon Books, 1971.

Buel, Richard. *Securing the Revolution: Ideology in American Politics, 1789–1815.* Ithaca: Cornell University Press, 1972.

Bullock, Charles J. "The Finances of the United States from 1775 to 1789, with Especial Reference to the Budget." *Bulletin of the University of Wisconsin* (Economics, Political Science, and History Series), I (June, 1895), 117–273.

Burnett, Edmund Cody. *The Continental Congress.* New York: W. W. Norton & Co., 1964.

————. "Note on American Negotiations for Commercial Treaties, 1776–1786." *American Historical Review,* XVI (April, 1911), 579–87.

Burns, Edward McNall. *The American Idea of Mission.* New Brunswick, N.J.: Rutgers University Press, 1957.

Buron, Edmond. "Statistics on Franco-American Trade, 1778–1806." *Journal of Economic and Business History,* IV (1931–32), 571–80.

Burt, Alfred LeRoy. *The United States, Great Britain and British North America, from the Revolution to the Establishment of Peace After the War of 1812.* New Haven: Yale University Press, 1940.

Callahan, North. *Henry Knox: General Washington's General.* New York: Rinehart, 1958.

Cantor, Milton. "Joel Barlowe's Mission to Algiers." *The Historian,* XXV (1963), 172–94.

Caughey, John Walton. *McGillivray of the Creeks.* Norman: University of Oklahoma Press, 1938.

Channing, Edward. *A History of the United States.* 6 vols. New York: Macmillan Co., 1905–1925.

Chinard, Gilbert. "Eighteenth Century Theories of America as a Human Habitat." *Proceedings of the American Philosophical Society,* XCI, No. I (February 25, 1947), 27–57.

————. *Honest John Adams.* Boston: Little, Brown & Co., 1933.

Chitwood, Oliver Perry. *Richard Henry Lee, Statesman of the Revolution.* Morgantown: West Virginia University Library, 1968.

Church, Henry W. "Corneille de Pauw and the Controversy over his *Recherches Philosophiques sur les Américains.*" *Publications of the Modern Language Association,* LI (March, 1936), 178–207.

Clark, Victor Selden. *History of Manufactures in the United States.* 3 vols. New York: McGraw Hill, 1929.

Coleman, Kenneth. *The American Revolution in Georgia, 1763–1789.* Athens: University of Georgia Press, 1958.

————. "Federal Indian Relations in the South, 1781–1789." *Chronicles of Oklahoma,* XXXV (Winter, 1957–58), 435–58.

Collier, Christopher. *Roger Sherman's Connecticut: Yankee Politics and the American Revolution.* Middletown, Conn.: Wesleyan University Press, 1971.

Combs, Jerald A. *The Jay Treaty: Political Battleground of the Founding Fathers.* Berkeley: University of California Press, 1970.

Crosskey, William Winslow. *Politics and the Constitution in the History of the United States.* 2 vols. Chicago: University of Chicago Press, 1953.

Crowl, Philip Axtell. *Maryland During and After the Revolution.* Baltimore: The Johns Hopkins Press, 1943.

Curti, Merle. *The Growth of American Thought.* New York: Harper and Row, 1964.

Curtis, George Ticknor. *History of the Origin, Formation, and Adoption of the Constitution of the United States.* 2 vols. New York: Harper and Brothers, 1854–1858.

Dangerfield, George. *Chancellor Robert R. Livingston of New York, 1746–1813.* New York: Harcourt, Brace, 1960.

Darling, Arthur Burr. *Our Rising Empire, 1763–1803.* New Haven: Yale University Press, 1940.

Davies, Wallace Evan. "The Society of the Cincinnati in New England, 1783–1800." *William and Mary Quarterly,* V, Ser. 3 (January, 1948), 3–25.

Deconde, Alexander. *Entangling Alliance.* Durham, N.C.: Duke University Press, 1958.

DePauw, Linda Grant. *New York State and the Federal Constitution.* Ithaca, N.Y.: Cornell University Press, 1966.

Dewey, Davis Rich. *Financial History of the United States.* New York: Longmans, Green and Co., 1909.

Diamond, Martin. "Democracy and *The Federalist*: A Reconsideration of the Framers' Intents." *American Political Science Review*, LIII (March, 1959), 52–68.

Dickerson, Oliver Morton. *The Navigation Acts and the American Revolution.* New York: A. S. Barnes, 1963.

Donahoe, Bernard and Marshall Smelser. "The Congressional Power to Raise Armies: The Constitutional and Ratifying Conventions, 1787–1788." *Review of Politics*, XXXIII (April, 1971), 202–11.

Downes, Randolph Chandler. *Council Fires on the Upper Ohio.* Pittsburgh: University of Pittsburgh Press, 1940.

————. "Creek-American Relations, 1782–1790." *Georgia Historical Quarterly*, XXI (June, 1937), 142–84.

Drake, Francis Samuel. *Life and Correspondence of Henry Knox, Major-General in the American Revolutionary Army.* Boston: S. G. Drake, 1873.

Echeverria, Durand. *Mirage in the West.* Princeton: Princeton University Press, 1957.

Eiseman, Nathaniel J. "The Ratification of the Constitution by the State of New Hampshire." M.A. thesis, Columbia University, 1938.

Elkins, Stanley and Eric McKitrick. "The Founding Fathers: Young Men of the Revolution." *Political Science Quarterly*, LXXVI (June, 1961), 181–216.

Ernst, Robert. *Rufus King: American Federalist.* Chapel Hill: University of North Carolina Press, 1968.

Farrand, Max. *The Framing of the Constitution.* New Haven and London: Yale University Press, 1913.

————. "The Indian Boundary Line." *American Historical Review*, X (July, 1905), 782–91.

Feer, Robert A. "Shays's Rebellion and the Constitution: A Study in Causation." *New England Quarterly*, XLII (September, 1969), 388–410.

Ferguson, E. James. "The Nationalists of 1781–1783 and the Economic Interpretation of the Constitution." *Journal of American History*, LVI, No. 2 (September, 1969), 241–61.

————. *The Power of the Purse; A History of American Pub-*

*lic Finance, 1776–1790*. Chapel Hill: University of North Carolina Press, 1961.

Field, James A., Jr. *America and the Mediterranean World, 1776–1882*. Princeton: Princeton University Press, 1969.

Fiske, John. *The Critical Period of American History, 1783–1789*. Boston and New York: Houghton, Mifflin Co., 1888.

Fleming, Denna Frank. *The Treaty Veto of the American Senate*. New York: G. P. Putnam's Sons, 1930.

Ford, Paul Leicester. *Bibliography and Reference List of the History and Literature Relating to the Adoption of the Constitution of the United States, 1787–1788*. Brooklyn: n.p., 1888.

————. *The Origin, Purpose and Result of the Harrisburg Convention of 1788*. Brooklyn: n.p., 1890.

Ford, Worthington Chauncey, ed. "The Federal Constitution in Virginia, 1787–1788." *Massachusetts Historical Society Proceedings*, XVII, Ser. 2 (October, 1903), 450–510.

Free, William J. *"The Columbian Magazine" and American Literary Nationalism*. The Hague: Montou & Co., 1969.

Frothingham, Richard. *The Rise of the Republic of the United States*. Boston: Little, Brown & Co., 1872.

Furnas, Joseph Chamberlain. *The Americans*. New York: G. P. Putnam's Sons, 1969.

Gerlach, Larry R. "Toward 'A More Perfect Union': Connecticut, the Continental Congress, and the Constitutional Convention." *Connecticut Historical Society Bulletin*, XXXIV, No. 3 (July, 1969), 65–78.

Giesecke, Albert Anthony. *American Commercial Legislation Before 1789*. New York: D. Appleton & Co., agents, 1910.

Gilbert, Felix. *To the Farewell Address*. Princeton: Princeton University Press, 1961.

Goddard, Henry Perkins. *Luther Martin: The "Federal Bull-Dog."* Baltimore: J. Murphy & Co., 1887.

Graham, Louis E. "Fort McIntosh." *Western Pennsylvania History Magazine*, XV, No. 2 (May, 1932), 93–119.

Green, Thomas Marshall. *The Spanish Conspiracy*. Cincinnati: R. Clarke & Co., 1891.

Greene, Evarts Boutell. *The Revolutionary Generation, 1763–1790*. New York: Macmillan Co., 1943.

Greene, Evarts Boutell and Virginia Draper Harrington. *American Population Before the Federal Census of 1790.* New York: Columbia University Press, 1932.

Grigsby, Hugh Blair. *The History of the Virginia Federal Convention of 1788.* Edited by Robert Alonzo Brock. 2 vols. Richmond: Virginia Historical Society, 1890–91.

Hall, Luella J. *The United States and Morocco, 1776–1956.* Metuchen, N.J.: Scarecrow Press, 1971.

Hall, Van Beck. *Politics Without Parties: Massachusetts, 1780–1791.* Pittsburgh: University of Pittsburgh Press, 1972.

Hamer, Philip May, ed. *A Guide to Archives and Manuscripts in the United States.* New Haven: Yale University Press, 1961.

Hammond, Bray. *Banks and Politics in America, from the Revolution to the Civil War.* Princeton: Princeton University Press, 1957.

Handlin, Oscar and Mary Flug Handlin. *Commonwealth: A Study of the Role of Government in the American Economy: Massachusetts 1774–1861.* New York: New York University Press, 1947.

Harding, Samuel Bannister. *The Contest Over the Ratification of the Federal Constitution in the State of Massachusetts.* New York: Longmans, Green & Co., 1896.

Harlow, Vincent Todd. *The Founding of the Second British Empire, 1763–1793.* 2 vols. New York: Longmans, Green & Co., 1952.

Hassler, Warren W. *The President as Commander-in-Chief.* Menlo Park, Calif.: Addison Wesley, 1971.

Hedges, James Blaine. *The Browns of Providence Plantation.* Cambridge: Harvard University Press, 1952.

Henderson, Archibald. "The Spanish Conspiracy in Tennessee." *Tennessee Historical Magazine,* III (December, 1917), 229–49.

Henkin, Louis. *Foreign Affairs and the Constitution.* New York: Foundation Press, 1973.

Henry, William Wirt. *Patrick Henry: Life, Correspondence and Speeches.* 3 vols. New York: Charles Scribner's Sons, 1891.

Hill, Helen. *George Mason, Constitutionalist*. Cambridge: Harvard University Press, 1938.

Hoffer, Peter. "The Constitutional Crisis and the Rise of a Nationalist View of History in America, 1786–1788." *New York History*, LII (July, 1971), 305–23.

Hofstadter, Richard. *The Progressive Historians: Turner, Beard, Parrington*. New York: Alfred A. Knopf, 1968.

Holbrook, Stewart Hall. *Ethan Allen*. New York: Macmillan Co., 1940.

Holst, Hermann Eduard von. *The Constitutional and Political History of the United States*. Translated by John J. Lalor and Alfred B. Mason. 8 vols. Chicago: Callaghan & Co., 1876–1892.

Horsman, Reginald. "American Indian Policy in the Old Northwest, 1783–1812." *William and Mary Quarterly*, XVIII, Ser. 3 (January, 1961), 35–53.

———. *Expansion and American Indian Policy, 1783–1812*. East Lansing: Michigan State University Press, 1967.

———. *Frontier Detroit, 1760–1812*. Detroit: n.p., 1964.

———. *The Frontier in the Formative Years, 1783–1815*. New York: Holt, Rinehart & Winston, 1970.

———. *Matthew Elliot, British Indian Agent*. Detroit: Wayne State University Press, 1964.

Howe, Mark Antony DeWolfe. *The Humane Society of the Commonwealth of Massachusetts*. Cambridge: Riverside Press, 1918.

Hume, Major Edgar Erskine. "Early Opposition to the Cincinnati." *Americana*, XXX (October, 1936), 597–638.

Hunt, Gaillard. *The Department of State of the United States, Its History and Functions*. New Haven: Yale University Press, 1914.

Huston, James Alvin. *The Sinews of War: Army Logistics, 1775–1953*. Washington, D.C.: U.S. Government Printing Office, 1966.

Innis, Harold Adams. *The Fur Trade in Canada*. Rev. ed. Toronto: University of Toronto Press, 1956.

Irwin, Ray Watkins. *The Diplomatic Relations of the United States with the Barbary Powers, 1776–1816*. Chapel Hill: University of North Carolina Press, 1931.

Jacobs, James Ripley. *The Beginning of the U.S. Army, 1783–1812*. Princeton: Princeton University Press, 1947.

James, James Alton. *The Life of George Rogers Clark*. Chicago: University of Chicago Press, 1929.

Jay, John. *Second Letter on Dawson's Introduction to "The Federalist."* New York: American News Company, 1864.

Jensen, Merrill. *The Articles of Confederation: An Interpretation of the Social-Constitutional History of the American Revolution, 1774–1781*. Madison: University of Wisconsin, 1940.

_____. *The Making of the American Constitution*. Princeton: Van Nostrand, 1964.

_____. *The New Nation: A History of the United States During the Confederation, 1781–1789*. New York: Alfred A. Knopf, 1950.

Johnson, Emory Richard, *et al. History of Domestic and Foreign Commerce of the United States*. 2 vols. Washington, D.C.: Carnegie Institution, 1915.

Kaplan, Lawrence S. *Colonies into Nation: American Diplomacy, 1763–1801*. New York: Macmillan Co., 1972.

Keith, Alice B. "Relaxations in the British Restrictions on the American Trade with the British West Indies, 1783–1802." *Journal of Modern History*, XX (March, 1948), 1–19.

Kenyon, Cecilia M. "Men of Little Faith: The Anti-Federalists on the Nature of Representative Government." *William and Mary Quarterly*, XII, Ser. 3 (January, 1955), 3–42.

King, Charles R. *The Life and Correspondence of Rufus King*. 6 vols. New York: G. P. Putnam's Sons, 1894 –1900.

Koch, Adrienne. *Jefferson and Madison*. New York: Oxford University Press, 1964.

Kohlmeier, Albert Ludwig. "The Commerce Between the United States and the Netherlands, 1783–1789." *Indiana University Studies in American History*, Study Nos. 66–68, XII (June, September, December, 1925), 1– 47.

Kohn, Richard Henry. "The Federalists and the Army: Politics and the Birth of the Military Establishment, 1783–1795." Ph.D. dissertation, University of Wisconsin, 1968.

Lewis, Benjamin Morgan. *A Register of Editors, Printers, and Publishers of American Magazines, 1741–1810*. New York: New York Public Library, 1957.

Libby, Orin Grant. *The Geographical Distribution of the Vote of the Thirteen States on the Federal Constitution, 1787–1788*. Madison: University of Wisconsin, 1894.

Looze, Helene Johnson. *Alexander Hamilton and the British Orientation of American Foreign Policy, 1783–1803*. The Hague: Mouton & Co., 1969.

Low, W. A. "Merchant and Planter Relations in Post-Revolutionary Virginia, 1783–1789." *The Virginia Magazine of History and Biography*, LXI (July, 1953), 308–18.

Lycan, Gilbert L. *Alexander Hamilton and American Foreign Policy: A Design for Greatness*. Norman: University of Oklahoma Press, 1970.

Lynd, Staughton. *Class Conflict, Slavery, and the United States Constitution: Ten Essays*. Indianapolis: Bobbs-Merrill Co., 1968.

McCormick, Richard Patrick. *Experiment in Independence: New Jersey in the Critical Period, 1781–1789*. New Brunswick, N.J.: Rutgers University Press, 1950.

McCoy, Samuel Duff. "The Port of New York (1783–1789): Lost Island of Sailing Ships." *New York History*, XVII (October, 1936), 379–90.

McDonald, Forrest. "The Anti-Federalists, 1788–1789." *Wisconsin Magazine of History*, XLVI (Spring, 1963), 206–14.

————. *E Pluribus Unum*. Boston: Houghton Mifflin Co., 1965.

————. *We The People: The Economic Origins of the Constitution*. Chicago: University of Chicago Press, 1958.

McLaughlin, Andrew Cunningham. *America and Britain*. New York: E. R. Dutton & Co., 1919.

————. *The Confederation and the Constitution, 1783–1789*. Vol. X of *The American Nation: A History*. Edited by Albert Bushnell Hart. New York and London: Harper & Brothers, 1905.

————. "The Western Posts and the British Debts." *Yale Review*, III (February, 1895), 408–24; IV (May, 1895), 58–79.

McLendon, R. Early. "Origins of the Two-Thirds Rule in Senate Action Upon Treaties." *American Historical Review*, XXXVI (1931), 768–72.

McMaster, John Bach. *A History of the People of the United*

*States From the Revolution to the Civil War.* 8 vols. New York: Appleton & Co., 1883–1913.

Main, Jackson Turner. *The Anti-Federalists: Critics of the Constitution, 1781–1788.* Chapel Hill: University of North Carolina Press, 1961.

—————. *Political Parties Before the Constitution.* Chapel Hill: University of North Carolina Press, 1972.

—————. "The Results of the American Revolution Reconsidered." *The Historian,* XXXI (August, 1969), 539–54.

—————. "Sections and Politics in Virginia, 1781–1787." *William and Mary Quarterly,* XII, Ser. 3 (January, 1955), 96–112.

—————. *The Upper House in Revolutionary America, 1763–1788.* Madison: University of Wisconsin Press, 1967.

Makinson, David H. *Barbados: A Study of North-American–West-Indian Relations, 1739–1789.* The Hague: Mouton & Co., 1964.

Malone, Dumas. *Thomas Jefferson As Political Leader.* Berkeley: University of California Press, 1963.

Malone, Dumas and Basil Rauch. *Empire for Liberty: The Genesis and Growth of the United States of America.* 6 vols. New York: Appleton-Century-Crofts, 1960.

Mason, Alpheus Thomas. *The States Rights Debate: Antifederalism and the Constitution.* Englewood Cliffs, N.J.: Prentice-Hall, 1964.

Miller, John Chester. *Alexander Hamilton and the Growth of the New Nation.* Harper & Row, 1964.

Miner, Clarence Eugene. *The Ratification of the Federal Constitution by the State of New York.* New York: Columbia University Press, 1921.

Mintz, Max M. *Gouverneur Morris and the American Revolution.* Norman: University of Oklahoma Press, 1970.

Monaghan, Frank. *John Jay.* New York: Bobbs-Merrill Co., 1935.

Montross, Lynn. *Reluctant Rebels—The Story of the Continental Congress, 1774–1789.* New York: Harper, 1950.

Morgan, Edmund S. "The Puritan Ethic and the American Revolution." *William and Mary Quarterly,* XXIV, Ser. 3 (January, 1967), 3–43.

Morison, Samuel Eliot. *John Paul Jones*. Boston: Little, Brown & Co., 1959.

————. *The Life and Letters of Harrison Grey Otis, Federalist 1765–1848*. Boston and New York: Houghton Mifflin Co., 1913.

————. *The Maritime History of Massachusetts, 1783–1860*. Boston and New York: Houghton Mifflin Co., 1921.

Morris, Richard B. "The Confederation Period and the American Historian." *William and Mary Quarterly*, XIII, Ser. 3 (April, 1956), 139–56.

Morse, John Torrey. *John Adams, Statesman*. Boston: Riverside Press, 1884.

Mott, Frank Luther. *A History of American Magazines, 1741–1850*. New York: D. Appleton & Co., 1930–1938.

Munroe, John A. *Federalist Delaware, 1775–1815*. New Brunswick, N.J.: Rutgers University Press, 1954.

Nettels, Curtis Putnam. *The Emergence of a National Economy, 1775–1815*. New York: Holt, Rinehart, and Winston, 1962.

Nevins, Allan. *The American States During and After the Revolution, 1775–1789*. New York: Macmillan Co., 1924.

Nussbaum, Frederick L. "American Tobacco and French Politics, 1783–1789." *Political Science Quarterly*, XL (December, 1925), 497–516.

————. "The French Colonial Arrêt of 1784." *The South Atlantic Quarterly*, XXVII (January, 1928), 62–78.

Nye, Russell Blaine. *The Cultural Life of the New Nation, 1776–1830*. New York: Harper and Row, 1960.

Olson, Gary D. "Between Independence and Constitution: The Articles of Confederation, 1783–1787." Ph.D. dissertation, University of Nebraska, 1968.

*The Parliamentary History of England from the Earliest Period to the Year 1803*. 36 vols. London: T. C. Hansard, 1806–1820.

Peckham, Howard Henry. *The War for Independence, A Military History*. Chicago: University of Chicago Press, 1958.

Perkins, Dexter. *The American Approach to Foreign Policy*. New York: Atheneum, 1968.

Peterson, Merrill. "Thomas Jefferson and Commercial Policy,

1783–1793." *William and Mary Quarterly*, Ser. 3, XXII (October, 1965), 584 –610.

Philbrick, Francis Samuel. *The Rise of the West, 1754–1830*. New York: Harper and Row, 1965.

Phillips, Howard J. "The United States Diplomatic Establishment in the Critical Period, 1783–1789." Ph.D. dissertation, University of Notre Dame, 1968.

Phillips, James Duncan. "Salem Ocean-Borne Commerce From the Close of the Revolution to the Establishment of the Constitution, 1783–1789." *The Essex Institute of Historical Collections*, LXXV (April, 1939), 135–58; LXXV (July, 1939), 249–74; LXXV (October, 1939), 358–81; LXXVI (January, 1940), 68–88.

Pitken, Timothy. *Statistical View of the Commerce of the United States*. New Haven: H. Howe and Co., 1835.

Pole, Jack Richon. *Foundations of American Independence: 1763–1815*. Indianapolis and New York: Bobbs-Merrill Co., 1972.

Prescott, Arthur Taylor, comp. *Drafting the Federal Constitution*. Baton Rouge: Louisiana State University Press, 1941.

Prucha, Francis Paul. *The Sword of the Republic: The United States Army on the Frontier, 1783–1846*. New York: Macmillan Co., 1969.

Ragatz, Lowell Joseph. *The Fall of the Planter Class in the British Caribbean, 1763–1833*. New York and London: Century Co., 1928.

Ramsay, David. *History of South Carolina: From Its First Settlement in 1670 to the Year 1808*. 2 vols. Charleston, S.C.: D. Longworth, 1809.

Reed, William Bradford. *Life and Correspondence of Joseph Reed, Military Secretary of Washington, at Cambridge*. 2 vols. Philadelphia: Lindsay and Blakiston, 1847.

Reeves, John. *A History of the Law of Shipping and Navigation*. Dublin: T. Burnside, 1792.

Reid, David S. "An Analysis of British Parliamentary Opinion on American Affairs at the Close of the War of Independence." *Journal of Modern History*, XVIII (September, 1946), 202–21.

Richardson, Lyon Norman. *A History of Early American Magazines, 1741–1789*. New York: T. Nelson and Sons, 1931.

Ritcheson, Charles R. *Aftermath of Revolution: British Policy Toward the United States, 1783–1795*. Dallas: Southern Methodist University Press, 1969.

Roche, John P. "The Founding Fathers: A Reform Caucus in Action." *American Political Science Review*, LV (December, 1961), 799–816.

Rossiter, Clinton. *1787: The Grand Convention*. New York: Macmillan Co., 1966.

Rowland, Kate Mason. *The Life of George Mason, 1725–1792*. 2 vols. New York and London: G. P. Putnam's Sons, 1892.

Rutland, Robert. *George Mason, Reluctant Statesman*. Charlottesville: University Press of Virginia, 1961.

————. *The Ordeal of the Constitution: The Antifederalists and the Ratification Struggle of 1787–1788*. Norman: University of Oklahoma Press, 1965.

Saunders, Jennings B. *Evolution of the Executive Departments of the Continental Congress, 1774–1789*. Chapel Hill: University of North Carolina Press, 1935.

Schachner, Nathan. *Thomas Jefferson*. 2 vols. New York: Appleton-Century-Crofts, 1951.

Scharf, John Thomas and Thompson Westcott. *History of Philadelphia, 1609–1884*. 3 vols. Philadelphia: L. H. Everts and Co., 1884.

Schlesinger, Arthur Meier, Jr. *The Bitter Heritage*. Greenwich, Conn.: Fawcett, 1966.

Schouler, James. *History of the United States of America, Under the Constitution*. 7 vols. Rev. ed. New York: Dodd, Mead and Co., 1894 –1913.

Schuyler, Robert Livingston. *The Constitution of the United States*. New York: Macmillan Co., 1928.

See, Henri. "Commerce Between France and the United States, 1783–1784." *American Historical Review*, XXXI (July, 1926), 732–52.

Setser, Vernon G. *The Commercial Reciprocity Policy of the United States, 1774–1829*. Philadelphia: University of Pennsylvania Press, 1937.

Singer, Charles Gregg. "South Carolina in the Confederation." M.A. thesis, University of Pennsylvania, 1941.

Smith, Charles Page. *James Wilson, Founding Father, 1742–1798.* Chapel Hill: University of North Carolina Press, 1956.

Smith, Donald Lewis. *John Jay.* New York: Columbia University Press, 1968.

Smith, Page. *John Adams.* 2 vols. Garden City, N.Y.: Doubleday and Co., 1962.

Smith, William Henry, arr. *The St. Clair Papers. The Life and Public Services of Arthur St. Clair, Soldier of the Revolutionary War.* 2 vols. Cincinnati: R. Clarke and Co., 1882.

Sparks, Jared. *The Life of Gouverneur Morris, with Selections from His Correspondence and Miscellaneous Papers.* 3 vols. Boston: Gray and Bowen, 1832.

Spaulding, Ernest Wilder. *His Excellency George Clinton, Critic of the Constitution.* New York: Macmillan Co., 1938.

––––––. *New York in the Critical Period, 1783–1789.* New York: Columbia University Press, 1932.

Stackpole, Edouard A. *The Sea Hunters.* New York: J. B. Lippincott Co., 1953.

Steiner, Bernard Christian. "Connecticut's Ratification of the Federal Constitution." *American Antiquarian Society, Worcester, Massachusetts, Proceedings,* XXV (1915), 70–127.

Stevens, Wayne Edison. *The Northwest Fur Trade, 1763–1800.* Urbana: University of Illinois Press, 1928.

Stille, Charles Janeway. *The Life and Times of John Dickinson, 1732–1808.* Philadelphia: Historical Society of Pennsylvania, 1891.

Stinchcombe, William C. *The American Revolution and the French Alliance.* Syracuse, N.Y.: Syracuse University Press, 1969.

Stourzh, Gerald. *Alexander Hamilton and the Idea of Republican Government.* Stanford: Stanford University Press, 1970.

Stover, John F. "French-American Trade During the Confederation, 1781–1789." *North Carolina Historical Review,* XXXV (October, 1958), 399–415.

Stuart, Graham Henry. *The Department of State.* New York: Macmillan Co., 1949.

Studenski, Paul and Herman Krooss. *Financial History of the United States.* New York: McGraw-Hill, 1952.

Sumner, William Graham. *The Financier and the Finances of the American Revolution.* 2 vols. Reprint of original publication, 1891. New York: Augustus M. Kelley, 1968.

Thompson, Richard Wigginton. *The History of Protective Tariff Laws.* Chicago: R. S. Peale and Co., 1888.

Tenholme, Mrs. Louise (Irby). *Ratification of the Federal Constitution in North Carolina.* New York: Columbia University Press, 1932.

Trescot, William Henry. *Diplomatic History of the Administrations of Washington and Adams, 1789–1801.* Boston: Little, Brown & Co., 1857.

Van Alstyne, Richard Warner. *American Diplomacy in Action.* Stanford: Stanford University Press, 1947.

————. *The Rising American Empire.* New York: Oxford University Press, 1960.

Van Doren, Carl. *The Great Rehearsal.* New York: Viking Press, 1948.

Varg, Paul A. *Foreign Policies of the Founding Fathers.* East Lansing: Michigan State University Press, 1962.

Walker, Joseph Burbeen. *Birth of the Federal Constitution.* Boston: Cupples and Hurd, 1888.

Ward, Harry M. *The Department of War, 1781–1795.* Pittsburgh: Pittsburgh University Press, 1962.

Warren, Charles. *The Making of the Constitution.* Boston: Little, Brown & Co., 1928.

Watlington, Patricia. *The Partisan Spirit: Kentucky Politics, 1779–1792.* New York: Atheneum, 1972.

Weeden, William Babcock. *Economic and Social History of New England, 1620–1789.* 2 vols. Boston and New York: Houghton Mifflin Co., 1891.

Weigley, Russell Frank. *History of the United States Army.* New York: Macmillan Co., 1967.

Wesley, Edgar B. "The Military Policy of the Critical Period." *Coast Artillery Journal,* LXVIII (April, 1928), 281–90.

Whitaker, Arthur P. "Alexander McGillivray, 1783–1798." *North Carolina Historical Review,* V (April, 1928), 181–203.

_____. "Alexander McGillivray, 1789–1793." *North Carolina Historical Review*, V (July, 1928), 289–309.

_____. "Spain and the Cherokee Indians, 1783–1793." *North Carolina Historical Review*, IV (July, 1927), 252–69.

_____. *The Spanish-American Frontier: 1783–1795.* Boston and New York: Houghton Mifflin Co., 1927.

_____. "Spanish Intrigue in the Old Southwest: An Episode, 1788–1789." *The Mississippi Valley Historical Review*, XII (September, 1925), 155–76.

Whitney, Janet (Payne). *Abigail Adams.* Boston: Little, Brown & Co., 1947.

Winsor, Justin, ed. *The Memorial History of Boston, Including Suffolk County Massachusetts, 1630–1880.* 4 vols. Boston: J. R. Osgood and Co., 1880–1881.

Wood, George Clayton. *Congressional Control of Foreign Relations During the American Revolution, 1774–1789.* Allentown, Pennsylvania: H. R. Haas and Co., 1919.

Wood, Gordon S. Book review in the *William and Mary Quarterly*, Ser. 3, XXIV, No. 4 (October, 1967), 632–37.

_____. *The Creation of the American Republic, 1776–1787.* Chapel Hill: University of North Carolina Press, 1969.

Wright, Benjamin Fletcher. *Consensus and Continuity, 1776–1787.* New York: W. W. Norton and Co., 1967.

Wriston, Henry Merritt. *Executive Agents in American Foreign Relations.* Baltimore: Johns Hopkins Press, 1929.

Young, Alford. *The Debate Over the Constitution, 1787–1789.* New York: Rand McNally, 1965.

Young, Alfred Fabion. *The Democratic Republicans of New York.* Chapel Hill: University of North Carolina Press, 1967.

Zahniser, Marvin. *Charles Cotesworth Pinckney.* Chapel Hill: University of North Carolina Press, 1967.

# Index

Adams, Abigail, 133
Adams, John: and Britain, 10, 54–55, 66, 97, 99, 132–33; fears war, 12; and Treaty of Paris, 12; and Tripoli, 40–41; and foreign debt, 46; and U.S., 46, 71, 127; and Anglo-American commerce, 67; on Orders in Council, 68–70, 79; and constitutional reform, 69 *n*, 71; fears subversion, 100; and French trade, 109; and foreign press, 113; mentioned, xiii *n*, 85, 94, 154, 166, 202
Adams, Samuel, 100, 194
Agriculture: before 1776, p. 53; and Orders in Council, 60, 61 *n*, 73, 75, 76, 192; and surplus farming, 60 *n*, 61, 192 *n*; in ratification campaign, 192
Algiers: and Spain, 38; and U.S., 40, 42, 208, 209; Dey of, 50; and England, 99, 100; mentioned, 112, 174, 189. *See also* Barbary pirates
Allen, Ethan and Ira, 103
Amis, Thomas, 24, 31
Annapolis Convention: described, 91–95; and absent delegations, 93; and Annapolis Report, 93–94, 137, 146

Antifederalists. *See* Federalists; Ratification campaign
Army: inadequacy of, 15–18, 48, 104; and Constitution, 49; discussed at Philadelphia, 143–45; after 1789, pp. 210–14. *See also* Constitutional Convention; Constitutional reform
Articles of Confederation. *See* Confederation government; Constitutional reform
Artisans: and shipbuilding, 64, 73
Austria, 89 *n*

Balance of trade. *See* British West Indies; Fiscal problems
Bancroft, George, xii, xiii *n*, xv, xvi
Barbary pirates: in historical accounts, xii *n*; raids of, 36–40, 38 *n*; negotiations with, 40–42, 208–209; and union, 48; and Britain, 99, 100; mentioned, 27
Barclay, Thomas, 40, 41 *n*
Barlow, Joel, 119, 120
Beard, Charles, xiv, xv
Bemis, Samuel Flagg, 6
Bentley, Arthur F., xiv
*Betsey*: seized by pirates, 38
Blount, William, 210

249

Border disputes: with Britain, 8–9; with Spain, 22, 25–32
Boston: and West Indies, 72; petitions for commercial aid, 73; on Shays's Rebellion, 102
Boudinot, Elias, 201
Bowdoin, James, 81, 145
Brant, Joseph, xii *n*, 20, 35–36, 211–12
Britain. *See* Great Britain
British East India Company, 62
British West Indies: importance of, 53 *n*, 66, 147, 191 *n*; and U.S., 54, 56–57, 57 *n*, 58, 61, 65; after 1789, pp. 214, 219
Brown, Robert E.: on the Constitution, xv
Bryan, George, 60, 72 *n*, 74 *n*, 194, 203 *n*
Buffon, Georges Louis Comte de, 125 *n*
Burt, Alfred A., 6 *n*
Butler, Pierce, 156 *n*, 157, 164, 203

Canada: and West Indies, 58; and Shaysites, 102; and Vermont, 103–104. *See also* Fur trade
Carleton, Guy, Lord Dorchester, 7
Carmarthen, Lord, 67, 68
Carmichael, William, 125
Carroll, Daniel, 153, 156 *n*, 203
Cathcart, James, 39
Channing, Edward, xii *n*, xiii *n*, xiv
Chesapeake Bay, 64
China, 214, 217
Clark, George Rogers, 18, 24
Class conflict, xiii, xiv, xvi. *See also* Shays's Rebellion
Clinton, George, 7
*Columbian Magazine,* 119
Commerce, xiii *n*, 92. *See also* Foreign commerce
Condorcet, marquis de, 116, 127 *n*
Confederation government: accomplishments of, xvi, xvii; and foreign debt, 45; and British orders, 66–68, 84–95; and foreign affairs,

70; and foreign commerce, 74; and report on commerce, 86, 88–90; and Monroe Committee report, 94; and quorum problem, 128–29; and committee system, 152–53; location of, 153; and isolationism, 153–54. *See also* Constitutional Convention; Constitutional reform
Congress. *See* Confederation government
Connecticut, 82, 89, 148
Constitutional Convention: on defense, 142–45; on foreign commerce, 146–51; on slavery, 148–50; its Committee of Detail, 148 *n*, 150, 155, 156, 158; its compromise on commerce, 150; federal powers of, 152; and executive power, 152–59; on treaties, 155–58; its Committee on Remaining Business, 156 *n*; and presidential council, 160–61; and citizenship requirements, 163–65
Constitutional reform: and treaty enforcement, 14–15, 48, 55, 68, 142, 143, 151, 194; and court of appeals, 15; and national defense, 47–51, 104, 142–43, 150; and federal troops, 50; and foreign commerce, 52, 55, 67–69, 71–74, 74 *n*, 75–95, 127, 135, 143, 146–51, 194, 204 *n*; and protective tariff, 77–79, 138–39; and national pride, 13, 78, 96, 127, 133–41; southern opposition to, 87; and Annapolis Convention, 91–95; and branches of government, 92 *n*; on defense, 208–14, 219; on commerce 214–19. *See also* Confederation government; Constitutional Convention; Ratification campaign; States
*The Contrast,* 120
Coxe, Tench, 74, 138, 175
Creek Indians, 4
Cumberland, 211

Dane, Nathan, 75 *n*, 94
*Dauphin*, 38
Davie, William, 178, 192, 203
Decatur, Stephen, 209
Defense. *See* Army; Barbary pirates; Constitutional reform; Great Britian; Navy; Northwest; War
Delaware, 87
Denmark, 44, 89 *n*, 107 *n*
Department of State, 162 *n*
DePauw, Corneille, 124
Dickinson, John, 149, 156 *n*, 161, 175, 203
Dissolution of union: in historical accounts, xiii; encouraged by Britain and Spain, 23, 24, 26, 35–36; west of Appalachians, 23, 33–36, 130; and Jay-Gardoqui talks, 33, 34, 48; opposed by Hamilton and Ramsay, 33; its impact on reform, 139; in ratification campaign, 188–89, 195
Dunlap, William, 120 *n*

Ellsworth, Oliver, 160, 164, 185, 190
England. *See* Great Britain

Fallen Timbers, 212–13
Farmers. *See* Agriculture
*The Federalist*: 169 *n*, 170–73
Federalists: differentiated from Antifederalists, xiv-xvii, 60–61, 61 *n*, 87 *n*, 88, 95, 101 *n*, 145 *n*, 177 *n*, 201–205; after 1789, p. 218. *See also* Ratification campaign
Federal revenue: in historical accounts, xii, xiii *n*; and national credit, 45; and Congress, 45; and foreign debt, 45 *n*; and national security, 45–47; in 1786, p. 139; remedied at Philadelphia, 143; under new Constitution, 208
Feer, Robert A., xv, 95 *n*
Fiscal problems: and national defense, 15–16, 44–45; and negotiations with Indians, 18–19; and

Jefferson, 42 *n*; and balance of trade, 65, 66, 76, 78, 214; and specie, 73, 76, 78; and imbalance of trade, 78; mentioned, xii *n*, 91. *See also* Foreign commerce; Foreign debt
Fiske, John, xii, xiii *n*
Fitzsimons, Thomas, 74, 203
Floridablanca, Count of, 26–27
Foreign commerce: in historical accounts, xii, xiii *n*, 56–57, 57 *n*; and Mediterranean, 36–40; with West Indies, 56–58, 85; hurt by British orders, 57 *n*, 58–66, 60 *n*, 85; with France, 65; with East Indies, 65; with China, 65–66; reliance on England, 98; after 1789, pp. 214–19. *See also* Constitutional Convention; Constitutional reform; Ratification campaign; Treaties
Foreign debt: in historical accounts, xii; to Spain, 27; as source of danger, 45–47, 122, 175, 177, 182; to France, 128
Foreign opinion of the U.S.: in historical accounts, xii *n*; hostility in, 97, 105, 113–15, 123–25; on lack of quorum, 128; on Constitution, 207. *See also* Ratification campaign
France: seen as menace, 46, 106–11, 114, 122, 154; supports Spain against U.S., 106, 108; her trade policy, 109–10, 115 *n*, 137, 217; mentioned, 3–4, 14, 37, 209
Franklin (state): 5 *n*, 211
Franklin, Benjamin: 38, 99, 114, 125–26, 132, 163–64, 202
Frederick the Great, 130
French West Indies, 85, 110, 137
Freneau, Philip, 119
Fur trade, 5–6, 9–11, 174

Gardoqui, Diego de. *See* Jay-Gardoqui talks
Genêt, Edmund, 218
George III, 66–67, 97, 130

Georgia, 4, 50, 59 *n*, 75, 81, 146, 147, 181
Gerry, Elbridge, 104, 111–12, 112 *n*, 140, 144–45, 153, 158, 159, 164, 165
Gilbert, Felix, 109 *n*
Grayson, William, 44, 103, 203
Great Britain: her forts in U.S., 5–11, 20, 98–99; and Indians, 19, 20–21, 35–36, 105; blocks access to lakes, 24; and U.S., 66–67, 97–98, 105, 123 *n*, 137, 177, 183; her trade restrictions, 80–83, 99, 214–19; importance of, 98, 217–18; and pirates, 99, 105; accused of subversion, 100–105; and Vermont, 104; demands ambassadors, 123; and Jay's Treaty, 212–14; after 1789, pp. 217–18. *See also* British West Indies
Greenville, Treaty of, 213
Grenville, Lord, 67, 68

Hamilton, Alexander: and treaty, 13; at Annapolis, 93; and Vermont-British connection, 103; at Constitutional Convention, 142, 145, 164, 165; in ratification campaign, 171, 192; after 1789, p. 218; mentioned, 153, 155, 172 *n*, 173, 203, 210
Hancock, John, 128, 203
Hanson, Alexander, 175, 188
Harmar, Josiah, xii *n*, 7, 17–18, 125, 128, 212
Henry, Patrick, 193
Higginson, Stephen, 153, 159, 202
Hofstadter, Richard, xvi *n*
Holland. *See* Netherlands
House of Representatives: on treaties, 155–57, 172; on war, 158–59; on citizenship requirement, 164–65
Humphreys, David, 118–19, 125

Indians: raids by, 19, 23, 139, 181; their attempts at confederation, 18, 20, 23, 36; mentioned, xii *n*, 4, 17 *n*, 18, 36, 91, 211–12. *See also* Treaties
Iredell, James, 172 *n*, 176, 183, 203
Innes, Harry, 210
International law, 45, 142

Jay-Gardoqui talks: in historical accounts, xii, xiii *n*; described, 25–32; Gardoqui's instructions regarding, 26; Jay's role in, 28–30 *n*, 32–33 *n*, 197; effects of. 33. 94. 157; and aid against pirates, 107 *n*; mentioned, 210
Jay, John: talks with Gardoqui, 25–32; and disunion, 34; and Orders in Council, 79, 83; and three-branch government, 92 *n*; and subversion, 107, 162; in ratification campaign, 172–75, 188, 202; mentioned, 8, 12, 13. 42, 48–49, 94, 107, 113, 152, 155, 197
Jay's Treaty, 213
Jefferson, Thomas: and Spain, 25, 31–32; and Mediterranean, 37; and Barbary, 38, 43; enlists Mathurins, 42; and measures against Britain and France, 43; and collective security, 43–44; and Orders in Council, 76; and England, 98; and subversion, 100; and Shays, 102; as minister to France, 110, 132; and propaganda, 126–27; and isolationism, 154; on Constitution, 206; mentioned, 202, 204, 210, 211 *n*
Jensen, Merrill, xiv, xvii, 57 *n*
Johnson, William S., 87 *n*, 156, 202
Jones, John Paul, 38, 43

Kentucky, 130, 197, 210, 213
Kenyon, Cecilia, 204
King, Rufus: and commerce reform, 92, 146; and Annapolis, 94; at Philadelphia, 148, 156 *n*, 157, 161, 165; mentioned, 39, 72 *n*, 79, 81, 87 *n*, 111–12 *n*
Knox, Henry, xii *n*, 6, 10, 15, 16, 134, 145, 176, 204, 212

Lafayette, Marquis de, 110, 115
Lamb, John, 41–42
Land ordinances, xvii
Land sales, 5
Law of Nations. *See* International
  law
Lee, Arthur, 153. 203
Lee, Henry, 27, 193
Lee, Richard Henry: and com-
  merce control, 87–88; and con-
  stitutional reform, 91; and Britain,
  97; and Europe, 115; mentioned,
  40, 197, 203
Livingston, Robert R., 61, 69, 153,
  172, 185, 201
Logan, Benjamin, 17
Logie, Charles, 99–100
Loyalists, 7, 101–102. *See also* Treaty
  of Paris

Mably, Abbé de, 69 *n*, 114, 127 *n*
McClurg, James, 201, 203
McDonald, Forrest, xiv, 59 *n*
McGillivray, Alexander, xii *n*, 23,
  34, 36, 210, 211 *n*
McHenry, James, 169 *n*, 203
McLaughlin, Andrew C., xii *n*, xiii
  *n*, xiv, xv
McMaster, John Bach, vii, viii *n*, xv,
  xvi
Madison, James: and treaty, 13 *n*,
  14, 48; and reform, 14, 92; and
  Spanish talks, 31; and Annapolis,
  92, 95, and Shays, 102; and national pride, 140; and interstate
  commerce, 146; and federal commerce control, 146; at Philadelphia, 151, 156–59, 161, 164, 165;
  and ratification, 170, 171, 179, 186,
  188; on nationalist mentality,
  204 *n*; and trade policy, 216–18;
  mentioned, 76, 88, 93, 126, 153,
  167, 173, 201, 209
Main, Jackson Turner, xiv, xvii, 60–
  61, 61 *n*, 201 *n*
Manufacturers: and federal com-

merce control, 77–79, 138–39, 215–
  16; mentioned, 99, 218
*Maria*, 38, 39
Marshall, John, 52, 139–40
Mathurins, 42
Martin, Luther, 145 *n*, 148
Maryland, 80, 84 *n*, 87, 89, 91–95,
  146
Mason, George, 75, 145 *n*, 149, 151,
  155, 161, 164, 165, 176
Massachusetts, 63, 80, 81, 82, 94,
  130, 187, 191. *See also* Boston;
  Nantucket
Mazzei, Philip, 127 *n*, 132 *n*
Mediterranean trade: and pirate
  raids, 36–40; value of, 37, 66; de-
  cline of, 65, 174
Mercer, John Francis, 153, 155
Merchants: and British orders, 62,
  73, 76, 112 *n*; petition for reform,
  72, 72 *n*, 74, 75, 201 *n*
Militia, 17, 144–45
Miró, Estaban, 22, 35, 214 *n*
Mississippi River: in historical accounts, xii *n*; closure of, 23–24;
  in Jay-Gardoqui talks, 25–32; in
  ratification debate, 197–98
Mohawk Indians, 4
Monroe, James: and Tory exiles, 7;
  and federal mutiny bill, 17; and
  Potomac and Hudson, 17 *n*; and
  Mississippi rights, 30; and Jay-
  Gardoqui talks, 30, 34; and federal control of commerce, 80–87,
  146; and British orders, 80, 187;
  and committee report of Feb-
  ruary 16, 1785, pp. 87 *n*, 88, 90;
  and commerce reform, 92; mentioned, 50, 153, 159, 193, 204 *n*
Montesquieu, 125 *n*, 130
Montmorin, Comte de, 108, 109 *n*
Morgan, Edmund, 82 *n*
Morocco, 38, 40. *See also* Barbary
  pirates
Morris, Gouverneur: at Philadelphia, 148–50, 155, 156, 158, 160,

163, 164, 165; mentioned, 79, 140, 148, 166, 202, 218
Morris, Richard B., xv
Morris, Robert, 58 *n*, 74 *n*, 203
Morse, Jedediah, 119
Moustier, Leonore F., 107–108 *n*, 124
Muhammad, Sidi, 40

Nantucket, 130
Naples, 43, 44, 89 *n*
Natchez, 22
National pride: in historical accounts, xii *n*, xiii, xiv *n*, xvi; its impact on reform, 50, 96, 133–41, 166, 195–96; described, 116–27, 128, 131–33; mentioned, 13, 43, 207. *See also* Ratification campaign
Nationalists. *See* Federalists
National unity. *See* Dissolution of union
Navy: inadequacy of, 16, 38–39, 42–43, 44, 144 *n*; lacks funds, 44–45, 63; under Constitution, 208–209, 210 *n*
Nelson, Horatio, 57–58
Netherlands: and pirates, 37, 107; and U.S. shipping, 38 *n*; and Algiers, 41; seen as menace, 47; jealousy seen, 112, 114; mentioned, 57.
Nettels, Curtis P., 6, 57 *n*, 58
New England: and shipbuilding, 63, 64; and whaling, 65; fears subversion, 102; in ratification, 183–84, 187; mentioned, 72
Newfoundland, 58, 59
New Hampshire, 80–81, 94, 184
New Jersey, 82, 148
New Jersey Plan, 92, 144, 146, 152, 155, 165
New York City, 64
New York State: and federal impost, 94, 135, 139; its chamber of commerce, 113, 139; mentioned, 4, 7, 81, 82, 94, 105, 185–86, 191 *n*

North Carolina, 80, 89
Northwest, xiii *n*, 5, 20 *n*, 21
Nova Scotia, 58, 59

Order of Malta, 44
Osgood, Samuel, 153, 159

Papal states, 89 *n*
Paper money, xii, xiii
Patriotism. *See* National pride
Peace of 1783. *See* Treaty of Paris
Pennsylvania, 81, 82, 89
Philadelphia Convention. *See* Constitutional Convention
Pinckney, Charles: at Philadelphia, 142, 145, 149, 150, 158, 160, 163; mentioned, 91, 111, 193, 203
Pinckney, C. C., 149, 150, 182, 203
Pinckney, Thomas, 203
Pinckney's Treaty, 213
Pitt, William, 54, 67, 97
Portugal, 38 *n*, 43, 44, 107 *n*, 115 *n*
Powers of Congress. *See* Confederation government
Pradt, Abbé de, 115
President of U.S., 152–61, 165
Price, Richard, 69 *n*, 113, 123–24
Proclamation of Neutrality, 218
Prussia, 154

Ragatz, Lowell, 57 *n*, 58
Ramsay, David, 176, 181, 193
Randolph, Edmund: at Philadelphia, 142, 145, 151, 163, 164; and ratification, 176, 179, 183, 188, 193; mentioned, 133 *n*, 146, 178
Ratification campaign: and Federalists, 167–69, 170, 174, 191–94, 200–201, 205–206; and Antifederalists, 168, 189, 190, 196–200; and national defense, 169, 170, 171, 174, 175, 176–90, 197–98; on national pride, 170, 171–72, 176, 193, 195–96; on treaty enforcement, 170, 174, 178; on union, 170, 175, 188, 195. *See also* Federalists

Raynal, Abbé, 124, 125, 126
Revenue. *See* Federal revenue
Rhode Island, 81, 89, 124, 189
Robertson, James, 34–35, 210
Roche, John P., xv, 204 *n*
Rush, Benjamin, 153, 186, 196, 203, 207
Russia, 89 *n*
Rutledge, John, 149, 151, 203

St. Clair, Arthur, 31, 32, 129, 212
St. Croix River, 8
Sardinia, 89 *n*, 107 *n*
Saxony, 89 *n*
Sebastian, Benjamin, 210
Secession. *See* Dissolution of union
Senate: on treaties, 33, 155 *n*, 156, 157, 163, 172, 197; on war, 159; on citizenship requirement, 163–64
Sevier, John, 35, 210
Shays's Rebellion: in historical accounts, xii *n*, xiii, xv, xvi; and reform movement, 95, 95 *n*, 139–40; and British subversion, 102, 104, 105, 190; mentioned, 144, 189, 205
Sheffield, Lord, 55, 56
Shelburne, earl of, 54
Sherman, Roger, 156 *n*, 157
Shipbuilding: before 1776, pp. 53, 63 *n;* and British orders, 62–65; 76; in the South, 64, 76; in ratification contest, 174; after 1789, p. 214
Shipping: and Britian, 52–53, 60, 73, 77, 85–86, 136; in the South, 59 *n*, 77; and Barbary pirates, 99; and ratification, 174, 191; after 1789, pp. 214, 218
Sicilies, 44
Singletary, Amos, 168 *n*
Slavery, 87, 147, 183. *See also* Constitutional Convention
Snow, Captain, 195
South: and shipping, 59, 59 *n*, 77; and shipbuilding, 64, 76; and federal commerce control, 75, 75 *n*,

76, 77 *n*, 84 *n*, 87, 87 *n*, 146–47, 193; and British orders, 76, 80, 81, 112 *n*; and trade, 76; and manufactures, 78; and Annapolis, 91–95; on Jay-Gardoqui talks, 94, 197; and national defense, 175–76, 179, 181–83, 186 *n*; and federal treaty power, 197. *See also* Slavery
South Carolina, 59 *n*, 64, 75–76, 78, 89, 147, 181
Spain: and the southwest, 21–23, 25; and New Orleans, 23–24; and Jay-Gardoqui talks, 25–32; and U.S. shipping, 38 *n*; and Algiers, 43; viewed as hostile, 105–106; and Barbary, 107 *n*; and U.S. trade, 112, 115 *n*; and Pinckney's Treaty, 213–14; mentioned, 35 *n*, 91, 211
States: and Congress, 3, 4, 5, 13–14, 18, 47, 151; and local rule, 80, 205–206; and Orders in Council, 80–83, 215; and federal commerce control, 88–89
Subversion: danger of, 7, 100, 101 *n*, 102–105, 154; as issue at Philadelphia, 162–66; in ratification campaign, 175, 188, 189, 190, 199
Sweden, 44, 107 *n*.

Tariff, after 1789, pp. 214–19. *See also* Manufacturers; States
Taxation. *See* Federal revenue
Temple, Sir John, 207
Tennessee, 130, 213
*Thompson*, 63
Thomson, Charles, 128, 169
Tonnage duties: after 1789, p. 215. *See also* States
Tories. *See* Loyalists
Trade. *See* Commerce; Foreign commerce
Treaties: violated by U.S., 3, 151; enforcement of, 3–15, 151–52; of Galphinton and Hopewell, 4, 211; with Indians 18–19; 213; of Stanwix, McIntosh, and Finney,

19, 36; of Pensacola and Mobile, 22; and two-thirds rule, 33, 197; of 1778, p. 37; commercial, 89, 89 *n*; of Holston, 154, 211; of New York, 211; of Greenville, 213. *See also* Barbary pirates, Ratification campaign

Treaty of Paris, 6, 9–13, 21, 128

Triangular trade, 53, 60

Tripoli, 40, 209. *See also* Barbary pirates

Tucker, St. George, 193, 203

Tunis, 209. *See also* Barbary pirates

Tuscany, 89 *n*

Two-thirds rule. *See* Senate

Union. *See* Dissolution of union

Venice, 43, 44

Vermont, 94, 103–105, 130

Virginia: 3, 64, 64 *n*, 80, 82–83, 84 *n*, 87, 94, 146–47

Virginia Plan, 146, 152, 155, 165

War: viewed as impending, 11, 20, 24, 78, 97–98, 218; and foreign debt, 45–46; and treaty enforce-ment power, 142; as issue at Philadelphia, 142–45, 158–59; and weakness, 186–87; with Barbary and France, 209. *See also* Ratification campaign

Washington, George: and defense, 16; and secession, 35; and national credit, 45; and reform, 48; his pride in U.S., 117, 134, 135; at Philadelphia, 159, 162; as president, 207, 208, 211, 215; mentioned, 27, 50, 94, 102, 147, 169 *n*, 174 *n*, 185, 197

Wayne, Anthony, 212–13

Webster, Noah, 120, 174 *n*, 175

Webster, Pelatiah, 177

West Florida, 22

West Indies, 174. *See also* British West Indies; French West Indies

Whaling, 53, 65

Wilkinson, James, 35, 210

Williamson, Hugh, 14, 48, 154, 156 *n*, 164, 178, 203

Wilson, James, 155, 156, 157, 161, 164, 165, 187, 203

Winthrop, James, 198–200